THE GREEN REPUBLIC

BY STERLING EVANS

The
Green
Republic

A CONSERVATION HISTORY OF COSTA RICA

UNIVERSITY OF TEXAS PRESS, AUSTIN

Requests for permission to reproduce material from this work should be sent to Permissions, University of Texas Press, P.O. Box 7819, Austin, TX 78713-7819.

∞ The paper used in this publication meets the minimum requirements of American National Standard for Information Sciences—Permanence of Paper for Printed Library Materials, ANSI Z39.48-1984.

Library of Congress Cataloging-in-Publication Data

Evans, Sterling, 1959–
    The green republic : a conservation history of Costa Rica / by Sterling Evans. — 1st ed.
        p.   cm.
    Includes bibliographical references and index.
    ISBN 0-292-72100-5 (cloth : alk. paper)
    ISBN 0-292-72101-3 (pbk. : alk. paper)
    1. Nature conservation—Costa Rica—History. 2. Nature conservation—Government policy—Costa Rica—History. I. Title.
    QH77.C8 E935   1999
    333.7'2'097286—ddc21   98-25495

To Charley Stansifer
whose knowledge of Costa Rica is matched only by his love for its
people and their history.

CONTENTS

FIGURES

TABLES

PREFACE

Esta tierra pertenece a los costarricences,
algunos ya han muerto, otros todavía viven,
pero la mayoría aún no ha nacido.
                                Costa Rican saying

(This land belongs to the Costa Ricans,
some have already died, others are still
living, but most have not even been born.)

The vision exemplified in the above oft-quoted saying makes Costa Rica an intriguing case study in environmental history. Its implied message—that Costa Rica is a country with a mind for the future, a future based on the environmental well-being of its land and inhabitants—begs the question of how such a model developed and what measures have been instituted to ensure its success. More implicitly, this idea must be tested by tracing the successes and failures of the Costa Rican conservation experience. Such analysis is the goal of this work. Does Costa Rica live up to its nickname "the garden of the Americas?" Does it embody what *New York Times* writer John Oakes in 1988 called the "greening" of the region? Is it on the path of what a conference that same year concluded was toward a *Centroamérica verde?*[1] Is Costa Rica a "green" republic?

To attempt answering such questions, this study seeks to track the history of conservation efforts in Costa Rica via analysis of its national parks and other protected areas. The focus of the book will be to examine how Costa Rica came to establish its conservation system, which today includes over 25 percent of the country's terrain. It will describe the system, discuss the key leaders involved, and analyze conservation in light of what it was in response to: rapid environmental destruction of tropical ecosystems due to the expansion of export-related agricultural commodities. How is this agricultural modernization different from past agricultural experiences and how has it affected conservation efforts? What conservation measures or agricultural practices from the nineteenth and early twentieth centuries influenced conservation patterns? How and why were national parks and biological reserves proposed and designated? Who has been behind them? Why and how did these individuals become involved in their country's conservation movement? What has been the overall impact of conservation on the nation's environmental well-being, economy, and education? What challenges have conservationists had to confront; what goals and dilemmas await them? Just as important, the study will ask what Costa Ricans have said and are saying about these conservation concerns. Emphasis will be placed on policy reactions—laws and decrees and how they came about.

Only two other works approach this subject in book form. The first, Luis Fournier's *Desarrollo y perspectiva del movimiento conservacionista costarricense* (1991), lists some of the early conservation policies and discusses the beginning of Costa Rica's conservation movement. Dr. Fournier is a botanist at the University of Costa Rica and has been a longtime conservation proponent. But while written from the perspective of someone who was actively involved in policy making, the book is a rather short condensation of conservation laws and the people behind them, with little analysis or in-depth discussion. Fournier's intent for the book was to be introductory—he provided directions for future research for which I am forever grateful.

The other book is David Rains Wallace's *The Quetzal and the Macaw: The Story of Costa Rica's National Parks* (1992). Wallace's work is limited, however, to the "story" of national parks only, includes no archival data, and does not put national park development in the larger context of Costa Rican conservation history. Its strength lies in the interviews Wallace incorporated into the book's narrative—interviews that were useful here since the voices of the people involved (some of whom I also interviewed) are important and should be heard in this conservation history.

I have attempted to be broader in historic range, more comprehensive in conservation policy making, and more reliant on archival records and newspapers than *The Quetzal and the Macaw* intended to be. I have also drawn on many articles and essays written by Costa Ricans and others that pertain to individual aspects of conservation policy. Those sources helped greatly in piecing together the larger picture.

To limit the scope of the project, "conservation" here will imply the creation of governmental and private areas of land (national parks and monuments, biological reserves, wildlife refuges, indigenous reserves, and private ecological reserves) that have been set aside for long-range preservation. This project will not address in any great length such environmental concerns as pollution, urban sprawl, toxic wastes, air and water quality, sanitation, or human health issues. These important matters have a literature all their own and exceed the boundaries of this particular conservation history. Nor is this work a comparison of Costa Rican conservation efforts with those of other republics in the region. Rather, *The Green Republic* is an attempt to synthesize diverse elements of Costa Rica's past (natural history, government, education, etc.) to evaluate the successes and failures of the nation's conservation system.

Luis Fournier has written that "in reality, we are no longer just a few people clamoring for a rational use of this environment, and what in the past for many was merely a romantic or utopian dream, has been transformed into something vital for the future of the country, and is coming to be understood by a greater number of Costa Ricans."[2]

The intent here is to follow the development of this Costa Rican pattern of thinking. Disagreement exists whether this is a long, historic phenomenon—predating and including the colonial era—or if it is a recent product of late-twentieth-century scientific understanding. Some scholars point to the ecologically sustainable ways of pre-Columbian native peoples in Costa Rica as a base for an enduring environmental awareness.[3] Others note that farmers in the colonial and early national eras practiced responsible agriculture and thus continued conscientious land use patterns.[4]

Some researchers, however, suggest that environmental awareness has resulted only in the past twenty-five years. Estrella Guier, the director of environmental education at UNED (the Universidad Estatal a Distancia, usually translated as the National Open University), remarked: "It is only recently that a conscience among some towards a rational and balanced exploitation of natural resources has been created." Luis Fournier agrees: "Fortunately in the [1970s] . . . in Costa Rica there has been a change of attitude in the people . . . with respect to the problem of the environment."[5]

Both sides will be examined here. But *has* Costa Rica managed its natural resources rationally, and if so, what mechanisms (structural and attitudinal) have proven successful and are in place to continue the trend?

To address these concerns, this book is divided into two parts. Part I concerns Costa Rica's history of conservation; Part II, the country's framework for what will be called "building a green republic." Emphasis in Part I is placed on such issues as the legacy of tropical research, the environmental dilemma of Costa Rican agriculture, and the conservationist response via public lands management—especially stressing the role national parks have played in the Costa Rican conservation strategy (Chapters 1 through 5). Surprisingly, a large percentage of public land was protected during the severe economic crisis of the early 1980s. Reporting how this unique, perhaps paradoxical, experience transpired is discussed in Chapters 6 and 7, and the government's push to restructure and decentralize conservation efforts in the late 1980s and 1990s is discussed in Chapter 8.

Part II examines other aspects of Costa Rica's conservation experience and how they apply to the structure in place for the future. Chapters 9 and 10 analyze the important roles played by environmental education and nongovernmental organizations. *Campesino* and indigenous movements are important dimensions of the overall story and are included in Chapter 10. And more recent phenomena such as ecotourism and biodiversity inventorying are discussed in Chapters 11 and 12.

The study, however, would be terribly remiss and blind to the facts if it omitted a discussion of the serious challenges facing Costa Rica's conservation system. What is often called "the grand contradiction" is the paradox of Costa Rica's development of extraordinary national parks simultaneous to massive deforestation in unprotected areas. The fact that only since 1969 more than 25 percent of Costa Rica has been protected in one form or another must be balanced with the fact that over 60 percent of the country is deforested and that the rate is growing by 4 percent a year. Equally disturbing is that 17 percent of the land is composed of highly degraded or seriously eroded soil, rendering it almost useless for agriculture or for reforestation.

Keeping matters in perspective, however, is important. Where things are now is less important than the direction in which they are going. And therein lies the hope for Costa Rica. The people of Costa Rica have been motivated for a change in direction to preserve their natural heritage. The history of how this occurred merits attention and is the underlying purpose of this work.

In his conservation history of Mexico, Lane Simonian has written that environmental history should become "more international" in scope. "In many places, people have fought to protect nature," he continues, and "their stories should be told."[6] What follows is the account of many who have worked to make Costa Rica a green republic—a country that conserves natural resources for those who have yet to be born.

ACKNOWLEDGMENTS

This book is indebted to the visionary people of Costa Rica who have striven with fierce resolve to protect their peaceful corner of the tropical world. The author is grateful to the various individuals who agreed to be interviewed in conjunction with research for this study. Among them are Karen Olsen de Figueres, former president Rodrigo Carazo, Mario Boza, Alvaro Ugalde, Gerardo Budowski, Luis Fournier, Alexander Bonilla, Roxana Salazar, María Eugenia Bozzoli, Eric Ulloa, Jorge Cortés, Alvaro León, Mario Alvarado Sánchez, and Anselmo Flores Reyes. They gave willingly and generously of their time (most on short notice) to open their homes or offices to me.

The staff at the National Archives in Zapote was especially friendly and helpful. I sincerely appreciate all the assistance given to me there by Joel Fallas, Danilo Meléndez, and, especially, Orlando Castillo, who shared not only his expertise of the archival system but also his time as a sounding board for some of my ideas. Equally cheerful were staff members at the Archives of the Legislative Assembly in San José. There Olman Madrigal was of great assistance, and the department chief, Leonel Núñez Arias, practically held my hand as I groped to understand the bewildering legislative strata of forestry policy.

Staying in Costa Rica is always a pleasure. People like Zoraida Aparicio, Marta Alvarado, Carl Stanley, and Xenia Murillo made extended stays ever the more enjoyable. (And extra thanks go to Marta and Xenia, who helped entertain my daughter so well during afternoons in summer 1996.) A special thanks to Willy Solano should be expressed for his personal tour of north-central Costa Rica back in 1992 and for his friendship over the years.

Stateside there are many people who have greatly assisted me and have had a hand in shaping this study. Special appreciation goes to the thesis "team" at the University of Kansas where this project originated: Charles Stansifer (my thesis director who gave countless hours of time and much advice and to whom this book is logically dedicated), Donald Worster (whose work and courses motivated me to continue pursuing the study of environmental history), and Philip Humphrey (whose class and discussions on biodiversity helped stimulate research for this project). When the thesis turned into the dissertation, professors Stansifer and Worster continued to stay on and to be actively involved in the process of finalizing it. I equally appreciate the time, advice, and recommendations of the other three readers, Elizabeth Kuznesof, donna luckey, and John Augelli, whose input strengthened the final manuscript. Likewise, thanks go to Scot Vink, an undergraduate research assistant, former student of mine, and close friend who accompanied me on two different trips to Costa Rica and assisted me in many ways.

My parents deserve special recognition for very actively opening my world to the joys of travel, camping, hiking, and visits to national parks when I was a boy (and for putting up with me on such trips when I was assuredly an unpleasant junior high traveler!). They have warmly encouraged me in all research endeavors. Also I thank John and Jeanne Goodman, whose tropical ecology trip to Mexico and Central America stimulated my interest in this area when I was an undergraduate student and is in great part the reason for my career direction now.

For the final product I am indebted to Wendy Johnson, who used her cartographic magic in reproducing the maps and figures here. It has been a pleasure working with the staff at the University of Texas Press. Shannon Davies has directed this project in a warm and professional manner. I thank her and the Press for taking such great interest in publishing works on environmental history. Lane Simonian and Darryl Cole-Christensen, the outside readers for the Press, offered very valuable assessments on ways to improve the manuscript. It is I, however, who remain solely responsible for any errors or omissions in the book.

Finally, a very special thanks goes to Sheri Little Evans (who knows more about writing than I ever will) for her incredible patience and unwavering support through the many stages of this project. I am also indebted to our daughter, Alex, who hastened the book's completion with her wonderful interludes of fun, play, and "stories" and who always seemed to tolerate why "Daddy's working the buttons."

S.E.

Edmonton, Alberta

THE GREEN REPUBLIC

Introduction

Costa Rica is . . . something of a model in Latin America. The enormous ecological variety encompassed in such a small area makes the country a tropical laboratory.

Carolyn Hall, *Costa Rica*

The Costa Rican Uniqueness Factor

The first thing to understand about Costa Rica's environmental history is how the country is so specifically different in many ways from the rest of the world. A preliminary glance reveals that Costa Rica is one of the least impoverished countries in the Third World, has the highest per capita income in Central America, maintains one of the highest literacy rates in the world (98 percent, according to some), and leads Central America in elementary and higher education. Likewise, with the possible exception of Cuba, Costa Rica enjoys the best federal health care coverage in the Western Hemisphere and has one of the highest life-expectancy averages (seventy-four years) and one of the lowest infant mortality rates in Latin America.[1]

Remarkably, Costa Rica has no military. Abolished in 1948 under the reform platforms of José Figueres, the government converted army fortresses into museums and freed federal funds for other endeavors—a stance that has been warmly supported by the people of Costa Rica. The country does, however, maintain active national police units (the Civil and Rural Guards), and nine government agencies control their own security forces. Some units receive military training, but there is no central command structure to enable them to assert undue influence over civilian society, as is frequently the case elsewhere in Latin America. Moreover, the head of the units is appointed by each new president every four years (with constitutionally prohibited reelections), further precluding the chance for military *caudillos* to establish a power base. Echoing the sentiment of many who call Costa Rica the "Switzerland of Central America," Gabriel Ureña has suggested that militarism ("that political plague of other countries in Latin America") could not prosper here where "law, peace, and a respect for human dignity are sacred precepts."[2]

Pertinent to this work, of course, is the fact that Costa Rica has developed one of the most complex systems of protecting natural areas in all of Latin America. And protecting wildlands means protecting species that Costa Rica has in incredible abundance. Flying, roaming, or swimming through the country are 850 species of birds, 220 species of reptiles, 160 species of amphibians, 280 species of mammals (almost half of which are different species of bats), and 130 species of freshwater fishes. Even more impressive is the diversity within the plant kingdom. There are approximately 9,000 species of vascular plants (4 percent of the world's total), of which 1,200 are different species of orchids and 1,200 are different species of hardwood trees. In some places the trees grow at a density of 200 or more species per acre.[3] The number of insect species is another story. Already numbered in the tens of thousands, research entomologists continue to discover thousands of previously unidentified species from the tree canopies of Costa Rica's many tropical forests.

The National Biodiversity Institute (see Chapter 12) is working to inventory Costa Rica's biological species. Insect collectors were bringing in some 100,000 specimens a month in 1990 when the director asked that they try to restrain themselves![4] What makes this biological information of such interest is that the high speciation occurs in so small an area. Costa Rica, a country of only 19,600 square miles (just smaller than West Virginia), is only 250 miles long and 150 miles wide at its widest point (see Figure 1). Yet the number of plant and animal species there is greater than that of the United States and Canada combined.

Costa Rica's phenomenon in biodiversity can be explained in large part by the country's unique geological history. Formed during the Pliocene (only three to four million years ago), an uplift united a small archi-

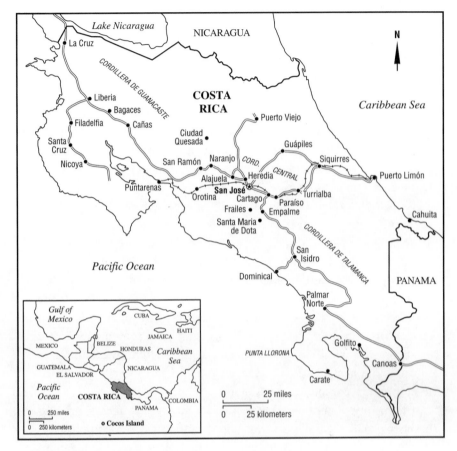

Figure 1. The Republic of Costa Rica (map by Johnson Cartographics, Edmonton, Alberta)

pelago to become a land bridge between North and South America. Costa Rica is located in the middle of this region, which geographer Carolyn Hall refers to as the only place in the world that is "both interoceanic and intercontinental." Noted Swiss biologist Henri Pittier, who studied and worked in Costa Rica in the late nineteenth and early twentieth centuries, was one of the first scientists to discern that such a meeting point allowed the free transfer of species from north to south. The transcontinental meeting point, then, greatly enriched the flora and fauna of the isthmus, an accepted theory referred to by another scientist as being that of a "biological bridge [and] filter." [5]

But the abrupt variations in topography and climate played an even greater role in species diversification in Costa Rica. What Hall has called a "great complexity of surface land forms" includes three distinct mountain ranges (the Central, Guanacaste, and Talamanca cordilleras), which climb up to 6,000 feet elevation, and five major natural areas (Central Valley, Northern Wet Caribbean, Dry Pacific, Southern Wet Pacific, and Southern Wet Caribbean). Hall explains that the different "microclimates" that developed in each region produced "an ecological diversity peculiar to the world's tropical, mountainous regions" where elevation bears greater responsibility than latitude for "rapid and qualitatively different environmental changes."[6]

Leslie R. Holdridge, an internationally respected forestry biologist who spent much of his adult life in Costa Rica, developed in the 1960s and 1970s a bioclimatic classification system of life zone ecologies for his adopted country. He identified twelve distinct life zones in Costa Rica (e.g., tropical dry forest, montane wet forest, etc.) based on temperature, rainfall, evaporation, humidity, and elevation. That these different life zones occur in such close proximity to each other in such a small area creates what has been termed a "biogeographical combination" or a "complex ecological mosaic" of species diversification. In evolutionary terms, a "riot of adaptations" occurred as plants and animals specialized to fit into such complex environments.[7]

The history of another species in Costa Rica, *Homo sapiens*, has also been shaped by the unique biogeography of the area. Dense tropical forests and steep mountainous terrain prevented a large pre-Columbian indigenous population from thriving in the area that is today Costa Rica. The exact number of native people who lived there prior to the European encounter is a topic of considerable academic contention. Estimates ranging from 27,000 to 400,000 are debated by anthropologists and historians, but one of the most respected authorities on the subject argues that an approximate figure of 80,000 reflects the most realistic precolonial population.[8] The population disparity received much attention in 1992 when Costa Rican president Rafael Calderón visited Spain and, in a press conference there, stated that Costa Ricans were proud of their Spanish heritage since so few Indians lived in the area at the time of European contact. The gaffe was picked up by the press. Native peoples and others were outraged in Costa Rica, but Calderón later complained that his statements were taken out of context.[9]

Whatever population figure is correct, the native people of Costa Rica were also a result of the isthmian land bridge—"descendants of the Meso-American and South American cultures who maintained inter-cultural contact," according to anthropologist Luis Tenorio. And scholars tend to agree that the population was sustainable to its tropical environment. "Sustainable," however, does not mean without any environmental impact. Archaeologists have shown that most forested parts of Costa Rica, including remote areas once thought to be primary forest, were burned for clearing by pre-Columbian peoples. The native population today is around 36,500—far less than in other parts of Central America—but the Indians share the country with approximately 3,000,000 other residents.[10]

Spaniards in the sixteenth century were not all that impressed with Costa Rica. Christopher Columbus may have thought the coastal areas scenically beautiful and held high hopes that riches there were awaiting his arrival (hence his naming of the area—Rich Coast), but gold and other minerals were not to be found in significant quantities and the humid, thickly forested terrain did not seem hospitable to early explorers and settlers coming from Spain's more temperate and dry regions like Castile and Extremadura. Hence, during the colonial era Costa Rica evolved quite differently than many other areas of the Spanish world. Far away, and not easily accessible from the *audiencia* (provincial) capital at Guatemala City, Costa Rica had little early agricultural development and, therefore, European settlement made less impact on the natural environment. Jean Carriere suggests that "because Costa Rica was a relatively poor, isolated and thinly populated corner of the Spanish Empire, the loss of forest cover associated with European settlement was limited." Carolyn Hall points out that only a few thousand Spaniards ever settled in Costa Rica between 1502 and 1821 but that the "poorest Spanish colony became the most prosperous republic."[11] Again, this unique feature of Costa Rica's past was largely due to its environment.

By the 1830s Costa Ricans discovered that the soil and climate of the volcanic montane region of Costa Rica's central valley was ideally suited for the production of coffee. At the same time, there was a growing world demand for the beverage that seemed to stimulate workers in industrial occupations. Hence, through the efforts of an English merchant named William LeLecheur (who introduced Costa Rican coffee to Great

Britain in 1843), a strong European market became well established for the new commodity. But coffee in Costa Rica is a unique example of how a developing agricultural product did not necessarily impair the environmental well-being of the countryside. While Carriere has referred to the coffee industry as Costa Rica's "first wave of deforestation," he also shows how most of the country remained under forest cover until the 1950s. Another study credits Costa Rica's "coffee monoculture" as being "a rare exception to the general rule of monocultures producing a dependent, stale economy and subsequent under-development. Coffee cultivation in mid-1800s Costa Rica established a social climate that encouraged strong development of natural sciences."[12]

Costa Rica accomplished such a feat by opening up trade patterns with a European market previously closed due to Spain's mandate for colonies to trade solely with the mother nation. This provided the stimulus for scientists to travel to Costa Rica to study its unique geography and later to instruct Costa Ricans about the more scientific end of their natural resources.

Equally important is the fact that most Costa Rican coffee growers farmed on small, family-owned *cafeteras* and were comparatively responsible land stewards as opposed to the elite landholders who practiced large-scale plantation monoculture (the *latifundista* experience typical in much of the rest of Latin America). Early twentieth-century tropical researchers Amelia and Philip Calvert observed that "the number of small landowners and coffee growers in Costa Rica is very great"—a "great advantage . . . in contrast with the conditions prevailing in the larger countries of that part of the world." They went on to explain that "where many own small pieces of ground, a much greater interest in the prosperous development of community and of peaceful progress exists than where there are only a few great landowners and the great mass of the population, having nothing to lose, are more indifferent and more easily drawn in the wake of political adventures." A middle class thus emerged that not only valued the land but established the base for a stable democracy that would force fewer pressures upon the natural environment.[13]

As Hall has suggested, Costa Rican agriculturalists soon discovered that their country's "large number of life zones" allowed the cultivation of "a much wider range of crops than would otherwise be possible at this latitude."[14] Bananas, Costa Rica's next agricultural boom, and other crops of the twentieth century, however, were not as friendly to the environment. But a basis was established for creating an environmental awareness by the very geographic makeup of the country. A cyclical pattern evolved: the geography that made Costa Rica unique led at first to the development of a different kind of agricultural society—one based on relatively small landholdings. Eventually, as agricultural conditions and international markets dictated, more and more forested land was turned into croplands, plantations, and pastures. This dangerous exploitation of natural resources, however, aroused a dormant ecological awareness in many Costa Ricans to address the need to protect what remained of the nation's natural heritage. Problems and solutions of this environmental model are examined below, but whether via its cultivated lands or its conservation areas, Costa Rica remains today a green republic—a country lush in tropical verdure and well established in environmental policy making.

An Overview of the Costa Rican National Park Experience

The words "model," "example," "beacon," "showcase," "prototype," "the ideal," and "wave of the future" have all been used repeatedly to describe Costa Rica's national park system. The descriptions are used to refer to the parks' diversity, number, size, management plans, beauty, and quickness in being established. The *United Nations List of National Parks and Equivalent Reserves*, by the International Union for the Conservation of Nature, listed no national parks or protected areas in Costa Rica as of 1970. Six short years later, however, a U.N. Food and Agricultural Organization study called *A Manual for National Parks Planning* referred to Costa Rica as a model on how to preserve natural areas and on how to create master plans to protect flora and fauna. By 1980 Costa Rica had more protected areas and more personnel working on conservation issues than any other Central American nation. Today it has a greater percentage of land designated as national parks or reserves than the United States, which would have to have an equivalent park system the size of Texas and Oklahoma to match Costa Rica's (see Figure 2).[15]

The figures today speak for themselves: 28 percent of Costa Rica is designated as legally protected land (11 percent in national parks, 4 percent in indigenous reserves, and 13 percent divided among biological re-

National Parks	Forest Reserves	Zonas Protectoras	Indigenous Reserves
1. Santa Rosa	29. Volcán Arenal	47. Maravillas	73. Matambu
2. Guanacaste	30. Taboga	48. Tenorio	74. Guatuso
3. Rincón de la Vieja	31. Cordillera Central	49. Arenal	75. Quitirrisí
4. Palo Verde	32. Matina	50. San Ramón	76. Zapatón
5. Barra Honda	33. Río Macho	51. Juan Castro Blanco	77. Barbilla-Dantas
6. Braulio Carrillo	34. Los Santos	52. El Chayote	78. Chirripó
7. Volcán Poás	35. Golfo Dulce	53. La Selva	79. Tayni
8. Irazú	36. Grecia	54. Acuíferos de	80. Telire
9. Tortuguero		Guácimo	81. Cocles
10. Chirripó	**National Wildlife**	55. Río Grande	82. Talamanca
11. La Amistad	**Refuges**	56. Cerros Atenas	83. Ugarrás-Salitre-
12. Cahuita		57. Tivives	Cabagre
13. Ballena	37. Isla Bolaños	58. Cerros de	84. Boruca-Térraba
14. Corcovado	38. Tamarindo	Turrubares	85. Coto Brus Guaymí
15. Isla del Coco	39. Ostional	59. El Rodeo	86. Osa Guaymí
16. Las Baulas	40. Curú	60. Cerros de Escazú	87. Abrojos-Montezuma
17. Manuel Antonio	41. Peñas Blancas	61. Río Tiribí	Guaymí
18. Guayabo (Nat. Mon.)	42. Barra del Colorado	62. Cerros de la	88. Conte Burica Guaymí
92. Bosque Diná	43. Tapantí	Carpintera	
94. Arena	44. Gandoca-	63. Cerros Caraigres	**Other Areas**
	Manzanillo	64. La Cangreja	
Biological Reserves	45. Golfito	65. Cerro Nava	89. Robert and
	46. Caño Negro	66. Río Pacuare	Catherine Wilson
19. Carara		67. Barbila	Botanical Garden
20. Hitoy-Cerere		68. Cuenca del Río Tuis	90. Junquillal Recreation
21. Cabo Blanco		69. Río Navarro/Río	Area
22. Isla del Caño		Sombrero	91. Horizontes
23. Marenco (private)		70. Río Banano	Experimental Station
24. Monteverde (private)		71. Tortuguero	93. Bosque Eterno de los
25. Lomas de Barbudal		Biological Corridor	Niños (private)
26. Islas Negritos		72. Las Tablas	
27. Isla Guayabo			
28. Isla de Pájaros			

Key to Figure 2.   (For a complete map of indigenous reserves, see page 210.)

serves, national forests, national monuments, and national wildlife refuges) (see Table 1).[16]

The Costa Rican park system is managed by SINAC (National System of Conservation Areas), a division of MINAE (Ministry of Environment and Energy). The protected areas are divided into three management types. Type I is "strict" protection (national parks, biological reserves, national monuments, natural reserves, and wildlife refuges) with these objectives: "to preserve species [and] to reduce human intervention in environments and ecological processes." These areas also include archaeological or historically significant sites (e.g., the prehistoric Indian ruins at Guayabo National Monument or the Filibuster War memorial at

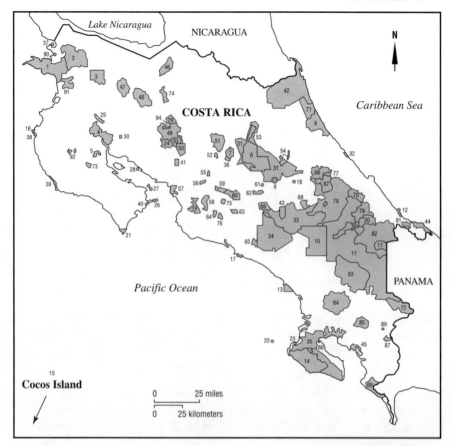

Figure 2. National Parks and Other Protected Areas of Costa Rica (adapted from Juan Diego López Ocampo and Rodolfo Meono Soto, *Guía verde de Costa Rica* [Alajuela, C.R.: Guías de Costa Rica, 1992])

Santa Rosa National Park). Over 11 percent of the total designated area is under this "strict" classification.

Type II includes forest reserves and protected zones whose objective is "partially to protect the biological diversity as they are open to exploitation of resources under certain conditions." They are managed for different degrees of multiple-use development (i.e., tourism, logging, etc.). They allow limited logging but were also established to protect important watersheds, wildlife, and forage. Type III consists of indigenous reserves for "the conservation of cultures and their environments and the protection of life systems in these communities and the way natural resources are used."[17] There are twenty-two Type III indigenous reserves.

Table 1.   Protected Areas in Costa Rica

Designation	No. of Acres	% of Total
1. National Parks	1,336,196	37.7
2. National Monuments*	3,624	.1
3. Wildlife Refuges	397,820	11.2
4. Biological Reserves	94,954	2.7
5. Forest Reserves	651,920	18.4
6. *Zonas protectoras***	426,730	12.0
7. *Humedales****	96,485	2.8
8. Indigenous Reserves	536,316	15.1
Total	3,544,045	100.0

*Includes two areas designated as "natural reserves."
**Protected watersheds, buffer zones, and biological corridors.
***State or provincially protected wetlands.
Source: SINAC records as of December 1995.

The Forestry Law of 1969 (and its various revisions since) outlines the differences in the designated protected areas. Article 74 legally defines "national parks" as "those regions or areas of historic importance that are set off by boundaries determined by executive decree and that for their scenic beauty or the national and international importance of their wildlife are to be set aside for the recreation and education of the public, for tourism, or for scientific research." National monuments are smaller areas (2,500 or fewer acres), have less diversity or less natural and historic value than national parks, or are areas protecting a specific resource. Biological reserves are "forest lands whose principal use is for conservation and research of wildlife and the ecosystems in which they exist." And national wildlife refuges are for "the protection, conservation, propagation, and management of wildlife species of flora and fauna."[18]

Some of the language in the Forestry Law reflected a utilitarian multiple-use perspective of conservation. The economic nature of Costa Rica's forest reserves (or national forests) is seen in Article 35-A of the 1990 revision, which defines them as "forests whose principal function is for the production of wood." Logging and recreation have been high management objectives. *Zonas protectoras* are defined as areas for "the protection of soil, regulation of hydrology, and conservation of watersheds." While these definitions are overtly economic in nature, one prominent conservationist acknowledges that the national forests are also the "lungs of the cities"—vital oxygen producers for so many aspects of the nation's health.[19]

The importance of the national parks (and other protected areas) is multidimensional. In the large sense, preserving the "natural and cultural heritage" of Costa Rica, as Mario Boza has identified the primary objectives of protected areas, seems like the obvious mission of the national parks. But in a country with such broad diversity of environments and life zones, and one so entrenched in agricultural and economic uses of the land, this is no small task. Costa Rica has responded to the challenge, however, by developing parks or preserves in all of its identified geographic zones (with the exception of the wet lowlands montane forest, which, according to Boza, has no representative natural or undeveloped areas remaining). The park service identified five management types of national parks to accomplish this goal: historical and archaeological, mountainous and volcanic, dryland forests, rainforests, and underground and submarine parks.[20]

The scientific value of this preservation system is probably immeasurable. Guanacaste and Santa Rosa national parks, for example, are the only large areas of protected tropical dry forests in the world. Poás Volcano is one of the world's few remaining active volcanoes with year-round access for scientific study. Likewise, maintaining as natural a state as possible for tropical plant and animal communities represents, as Luis Fournier put it, an "endless fountain of educational and research material for all age levels." It also is a "deposit of genetic material" that has scientific, medical, and economic potential. The genetic value of species protection in habitat protected by Costa Rica's parks and preserves (what Fournier refers to as "open-air laboratories") may keep the country in the scientific limelight for decades to come.[21] Furthermore, in the next fifty years these protected areas may be the only natural territories left in the entire country if development continues at its present rate. After a slide presentation on endangered tropical forests at a 1990 Legislative Assembly hearing to draft a new forestry law, Mario Boza (then vice minister of natural resources, energy, and mines) declared, "What you saw in the slides—the national parks—are what have saved any forests that are left at all."[22]

That Costa Ricans acknowledged this threat and acted quickly to save as much as they could in all of the representative geographic zones (save the one listed) exemplifies their awareness of the environmental welfare of the country and the foresight of many conservation-minded individuals. Their experience has also served as a regional model for an ecologically troubled Central America. Mario Boza and Rolando Mendoza wrote that "the subject of national parks is gaining in importance in other Central American countries due, to a certain extent, to the influence of Costa Rica." And former President Oscar Arias took the importance of the parks one step further to include a global responsibility: "Our system of national parks and wildlife areas protects individual ecosystems that are of vital importance not only for present and future generations of Costa Ricans, but for all humanity." [23]

Costa Rica's History of Conservation

Figure 3. Beach on the Caribbean at Cahuita National Park

A Legacy of Scientific Thought and Tropical Research

To those who with effort, caring and dedication from 1841 to 1941 established the basis for biological sciences in our homeland. May their labor be a permanent example for future generations.

Plaque at entrance of the
University of Costa Rica's School of Biology

Listed with the above message are the names of twenty-three professional biologists (some foreign and some Costa Rican) who have played a profound role in the conservation history of Costa Rica. Part of Costa Rica's uniqueness has been its historic ability to lure a significant number of foreign scientists and to establish a sound training system for local scientists to study and understand the nation's diverse natural history. Mario Boza, one of Costa Rica's leading conservationists, explained that "the diversity and wealth of Costa Rica's flora and fauna, as well as the majesty of its countryside, have attracted the attention of scientists and naturalists from all over the world since the mid-1800s."[1] The legacy of scientific investigation—indeed the drive to understand Costa Rica's biological uniqueness—was important in developing a national appreciation for conserving natural resources. Costa Rican biologist Luis Fournier acknowledged these links when he wrote that "Costa Rican ecological thought developed from the numerous observations about the country's natural history in the past century and early decades of this century by foreign and national naturalists."[2]

Tracing the history of interest in Costa Rican ecology and conservation goes back to the sixteenth century. Fernández de Oviedo, a Spanish naturalist who traveled to colonial Costa Rica in the 1700s, was one of the first to recognize the area's distinct biodiversity and warned against deforestation. But while there were other early decrees and proclamations for forest preservation and soil conservation in the 1770s and 1830s, there was not a base of support for conservation issues in Costa Rica until the final decades of the nineteenth century.

Largely ignored by the colonial government, Costa Rica by the time of independence was one of the poorest and least developed areas of the United Provinces of Central America. After separating from the federation, Costa Rica never had the wherewithal or the population to support higher education. There was virtually no national scientific or professional training. Charles Stansifer shows that by 1845 Costa Rica had no bookstores, hospitals, universities (elementary education was only marginal), research or scientific organizations, or even theaters. He goes on to say that the few scientifically trained persons in Costa Rica at this time were either Guatemalans, Nicaraguans, or Costa Ricans who had studied at foreign schools. A study by Luis Gómez and Jay Savage claims that European naturalists were at first more interested in studying the more geologically wealthy regions of Mexico and Peru because of world fascination with gold and silver. Clearly, Costa Rica's early national years were characterized by what the noted Costa Rican biologist Rafael Lucas Rodríguez has called a "slow development of modest and utilitarian understanding of Nature."[3]

Two events outside of Costa Rica, however, reversed forever the scientific community's disinterest in Costa Rica's tropical ecology: international demand for coffee and speculation of a trans-isthmus canal in lower Central America. Not only did the railroads, built to transport coffee beans to port, open up many unexplored areas of the country, but the coffee trade with Europe brought many foreigners to Costa Rica. Some were scientists who, because of sociopolitical repression and scientific stagnation in their home countries, were excited by the prospect of marketing their services in a new area and by the adventure of visiting a poorly understood biological region. One German scientist who visited Costa Rica in the early 1850s explained that Germany at that time was divided into competitive regional states governed by "reactionary police regime[s]." Thus for many professional researchers, the Americas "seemed like the place to go." Schools and fine arts developed more quickly with the advent of foreigners, triggering more communication and travel between Europe and Costa Rica. News of the country's vast diversity sparked interest for European naturalists to visit, and "those who came usually stayed."[4]

Toward the end of the nineteenth century, when a growing commercial interest emerged for constructing a Central American canal to connect the Atlantic with the Pacific, attention focused on Nicaragua, Costa Rica, and the Colombian province of Panama. Scientists were drawn to the region to investigate canal site possibilities. Two German naturalists, Moritz Wagner and Karl Scherzer, became enchanted with Costa Rica and stayed to research its natural history. According to one historian of the subject, their writings (especially *Die Republik Costa Rica*) "probably did more to draw European scientists [to Costa Rica] than any other work."[5]

One such scientist who followed was the Danish botanist Anders Sandre Øersted, who was the first to publish a detailed description of Costa Rican plants. Others were William More Gabb (from Great Britain), who studied Costa Rican geology, paleontology, and zoology; and Joseph Warscewicz (from Lithuania), who studied horticulture and ornithology and was the first to send bird collections to the most respected natural history museums of the time in Berlin and London. In the 1880s F. Ducane Godman and Osbert Salvin studied in Costa Rica and published their *Biologia Centrali-Americana,* one of the most complete biological works about the region up to that date. The German geologist and naturalist Karl Sapper also conducted investigations in Costa Rica, and the American ornithologist George N. Lawrence was the first to catalogue Costa Rican birds, listing 511 species—two-thirds of all Costa Rican bird species known today. The research of these scientists inspired even greater interest in Costa Rica abroad.

Two other German scholars who went to Costa Rica in the mid-1800s were more influential in the legacy of tropical research. Alexander von Frantzius and Carl Hoffman, both medical doctors, landed in Costa Rica somewhat by chance. Von Frantzius had been advised to move to the tropics to improve his health and Hoffman was intrigued by the adventure of exploring mountains. They both practiced medicine in Costa Rica and in their spare time climbed Poás and Irazú volcanoes, coming to know the ecologies of both mountains intimately and producing major collections of their flora and fauna. Historian Carlos Meléndez claims that these two German scientists initiated a prodigious era of the study of Costa Rican science.[6]

Alexander von Frantzius was the first scientist to catalogue Costa Rican mammals. He also wrote extensively on the native tropical plant life and through his botanical explorations and publications "made Costa Rica known to the scholarly world." He also produced the first academic work on Costa Rican climatology. Carl Hoffman, although far less published than von Frantzius (he only published three important articles on volcanoes), did become known for his taxonomy of Costa Rican plant and animal species (of which twelve bear his name today) and also sent impressive collections to Berlin. Hoffman served as an army surgeon for the Costa Rican forces in the battle against American filibuster William Walker in 1856. While in Guanacaste province in northwestern Costa Rica, he noted the unusual diversity of bats, which he collected and studied. His work in this area became the first scientific research of bats in Costa Rica.

Bringing new information to the scientific community, however, was not von Frantzius' most pronounced mark on Costa Rican ecological research; teaching natural history to Costa Ricans was. Later in life, von Frantzius opened a pharmacy, the back room of which was used as a laboratory and meeting place for students. Three such Costa Rican students, José Zeledón, Anastasio Alfaro, and J. F. Tristán (known as the "drugstore gang"), became close assistants, accomplished biologists, and early leaders in the effort to research tropical issues and educate others.

An important step in Costa Rica's favor—and a move that was unwittingly conservationist—was the government's spirited attempt in the mid-nineteenth century to improve the educational system. The University of Santo Tomás was founded in 1844 as a way to attract scholars and to educate professionals. But lacking enough local teachers and scientists, the government decided to recruit European educators to teach Costa Ricans.[7] The administrations of Jesús Jiménez and Tomás Guardia in the 1860s and 1870s invited many German and Swiss teachers. Many foreigners who came, however, left after short stays when they discovered that they were expected to spend more time teaching than doing research. One who stayed was Helmuth Polakowski, who became an expert in tropical botany.

The University of Santo Tomás was abolished in 1888 by President

Bernardo Soto. His influential and politically powerful minister of public instruction, Mauro Fernández, believed that no university could succeed without a strong secondary school system in place. He was actively involved in starting the challenging school Liceo de Costa Rica, changing education by making it sponsored by the state instead of by the church, enacting legislation to make education compulsory to the seventh grade, opening up high schools to women, and beginning an even stronger push to attract foreign teachers. Several more Swiss scholars accepted the challenge. One, Henri Pittier, was another individual who was destined to change the course of the country's biological thought and to begin what has been called the "golden age of Costa Rican natural history." Described as "determined, indefatigable and tyrannical," Henri Pittier had a bold "multidisciplinary approach to field biology." To acquaint himself seriously with the country, he climbed every volcano more than once, lived with different indigenous peoples, and collected as many specimens as he could to "amass a body of information unsurpassed to that date." He was intrigued and captivated by Costa Rica's biodiversity, calling the country the "botanical and zoological emporium of the continent."[8]

Pittier branched out from the confines of his own research to organize the National Agricultural Society and to create the National Observatory. He also recruited many other scientists to study in Costa Rica and with their help developed the largest herbarium in Latin America at the time. More important, he founded and succeeded in acquiring government funding for the Physical Geographic Institute (IFG, called the National Geographic Institute after 1914). This institute, soon to become one of the leaders of its kind in Latin America, was in charge of collecting biological data, managing the herbarium, recording all meteorological information, researching national agricultural problems, and, perhaps most important, accurately mapping the republic. All of these successes, unheard of in much of the rest of Latin America, created a national base to encourage scientific thought and to spur others to pursue research topics in Costa Rican natural history.[9]

Disagreeing with the government's 1904 decision to place the IFG under the auspices of the National Museum, Pittier moved to the United States and accepted employment with the U.S. Department of Agriculture. Capable scientists like Adolphe Tonduz, Carlos Wirklé, and George

Cherrie carried on Pittier's work in Costa Rica, and Anastasio Alfaro (one of von Frantzius' "drugstore gang") became the director of the museum and the IFG.

The National Museum, then, became the focus for scientific research. Alfaro, only twenty-two years old at the time he was appointed director, had the able help of José Zeledón. Zeledón was sent to study at the Smithsonian Institution in Washington, D.C., and established important liaisons with American scientists.

With these connections, the floodgates were now open for U.S. researchers to start pouring in to Costa Rica—a flow that never waned. Some of these biologists included Edward Cope and Edward Taylor in herpetology, and Philip and Amelia Calvert in entomology. The Calverts, who were primarily interested in studying the life histories of tropical dragonflies, traveled around Costa Rica for a year (May 1909 to May 1910) and ended up writing a comprehensive field biology study entitled *A Year of Costa Rican Natural History.* Concerned about what "transformations" in the land would occur in Costa Rica due to the Panama Canal (influx of people, more transportation, etc.), the Calverts wrote that the book's mission was to "leave for the future a picture of what the past contained." To do so, they studied with and received valuable local assistance from such scientists as Adolphe Tonduz, Henri Pittier, J. F. Tristán, C. H. Lankester, and José Zeledón and acknowledged the "liberal and enlightened Costa Rican government" for its recognition of the importance of studying tropical sciences. The government's attitude, coupled with Costa Rica's "high mountains, rushing rivers, great variety of climate and of natural products," they wrote, made "such wonderful inducements for naturalists and entomologists."[10] Swiss biologist Paul Biolley also made important contributions in entomology and malacology in these years. By 1914 Costa Rica had become the center of scientific research in tropical America.

Attracted to such a place in the 1930s was American botanist (and later ornithologist) Alexander Skutch. Skutch arrived in Costa Rica to extend his dissertation research on the leaves of banana plants but ended up staying for the next sixty years. In that time he homesteaded a small farm in El General Valley, meticulously studied the life histories of a variety of tropical birds, and researched many different plants. His work resulted in over 200 journal articles and a dozen books on topics ranging from ornithology and botany to tropical conservation and philosophy. Summing up why he and many others in his field were so enchanted with Costa Rica, and why he stayed for so many years, Skutch wrote that "in the mid-1930s Costa Rica was still largely unspoiled. Its population of less than half a million people was concentrated in the narrow Meseta Central. . . . Other advantages . . . were its political stability and the friendliness of its people. . . . Thus the naturalist working in some remote spot was not likely to have his studies suddenly interrupted or his thin lines of communication cut by a violent upheaval, as has happened to many in Latin America."[11]

Without a university or even an agricultural school (until 1926) to support professional research efforts, however, the period from the 1920s to the 1950s witnessed a decline in Costa Rican scientific study. Because field research was viewed by many as a pastime for the eccentric or the rich, few Costa Ricans became involved. An attempt in the 1920s to re-open a university hindered rather than helped these efforts because of a lack of trained faculty in the biological sciences. When the University of Costa Rica was finally established in the 1940s, the National Museum was placed under its direction; as a result of poor management, many of the specimen collections of earlier scientists were ruined.

Despite these setbacks, progress occurred with the establishment of the National School of Agriculture in 1926. Staffed with people like José Orozco (a sylviculturist who urged forest protection), José Arias (who developed an early conservation plan), and Rafael Chavarría (a conservationist-minded director), the school became instrumental in teaching farmers the proper use of controlled burning, prevention of erosion, and other soil conservation techniques. Luis Fournier writes that the School of Agriculture went on to play "a great role in helping form conservationist thought." One instructor there, Enrique Jiménez (educated in Belgium), taught with an awareness of environmental problems, later became Costa Rica's secretary of agriculture, and was instrumental in the passage of the Ley de Quemas (a law regulating controlled burns) to protect the forests.[12]

Progress also occurred in the 1930s and 1940s through the work of two exceptionally bright Costa Rican scientists: Alberto Manuel Brenes Mora and Clodomiro Picado Twight. Brenes, from San Ramón and educated at the Liceo de Costa Rica and at universities in Paris, Lausanne, and Geneva, became one of the country's most noted botanists. From 1902 to 1948 he was an active instructor at various San José schools and was an avid specimen collector. He discovered and wrote on many new species of plants and came to specialize in orchids. The Brenesia orchid was named in his honor by European taxonomists. He ended his long academic career as head of the National Museum's botanical section, maintaining a herbarium with thousands of specimens. Picado, educated at the Sorbonne, returned to his homeland to concentrate on the study of Costa Rican natural resources. He published hundreds of scientific articles, pioneered research on bromeliads, and wrote *The Poisonous Snakes of Costa Rica.* He has been called the "first Costa Rican academic biologist."[13] Unfortunately, Picado died at an early age in 1944 and never lived to be a part of the University of Costa Rica (UCR). His statue, however, graces the front lawn of the School of Biology at UCR as an inspiration to future biologists.

But while Picado conducted independent research and efforts of the National School of Agriculture centered primarily on conservationist farming practices, a professional outlet for scientific study and a center to train others in tropical research was still lacking. This changed in the 1950s with the expansion of UCR. In the early fifties Antonio Balli (an Italian biologist) and Rafael Lucas Rodríguez Caballero (a Costa Rican educated at the University of California) organized the biology department at UCR. Rodríguez, whom Luis Fournier has called a man with "great vision for the future," published a forward-looking work on areas in Costa Rica that he believed required protection.[14] He was also instrumental in working to have the biology department changed to become the School of Biology, a separate division at the university, in 1955. A full-time staff of professional biologists was hired, and Archie F. Carr, a herpetologist at the University of Florida, designed the curriculum. Carr spent years studying and lobbying for the protection of the green sea turtle (*Chelonia mydas*) that lays eggs on Costa Rica's northeast coast. The School of Biology became one of the best of its kind in Central America and has served as a springboard for research into tropical studies for Costa Rican and other Latin American students. It was dedicated to Dr. Rodríguez in 1979. A national wildlife refuge, established in Guanacaste province in 1977, also bears his name.

Another influential faculty member of UCR's School of Biology was Alexander Skutch, who taught there for many years. Increasingly over time, Skutch's beliefs in natural history and ecological harmony evolved into conservation advocacy. He decried how man "covers larger areas with his highways and constructions, destroys thriving forests to make cultivated fields and pastures for his beef cattle, contributes to the spread of deserts by over-exploiting arid lands, and poisons seas with his wastes." [15]

For Skutch, the study of natural history, tropical ecology, and conservation complemented his beliefs in ajimsa yoga regarding the sanctity of all life and the preservation of a harmonious balance of nature. According to Fournier, this "very special philosophy toward nature, of great significance from a conservationist point of view, without doubt influenced the [conservation] movement in Costa Rica." [16]

The University of Costa Rica is important in Costa Rica's conservation history in other ways. The National School of Agriculture (changed to the School of Agronomy) became a division of UCR and continued its instruction of conservation values. The Costa Rican zoologist Alvaro Wille (educated at the University of Kansas) developed the entomology section there, which likewise has become a valued, regional center for tropical issues. [17] UCR's law school also became actively involved in environmental policy through its Center for the Study of National Problems.

The momentum continued with the development of organizations promoting conservation issues in Costa Rica. In 1942 the Inter American Institute for Agricultural Sciences (IICA) was founded in Turrialba by the Organization of American States (OAS). It specialized in training individuals in agricultural sciences, forest conservation, and wildlife management. In 1972 the institute's board members voted to end affiliation with the OAS and to form an independent research and training organization with the new name CATIE—Centro Agronómico Tropical de Investigación y Enseñanza (Tropical Agronomical Research and Higher Education Center). It is headquartered in a campuslike facility with modern laboratories, classrooms, and library just outside of the city of Turrialba. CATIE has sponsored a wide variety of tropical agricultural programs over the years and has attracted a great number of national and international scientists and students to study sustainable tropical agronomy and forestry.

Dr. Leslie Holdridge, one of the early and most instrumental leaders at CATIE, was an instructor there for many years. He believed in rainforest preservation and later purchased a heavily forested tract of land ("La Selva") in the north-central part of the country that he used for more intensive study of tropical lowland systems. Moving to CATIE in 1952 to study under Holdridge's direction and to earn his master's degree in science was a Venezuelan graduate student named Gerardo Budowski. Budowski, who went on to Yale to pursue a doctorate in forestry, has used his knowledge of tropical ecosystems to promote conservation both in his adopted country of Costa Rica and in a variety of positions abroad. He became a CATIE instructor and later its director general, a scientist at UNESCO in Paris (where he organized the 1968 World Biosphere Conference), and for six years was the director general of the International Union for the Conservation of Nature (IUCN) in Switzerland. He is currently on the international board of trustees of the World Wildlife Fund, president of the World Ecotourism Society, director of natural resources at the University for Peace in Costa Rica, and still maintains ties with his "beloved" CATIE as senior advisor to the director general.[18]

In 1966 CATIE initiated a course on national parks and wildlife under the direction of Dr. Kenton Miller, a biologist from the United States who likewise came to appreciate very deeply Costa Rica's tropical environment and potential for conservation. He taught there for several years and later became an international authority on national park development. One of his CATIE students in the late 1960s was a Costa Rican named Mario Boza, who went on to spearhead the country's national park program. Boza had recently graduated from UCR with a degree in agronomy and had wanted to study teakwood production at CATIE.

Heeding the advice of his instructor Gerardo Budowksi, however, he got involved with Kenton Miller's national parks course, wrote a master's thesis on the development and management of a national park at Poás Volcano, and has been in the forefront of Costa Rica's conservation program ever since. He became the nation's first director of its fledgling national park service, natural resources advisor to President Rodrigo Carazo, university professor, founder and director of the conservation organization Fundación de Parques Nacionales, author of several books on Costa Rica's national parks, assistant director of the Ministry of Natural Resources, and currently is head of the Mesoamerican Biological Corridor Foundation, whose aim is to link conservation areas throughout Central America.

Through people like Leslie Holdridge, Gerardo Budowski, and Mario Boza, CATIE has actively influenced the scientific and conservation leadership of Costa Rica for over five decades and has had an impact on conservation in other tropical countries. In 1982 Craig McFarland, CATIE's director of the Wildlife and Watershed Program, conducted a survey to inventory the conservation strategies of other Third World nations (i.e., their national parks, provincial or state parks, national forests, biological reserves, watershed conservation, management plans, legislation, finances) to serve as a base data pool to improve CATIE's ability to understand the conservation needs in other nations.[19] Likewise, the center continues to attract many foreign students each year.

There have been other private sources of conservation in Costa Rica that have played large roles in the country's legacy of scientific thought. In the early 1950s American Quakers from Alabama, fleeing a militaristic U.S. government involved with the Korean conflict, were attracted to Costa Rica because of its abolition of the army and looked for a place to settle. They chose an area near Monteverde in north-central Costa Rica to practice low-technology agriculture and dairy farming. Much of the surrounding area had been deforested by local farmers, but the Quakers, under the leadership of Wilford Guindon, recognized the need to preserve forests on the mountainsides to protect the region's important watersheds. To that end they established an 800-acre reserve in a pristine montane environment that abutted their farms. Today the area is part of the Monteverde Cloud Forest Preserve, which protects habitat for many endangered species, including the well known resplendent quetzal (*Pharomacrus mocinno*).

In 1959 Archie Carr was influential in helping to found the Brotherhood of the Green Turtle and its subsidiary, the Caribbean Conservation Corporation (CCC), the first nongovernmental conservation organization in Costa Rica. Because of uncontrolled commercial turtle and turtle egg hunting, numbers of the giant reptiles had dropped to dangerously low levels and were threatened with extinction. Carr understood the urgency of the situation and the CCC set out to research the ecology of the turtle and to advocate protection of its most important nesting habitat at Tortuguero (meaning "place of the turtle") on Costa Rica's northern Caribbean coast. The organization's work culminated with the establishment of a protected area for turtles in 1970 that was enlarged into a national park (with carefully monitored visitation policies) in 1975. It continues to research, track, and count green turtle populations and has branched out into other regional conservation campaigns.

Dr. Carr's sons, Archie III and David—both of whom have spent considerable time conducting research on tropical conservation in Costa

Rica—are now at the helm of the CCC. They, along with Mario Boza and James Barborak (a U.S. biologist who started coming to Costa Rica in the 1970s as a conservation consultant) are leading the efforts of the Mesoamerican Biological Corridor, also known as the Paseo Pantera, or "Path of the Panther," project. A joint effort with Wildlife Conservation International (a division of the New York Zoological Society), it seeks to halt the fragmentation of biologically diverse habitats in a 1,500-mile greenbelt ranging from southern Mexico to Panama. Working to connect conservation areas with ecosystem corridors, however, also provides protection for important watersheds in the region—vital sources for water and flood control for thousands of Central Americans.[20]

Another organization, the Tropical Science Center (TSC), has also played an active role in Costa Rican conservation. TSC is a private consulting firm that was established in 1962 by three American biologists—Leslie Holdridge, Robert Hunter (a forester and land-use specialist), and Joseph Tosi (an agricultural scientist). TSC has assisted the IICA (CATIE) with many projects, developed a biological station at Rincón de Osa, organized conferences and training sessions, and worked for the creation of private biological reserves for field research and education.

TSC has left its largest mark in Costa Rican conservation history through its efforts to preserve the Monteverde Cloud Forest Preserve. TSC's connection to the Quakers' watershed conservation program stems from the work in the early 1970s of an ornithology graduate student from the United States named George Powell and his scientist wife Harriet Powell. The Powells were conducting dissertation research on birds of the Tilarán Mountains where they were "astounded" by the "extraordinary biological richness of the cloud forest" and "alarmed" by the threat posed to the area by hunters, land speculators, and squatters. In 1972 George Powell approached TSC for advice on establishing a nonprofit association to enable him to apply for and receive grants for purchasing and protecting the area. "We were immediately interested," Tosi explains, and after visits with Powell to the area "we were in agreement that the area warranted full protection." Over the next few years Powell and TSC set up the fund, received hundreds of thousands of dollars from international conservation organizations to acquire the land, and expanded the area into a 10,000-acre preserve. TSC became its managing agent and Powell served several years as its director.[21]

Today the Monteverde Preserve is one of the best-known parks in

Costa Rica. With the help of TSC and its offspring organization, the Monteverde Conservation League (in Canada), the preserve is now over 27,000 acres and continues to expand. Expansion has meant that squatters who moved onto the land to farm in the 1970s and 1980s had to move. The Monteverde Conservation League and the World Wildlife Fund raised funds to help offset the cost of relocating and resettling them by "selling" tracts of land to donors for twenty-five dollars an acre.[22]

In the early 1980s a TSC study group created a recommendation for Costa Rica's National Park Service to develop the Tilarán Mountain area into a national park that would include the Monteverde Preserve. While this recommendation was denied in 1981 due to "a lack of money to pay the numerous occupants" and landholders in the region, it remains a private nature reserve and open to the public. In 1995 over 50,000 people visited Monteverde despite the slow, rough mountain roads leading there. Plans to improve the roads were discussed but abandoned by TSC as a measure to limit tourist access and prevent overburdening the fragile mountain environment. Dr. Tosi boasts that Monteverde remains today as "one of the most efficient, well organized, and exemplary private reserves of its kind in the world." Its relatively small area is home to more than 2,500 species of plants, 100 species of mammals, 120 species of reptiles and amphibians, 400 species of birds, and tens of thousands of insect species.[23]

A spin-off of the Monteverde conservation strategy was the establishment of the Children's Rain Forest Preserve. Adjacent to Monteverde, this protected area is the result of a Swedish teacher's efforts to save unprotected areas surrounding the preserve that she observed were seriously threatened when she visited the site in the late 1980s. She returned to Sweden with these concerns and enlisted the help of her nine-year-old students. They started a fundraising drive to purchase thirty-five acres next to the preserve. The idea soon spread to other parts of Sweden and Europe, Great Britain, Canada, the United States, and Japan. Through the efforts of schoolchildren across the world, then, more than 17,500 acres are now protected and similar measures have started in other parts of the world. Joseph Franke has written that the program's success is "an example of how important conservation ideas often start small but have far-reaching effects."[24]

By the early 1960s research and instruction on tropical ecology were increasing in the United States. Scholars from six leading universities in this field (Michigan, Florida, Miami, Kansas, Harvard, and Washington) saw the need to consolidate efforts to develop a research field station in the tropics. Costa Rica was chosen as the site because of the number and proximity of its geographic zones, its broad biological diversity, and its politically stable government. In 1963 the consortium of these schools plus UCR formed the Organization for Tropical Studies (OTS). Its mission was "to provide leadership in education, research, and the wise use of natural resources in the tropics.[25]

The OTS has been accused of suffering from so-called "scientific imperialism" in its early years of existence. This "big stick" or "missionary" attitude was manifest in the fact that some U.S. and European scientists went to Costa Rica to show the locals what to do and how to perform research in their own country. Soon, however, OTS personnel learned to cooperate with the host government and have since included Costa Rican and other Latin American students and instructors in all research endeavors. Over the years more than 700 papers have been generated by OTS research, and many ecologists trained there have gone on to work for conservation issues or have become teachers themselves. It has been said that "almost every major figure in tropical biology today" has been associated with the OTS.[26]

These OTS instructors and students have made a profound impact on the conservation history of Costa Rica and other tropical places. Early OTS directors who had an innovative environmental vision for tropical education were Norman Scott and Donald Stone. Daniel Janzen, one of the first OTS students and later an instructor there, moved to Costa Rica and has spent much of his life researching and working to protect the tropical dry forest environment in Guanacaste. Another shining example of an OTS product is Rodrigo Gámez, a plant virologist, former molecular biology professor at UCR, and past natural resources advisor to President Oscar Arias. Gámez, an OTS board member in the early 1990s and currently director of Costa Rica's National Biodiversity Institute, stated, "My association with the OTS helped open my eyes to the importance of biological diversity, particularly for a country like Costa Rica. From trying to figure out what all those *gringos* [were] doing down there, many Costa Ricans have developed a greater appreciation of the nation's biological wealth. The OTS has played a crucial role in providing credibility for conservation."[27]

A big boost to the organization occurred in 1968 when Leslie Holdridge sold his property known as "La Selva" to the OTS. La Selva was an island in an area subjected to increasing timber and cattle pressures near Puerto Viejo in northeastern Costa Rica. It became the OTS's biological station and center of tropical research. While only four and a half square miles in size, La Selva has half as many species as all of California, including 320 species of trees, 394 species of birds, 143 species of butterflies, 122 species of reptiles and amphibians, 104 species of mammals, and 42 species of fishes.[28]

In the 1980s La Selva was expanded to border Braulio Carillo National Park (the combination of which has been identified by UNESCO as a World Biosphere Reserve). The expansion ensured the seasonal migration of species within the different parts of the ecosystem, an activity that was being seriously threatened by increased logging and cattle grazing in the region. Along with international conservation and philanthropic organizations, the OTS actively participated in the campaign for the expansion, which resulted in the creation of a *zona protectora* by the Costa Rican government. Rodrigo Gámez stressed the importance of such a zone when he wrote, "We cannot put fences around the parks and reserves and forget about what happens outside them."[29]

The creation of the *zona protectora* attracted even more local and international scientists to La Selva. Research usage increased fourfold, with the number of individual researchers there increasing by 257 percent in just six years. Laboratory and lodging facilities expanded, and by 1990 an average of twenty researchers a day were studying at La Selva. Fully half of all OTS usage is by Costa Rican biologists and students, and Costa Ricans are on the staff of every OTS project. Likewise, the OTS has provided its services to its host country on many occasions. In 1983, for example, Harvard biologist Charles Schnell sponsored an OTS biological inventorying project for the newly created Chirripó National Park.[30]

The OTS maintains two other biological field stations besides the one at La Selva. One is in Guanacaste near Palo Verde National Park and is used by biologists studying tropical wetlands ecology. The other is at Las Cruces, Coto Brus (near the village of San Vito)—a tropical forest setting in extreme southern Costa Rica. Las Cruces was started by Florida horticulturists Robert and Catherine Wilson, who moved to Costa Rica in 1963 to try their luck in tea and coffee farming. When those ventures did not pan out, the Wilsons decided to start a botanical garden as a way of leaving a tropical legacy for future generations to enjoy. After a series of setbacks and failures and having nearly exhausted their own financial resources, they looked to the emerging OTS for help. In 1973 they donated the twenty-five-acre botanical garden to the OTS, but Robert Wilson maintained control of it. Darryl Cole-Christensen, a resident of the area at the time, explained that "the first years of OTS custody were characterized by apparent failure of the garden. Everywhere there was evidence of collapse, greenhouses literally falling down, weed encroachment . . . every evidence of the imminent end of the dream."[31]

But the Wilsons and OTS continued their work and turned the garden into a successful venture, "a fine achievement of tenacity and commitment," as Cole-Christensen related. Due to Robert Wilson's failing health, the OTS assumed full maintenance of the garden in 1986. Surrounded by a 342-acre forest reserve, it has since served as a center for botanical, agro-ecological, and horticultural research and is used for scientific training and public education. Regional plant species that are threatened with habitat loss and extinction are preserved there for future reforestation projects. Besides tropical palms, bromeliads, ferns, heliconias, marantas, and many other plants, the Wilson Garden is home to hundreds of species of birds and other animals. Trails through the rain forest are also open to visitors. It is managed today by biologists and long-time proponents of Costa Rican conservation efforts Luis Diego Gómez and Gail Hewson.[32]

Today the OTS, as a whole, is a consortium of fifty-two U.S. and Costa Rican universities. The mutual advantages of its being located in Costa Rica were summed up by current OTS co-director David Clark: "The most important of OTS' experiences . . . is the long history of positive relations it has enjoyed with its host country . . . from the ease in which research permits can be obtained to the willingness of talented Costa Rican biologists to collaborate in joint projects. . . . For its part, Costa Rica has benefited ecologically, educationally, and scientifically from the relationship."[33]

Other important figures in Costa Rican conservation history emerged in the 1960s and 1970s. Biologists like Luis Fournier, Sergio Salas, Gary Stiles, W. L. Ramírez, and Alexander Bonilla all represent part of the result of Costa Rica's scientific legacy. Others advocated conservation and changes in policies by becoming involved in government agencies. Scientists like Mario Boza, Rodrigo Zeledón, Carlos Quesada, Alvaro Ugalde, Rolando Mendoza, and Tobías Ocampo are among those who represent Costa Rica's emphasis on science. Much of the work of these scientists was financed through CONICIT (Consejo Nacional de Investigaciones Científicas y Tecnológicas), which is similar to the National Science Foundation in the United States. Established by the government in 1973, CONICIT has assisted scientists by funding both large- and small-scale programs. The government's support of CONICIT is another reflection of the nation's understanding of the importance of scientific inquiry.

While the percentage of Costa Ricans who are scientists is small (and of those, the percentage of field biologists even smaller—which is typical of most, if not all, countries of the world), interest is there, numbers are growing, and a strong educational system is in place to foster scientific thought and conservationist policies well into the future. The Gómez and Savage study concludes that Costa Rica now has a cadre of biologists whose orientations have been shaped by the new theoretical ecology, the ecological movement, and the stimulus of the OTS. Through their efforts, Costa Rica has a solid scientific base in its CONICIT, its universities, and the National Museum.[34]

Knowing as much as possible about the natural environment, how ecosystems are interrelated, and how they affect humans (as well as how we affect nature) is the key to understanding why and how to protect it. The beginning of this understanding, notes Gerardo Budowski, was the country's physical geography itself—"forests and volcanoes" and later "a friendly, democratic republic" that made Costa Rica an enticing destination for foreign scientists.[35] Calling it the "sweat equity donated by hundreds of scientists and volunteers," a 1995 report summed up this sentiment: "When conducting experiments, donor agencies and scientists want to reduce risks and variables. Costa Rica has the advantage. . . . Conservation is hard enough under the best of circumstances. Who wouldn't choose to work in a country where there is an abundance of habitats, experts, laboratories, libraries, institutions, and communications facilities that can contribute to the success of a project? Perhaps more important, one can start a lengthy project here, work in relative security, and know that a coup, famine, or government expropriation won't rub out years of data."[36] But if the number of Costa Ricans with advanced degrees in the biological sciences is small, the number of Costa Ricans who support conservation is large. Most may not actively lobby for ecological issues, but many do support the causes that will preserve their natural heritage. This support is rooted in the legacy of Costa Rica's emphasis on tropical science and is manifested in society today.

2 *The Environmental Problem*

From the beginning of humanity, man has maintained a close contact
with nature and has obtained from it the necessary resources for
his subsistence.

Luis Fournier Origgi, *Recursos naturales*

The Historical Setting of Deforestation

The point at which dependence on the natural environment becomes
exploitation of the natural environment is the problem addressed in this
chapter. Today a large percentage of Costa Rica is deforested and suffers
from erosion and habitat loss for many species of flora and fauna, including a large number of endemic species (ones native to that area and
not found elsewhere). Exactly how this scenario unfolded deserves careful, historical study to understand the dilemma and Costa Rica's responses to it.

Costa Rica's unique geography forged a distinct land-use pattern for
native people and European settlers. Some anthropologists have argued
that indigenous people who inhabited Costa Rica for at least 10,000 years
before the arrival of Spaniards did little to deteriorate the natural environment.[1] Indians recognized the areas where not much would grow and
did little to alter that land's condition. In fact, Indians primarily developed agriculture in only four of Costa Rica's twelve life zones and limited
cultivation to such local crops as yuca (manioc), chilies, tomatoes, beans,

corn, avocados, *pejibayes,* and other native fruits and vegetables. Likewise, they fished, hunted native animals, and gathered wild fruits and nuts. Carolyn Hall explains that "Indians exploited the natural environment while simultaneously conserving its potential resources."[2]

In order to conserve, the Indians learned resource management techniques. They cleared forests by burning small parcels (a practice referred to as swidden agriculture) and, to guard against erosion during the rainy season, seeded the areas with various plants to provide a permanent cover. Their small, stable population necessitated subsistence farming only—producing enough food for the family or basic community units. One study that compared archaeological evidence to present-day indigenous activities concludes that "it might seem like a paradox that we consider the Indians as conservers of their environment because it was precisely from their system that we inherited the custom of burning terrain and even the practice of hunting, fishing, and gathering, or in other words, a production economy that is also extractive and exploitative."[3]

The Spanish agricultural experience in Costa Rica, however, was exploitative in a different way. Early settlers not only gathered and cultivated native products but soon introduced such European commodities as sugar cane, citrus fruits, cereal grains, and livestock—what Carolyn Hall terms "ecological colonialism" and Alfred Crosby calls "the Europeanization" of the flora and fauna. Crosby includes Costa Rica in his list of "NeoEuropes" that were characterized by "biological expansion" or "ecological imperialism" in colonized parts of the world. Put in another way, as a different study suggests, the Europeanization process can be defined as "an amalgam of what they [the settlers] discovered, what they introduced, and what they fashioned for themselves."[4]

Because the colonizers considered Indian ways inferior (less productive) to European agriculture, they initiated a slow, continuous deforestation process. The lands became dedicated to livestock grazing and to the cultivation of introduced crops, which disrupted the indigenous way of life in those regions. The comparatively few resident Indians in Costa Rica were not used as slaves nearly to the extent that they were in the more mineral-rich parts of the Spanish New World. Instead, they were pushed out of areas the European settlers wanted, or captured and sold as slaves for other parts of the Spanish Empire. Their "empirical knowledge of ecologically appropriate" agriculture, as Hall has described it, was ignored by whites and relegated to the small group of Indians isolated from colonial settlements.[5]

Environmental impact during the colonial era, however, remained limited due to Costa Rica's relative isolation and low population. While colonial farming practices were inappropriate for tropical environments, the crops produced were foodstuffs for a small colonial population at home or tobacco and cacao for local and regional markets. Early colonial agriculture (limited to the Central Valley) had relatively little impact on the land.

Everything changed in the late 1830s when coffee was found to thrive in some of Costa Rica's climatic zones. Many thousands of acres in sloped, cool terrain were cleared for coffee cultivation. What developed for Costa Rica was an agricultural export commodity with subsequent growth ramifications. The emergence of a coffee elite class meant that large landholders dominated the coffee industry and an agro-export oligarchy of merchant elites controlled the trade of coffee to foreign markets. Both groups came to dominate politics competitively and advocated increased production. Unlike many parts of newly independent Latin America, however, this trade was controlled by local Costa Ricans and not by foreign interests. As demand increased, the elite were motivated to turn more and more acres of previously undisturbed forest into coffee fields. Since 1845 (the beginning of the coffee trade with Great Britain), the government of Costa Rica provided further incentives for these efforts through lucrative tax breaks to the growers. For more than forty years thereafter coffee was virtually Costa Rica's only export product.

But in Costa Rica an incipient conservation awareness was already starting to emerge. Not all farms were large landholdings, but small or large, as Luis Fournier notes, the scale of agricultural deforestation in those years had "little marked effect on the environment." The Spanish and Costa Rican growers had "enough ecological sense to settle in regions where the soil and climate were sufficiently satisfactory for agricultural activities."[6]

Likewise there were early calls for conservation. As far back as 1775 the Spanish governor of Costa Rica, Juan Fernández de Bobadilla, issued a proclamation to discourage controlled burns on the basis that too much land was being cleared and causing soil sterility. In 1833 and 1846 there were decrees regarding forest preservation (the latter pertaining to forest cover near cities). In 1888 a decree to protect watershed areas in mountains was announced, and by the early twentieth century there were calls for a national forestry code. Hunting laws were enacted by 1853 as a means to conserve wildlife. And, very important, a further deterrent to environmental degradation was Costa Rica's low population, which in the early years of statehood was less than one person per square mile.[7]

On the other hand, the advent of the banana industry toward the end of the nineteenth century and first few decades of the twentieth signaled an even greater agro-export phenomenon with greater environmental consequences. Unlike coffee, banana plants grow in low, humid zones, can be harvested year round, and are less susceptible to yield variations. For these reasons, and because there was a robust market in the relatively nearby United States, bananas were introduced into Costa Rica's Caribbean lowlands in the late 1870s. They thrived there and came to dominate the agricultural landscape of lowland Costa Rica.

A major difference between the two industries is that banana production requires a large, capital-intensive labor and transportation infrastructure. This discouraged small farmers from entering the banana business and opened the door to foreign multinational corporations. Such was the case in Costa Rica, where the United Fruit Company came to monopolize the banana scene. Boston businessman Minor C. Keith completed the International Railroad of Central America and helped found United Fruit in 1898 as a means of bringing bananas to a rapidly growing U.S. market. But because absentee landowners have significantly less contact with the land and are more interested in a good return on their investment than in ecologically sensible agriculture, the banana industry became damaging to the Costa Rican environment.

Banana growers (*bananeros*) practiced continual forest removal to raise banana plants since a banana field's productive life is limited to seven years. More destructive were Sigatoka and Panama disease (caused by the soil fungus *Fusarium oxysporum*), which rendered banana fields infertile and caused the *bananeros* to clear more forest for plantations. The diseases forced United Fruit to abandon most of its Caribbean lowland banana fields by 1940 and move operations to the Pacific Coast near the town of Golfito. United Fruit records show that from 1900 to 1965, nearly 185,000 acres of forest were cleared for bananas. From 1966 to 1990, however, the pace of deforestation greatly quickened with estimates as high as 153,000 acres *a year*—representing up to 11 percent of Costa Rica's annual deforestation. Some 96,000 acres (10 percent of which was primary forest) were cleared for banana plants in the six-year period from 1986 to 1992 alone.[8]

Clearing land for banana fields, however, is only part of the banana deforestation picture. Where before there were cart roads, railroads—on the Atlantic side by 1890 and on the Pacific side by 1930—were constructed to haul bananas to port and opened up new areas to developers. Cattle ranches were needed to feed the growing number of plantation workers. And when plantations were abandoned, like the ones near Limón by 1940 and near Golfito by the early 1980s, banana workers flocked to the countryside to settle, farm, and eke out a living in the forest. A study by William Holliday concludes that with the impact of these infrastructure and social developments, deforestation due to banana expansion accounted for up to 20 percent of Costa Rica's total annual deforestation rate.[9]

Other agricultural changes starting in the 1950s (referred to as the "era of transformation") hastened deforestation in Costa Rica.[10] Up until this point, the "dessert crops" (coffee, bananas, and to a lesser extent sugar, cacao, and tobacco) dominated agro-export production. The postwar world economy, however, affected Costa Rican production. European and North American demand for Costa Rica's products fell after World War II because other tropical regions, such as Africa and Southeast Asia, began vigorously competing on the world market. In the late 1940s and early 1950s African palm trees were introduced in Costa Rica on former banana plantation land. The trees were planted to begin a palm oil industry (for the manufacture of margarine and other products) and as a way to diversify the agricultural economy. Like bananas, this exotic species thrived but required capital-intensive management.

Likewise, the sharp decline in world coffee prices in 1958 affected development patterns. Coffee, long Costa Rica's sole means of economic leverage in the world import-export arena, nevertheless was always vulnerable to demand and at the mercy of foreign land speculators and financiers. The government responded with its program of *desarrollo hacia adentro* (internal development) to promote manufacturing and encourage other agricultural industries to develop in Costa Rica.[11]

One commodity that emerged in the 1960s and 1970s was cattle. Since the colonial years when Spanish settlers introduced domestic livestock to the Central Valley, cattle have thrived on the lush valley grasses and have supplied beef for local markets. In 1855 Carl Hoffman described how the valley was "perfect for cattle." The "superabundant meadows, eternally green, fresh, and maintained by the cool temperatures and daily showers," he wrote, were the ideal "natural conditions [that] have given to industrious men [the means] to establish a great cattle business."[12]

The cattle business, however, remained limited to providing beef for local and regional consumption until the 1970s. Then an exponentially growing North American market, strongly rooted in the need to supply fast-food restaurant chains with hamburger due to a sharp shortage of cheap cuts in the United States, encouraged Central American countries to expand ranching interests. Costa Rican farmers, ranchers, and speculators leapt at the opportunity, especially after discovering that the Asian zebu breed of cattle was so well adapted to the terrain and climate of Costa Rica. One of the oldest living species, the zebu (with the easily recognizable hump between its shoulders and large, floppy ears) has lived for millions of years in India and is considered to be the most widely distributed breed of cattle on earth today. In a 1969 article, the San José newspaper *La Prensa Libre* explained to its readers why they were seeing such dramatic increases in the number of zebu around the country. Calling it the "ideal bovine for the tropics," the article related how zebu have great resistance to tropical diseases, are able to move their flexible skin to shake off pesky insects and to eliminate excess heat (unlike European breeds), and can easily graze on steep slopes. That zebu are not susceptible to hoof and mouth disease made U.S. import approval possible and gave meat dealers the green light to wholesale the beef to the hamburger chains.[13]

Zebu cattle seemed to be a perfect match for Costa Rica and by 1986 the country was the top beef producer in Central America—89 million tons, of which 36 million tons were exported. Ninety-six percent went to the United States, which received more beef from Costa Rica than from any other Central American country. In the late 1970s the U.S. Department of Agriculture policy on fixed quotas allowed for a staggering 9.8 percent of all imported beef to be from relatively tiny Costa Rica.[14] Cattle raisers there worked hard to meet the annual challenge.

By the 1980s, however, this "volatile dependence" on the United States, as Susan Place explained it, became hostage to a "fluctuating market" and to the whims of the U.S. Congress, which established and changed (lowered) these import quotas. The emphasis on exporting beef triggered a variety of social and environmental consequences. One was the significant drop in locally consumed beef. Simply stated, there was less meat available due to the push to raise cattle for export. Local prices for dairy products and beef subsequently climbed, which lowered the overall standard of living for the nation. To illustrate the dilemma, the scarcity of local beef was especially noted by the McDonald's hamburger chain in Costa Rica, which in 1977 had to import 140,000 pounds of meat a month from Guatemala.[15]

The powerful Cámara de Ganaderos (Cattlemen's Trade Association) lobby was extremely influential in gaining and maintaining governmental support for export production. The government provided such generous tax and credit incentives to ranchers that many dairy farmers switched to raising zebu for beef. The number of cattle raised in Costa Rica tripled in three decades: from 607,850 head in 1950 to 2,050,350 head in 1985.[16]

This kind of cattle industry requires massive amounts of pasture. Not exactly a prairie republic, Costa Rica had to create pastureland through systematic deforestation efforts. By 1980 over 6,500 square miles, or about one-third of the country, had been converted to pasture. More important, according to land use capability (LUC) studies, only 9 percent of Costa Rica is ecologically fit for pastureland. Julio Calvo, a forester at Costa Rica's Institute of Technology, argues that this land is "suffering from erosion and loss of productivity owing to inappropriate management." Geographer George Guess suggests that because of erosion, Costa Rican pastureland "works towards its own obsolescence with tragic efficiency." LUC studies have identified 54 percent of the damaged land as land that could have been used for annual crops.[17]

More alarming than these figures for pastureland is the rate of forest loss. Costa Rica in the 1980s was losing 4 percent of its forested land a year—a rate that was higher than elsewhere in the Western Hemisphere, despite the more publicized information on deforestation from the Brazilian Amazon. (El Salvador, Haiti, and Cuba have even less percentage of remaining forest cover, but because not much forest is left, the rate of deforestation has slowed in those countries.) Former Costa Rican president and Nobel Peace Prize winner Oscar Arias admitted that "we deplore the sad leadership we possess in destroying our forests. No country in Latin America has a higher rate of deforestation than ours; less than five

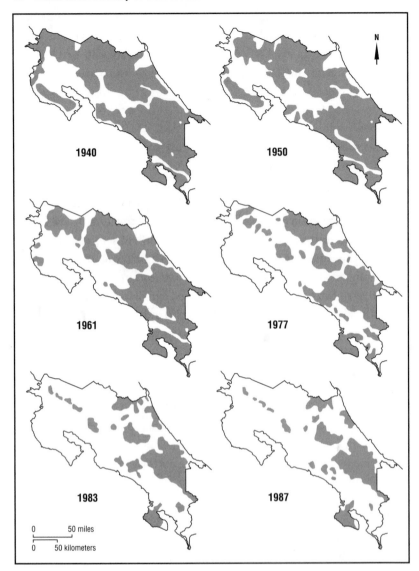

Figure 4.   Costa Rican Deforestation over Time (shaded areas represent forest cover) (*source:* Fundación Neotrópica)

percent of the nation's dense forests exist outside protected areas." As late as 1950, 90 percent of the country remained in forest cover, but by 1990 the figure had dropped to only 25 percent (see Figure 4). In turn, 17 percent of Costa Rica's land was degraded, with an estimated 680 million tons of topsoil a year being washed away.[18]

While much of this loss was due to expansion of agriculture and pas-
turelands, which increased by 250 percent from 1950 to 1984, the timber
industry is also responsible for massive deforestation. In fact, it was the
timber industry that first opened up many forests for agricultural development by constructing roads into previously inaccessible areas and
clearing land for fields. By the late 1980s there were 17,000 miles of roads
in Costa Rica, more than in any other Central American nation.[19] What
B. E. Lemus calls the "forest industrial complex" is big-business timber-
ing, most of which occurs on private land. However, because of imprecise
surveying efforts, poorly delineated boundaries, and underbudgeted enforcement measures, logging (and the resultant pasturing) has occurred
inside protected areas as well. And instead of using a plan of selective
cuttings in forest reserves, timber companies have been clearcutting large
tracts of densely forested areas for short-term economic rewards. Two-
thirds of all harvested timber is consumed as fuel and much is wasted, as
Carolyn Hall points out, due to "deficiency of extractive methods and
the lack of industries to use the poorer quality wood." Such waste and
nonsustainable harvests are fast resulting in a situation that some fear
could make Costa Rica have to import wood for domestic use by the
year 2000.[20]

Along the roads made to haul timber out of the backcountry came
squatters—poor settlers called *precaristas* (literally, those in a precarious
situation, living on the edge)—looking for land to farm and a way to feed
their families in newly deforested areas. Colonizing farmlands in the
tropical forests by such people was nothing new in Costa Rica. In the
1930s Alexander Skutch observed squatters moving into the El General
Valley who were "eager to take possession of as much land as [they] could
for this sort of agriculture." The squatters, he wrote, were "obliged by law
to clear and plant at least half [their] area" and during each dry season
"renewed [their] attack upon the dwindling forest." He reminisced that
"January and February were the chief months when the woods were
levelled. . . . Before they felled the tall trees, the laborers cleared away all
the underbrush with their machetes. This made the forest parklike and
most inviting. . . . Soon the big trees were attacked and overthrown, the
noble forest reduced to a scene of chaos and ruin."[21]

The *precaristas* of the 1960s, 1970s, and 1980s practiced similar agricultural techniques, although most used fire instead of an ax to clear the
forest. The colonizers came out of the interior of the country and mi-

grated toward the coasts. In 1961 the Law of Lands and Colonization (similar to the Homestead Act in the United States and discussed in more detail in Chapter 3) was enacted. It established the Institute on Lands and Colonization (ITCO) to aid the *precaristas* and imposed sanctions on landowners retaining uncultivated acres. ITCO encouraged migration in the early 1960s to "improve" virgin "farm" land. But while the majority of *precaristas* squatted on land designated as farm areas, they did not settle solely on private land. The conservation organization Fundación Neotrópica reported that a staggering 25 percent of federally protected land was invaded at one time or another. Cropland and cattle pastures were established before the government could react and, in many cases, before it even knew. Likewise, some *precaristas*—without permission from the landowners—occupied and attempted to farm plantation land belonging to foreign owners.[22]

By the 1980s, colonization was becoming a significant economic, sociological, and environmental problem. Some estimates suggested that one-sixth of all Costa Rican families were *precaristas*.[23] Making a long-term, better living for their families, however, in many cases did not materialize. Cleared land and supplies were bought on credit. Interest rates and principal became difficult to pay when prices and demand for agricultural commodities dwindled. Price policies set far from where the *campesinos* worked dictated production needs without the squatters' knowledge or ability to change crops. An even greater setback was erosion. Crops could be grown for only three to five years, after which many peasant families were forced to sell out to large real estate firms which, in turn, sold the land to ranchers for use as pasture. Intensive grazing made the land suitable for only four to six years more before rendering it completely degraded. Meanwhile, the *precaristas* searched for and moved to new frontiers, renewing the destructive cycle.

To be fair to the squatters, it is important to note that not all research shows *precarismo* to have had a negative impact. Beatriz Villareal maintains that in 1973 (near the height of the *precarista* period) the squatters represented only 8 percent of the rural population. Daniel Janzen has argued that "squatters have never been a problem on government or private land under conspicuous use" and that at Guanacaste National Park (a preserve that Janzen was instrumental in establishing) squatters would only take marginal land. Likewise the OTS in 1984 began an environmental education program for squatters living near its La Selva biological station that was aimed at "treating them as friends and neighbors and not as invaders." A similar approach was used at Monteverde. There the World Wildlife Fund and the Canadian-based Monteverde Conservation League sold tracts of land to *precaristas* for twenty-five dollars an acre to help them relocate away from endangered tropical rainforests.[24]

Overall, the impact of deforestation an Costa Rica is indeed multifaceted. There is not only the obvious loss of trees and therefore timber, but also the loss of wildlife habitat (especially of threatened and endangered species), scenic value, and watersheds. Deforestation also results in river silting (caused by erosion on cleared lands), disruption of fisheries and traditional fishing grounds, abnormal flood-drought cycles, riverbank erosion, heavy soil compaction (from cattle), and soil sterility that often leads to complete desertification of the area. An important 1972 study on the subject explained the desertification process by showing how forest areas that were cleared and not allowed to recover "never reached the climax stage [of succession]." The clearing caused a "reduction in organic matter and nitrogen removal of the original vegetation exposing the soil to full sunlight and to receive the full impact of rainfall." In turn, surface temperatures rose and humidity fell. If the area was burned, the deterioration process was magnified.[25]

The Agricultural Dilemma

Costa Rica's past experiences with land use have led to a late-twentieth-century agricultural dilemma. The problem teeters between agro-development (for short-term economic prosperity) and environmental conservation (for long-term protection of natural resources). The noted Latin American economist Raúl Prebisch refers to this dilemma as a "technical ambivalence" in which increased productivity has made an "enormous contribution to human welfare . . . but at the same time has had serious consequences for the biosphere."[26]

In addition to the negative environmental effects, deforestation in Costa Rica has caused serious economic problems. The decrease in watersheds meant a reduction in hydroelectric generating capability, thereby limiting the flow of electricity and reducing employment opportunities in some sectors of the economy. Soil sterility and overgrazed pastures have led to an overall loss of potential economic opportunities from sustainable agriculture. The problem was grounded in a widespread belief in abundance theory—a lack of acknowledgment of a renewable resource problem. The theory was defined by one study as that pattern of thinking in the 1960s and 1970s based on the belief "that Costa Rica had more than enough resources and that no shortages would develop." In contrast to nineteenth-century agricultural patterns, many Ticos (what Costa Ricans fondly call themselves) in the last forty years have believed that "basically the entire country was suitable for agriculture and livestock and that forests were only impediments to development." Deforestation, then, was seen as an "improvement" to the land. But what Ticos thought might be a "giant step towards modernization," wrote geographer John Augelli, in reality became a "minimum of socially desirable and environmentally adaptive components [resulting in] painful social and ecological costs."[27]

A landmark study of the banana problem in the Sarapiquí region of northeastern Costa Rica defines the environmental transformation as a six-step process: economic opportunity due to market expansion (in this case, Europe); the purchase or governmental concession of land (including rainforest that is "promptly cut down"); the importation of workers (historically from the British West Indies, but more recently from Nicaragua); the release of a large percentage of the workforce when their service is no longer required; the workers' usually unsuccessful search for other employment (and thus their search for land on which to grow subsistence crops); and the resultant forest invasions, which cause more deforestation. "In this way," the authors conclude, "Costa Rica, one of the world's showcases of conservation, is currently promoting a policy that actually encourages rainforest destruction."[28]

The three major banana-producing multinational corporations (United Brands [Chiquita], Standard Fruit [Dole], and Bandeco [Del Monte]) plus several other producers have all been dependent on chemical pesticides for increased harvest yields. These yields, however, have been accompanied by environmental and public health disadvantages. In a study entitled "Effects of Banana Expansion on Human Health and the Ecological System," University of Costa Rica scientists Leonardo Mata and Alfonso Mata summed up the situation by writing that "an environmental and sanitary disaster generated by the banana plantations" was the result of the industry's "predominant interest in the economics, over the ecology," of the crop.[29] Standard Fruit, for example, was using the fungicide DBCP (dibromochloropropane) in the early 1970s until it caused sterility in 2,000 workers. Similarly, according to the Mata and Mata study, 76 percent of all pesticide poisoning claims at the National Insurance Institute were filed by banana plantation employees. And in a different report, S. A. Lewis disclosed that by 1992 Costa Rica's pesticide use was seven times the world's per capita average, resulting in 250 to 300 cases annually of pesticide poisoning involving agricultural workers. He called the expansion of banana plantations "a model of modern, unsustainable agriculture."[30]

Banana production has also been the source of other forms of pollution in Costa Rica. A well-publicized case in point was in the early 1980s when scientists discovered that Cahuita National Park (the country's first protected coral reef on the southern end of its Caribbean coastline) was suffering from sediment runoff from nearby banana plantations in the Estrella River Valley. A graduate student in biology named Jorge Cortés investigated the situation and ended up writing his master's thesis on the sediment runoff that was endangering the coral environment. Heavy concentrations of iron, lead, copper, and other metals were flowing down the streams from the banana plantations into the Caribbean and were building up on the fragile reef. Cortés, now a marine biologist specializing in coral reefs at the University of Costa Rica, claims his work on the Cahuita crisis was aimed at "creating an awareness" for the danger involved to the marine ecosystem. But while the Estrella River Valley plantations were penalized and instructed to stem their chemical runoffs, Cortés claims that, having conducted a follow-up study at Cahuita in the mid-1990s, the situation is "even worse" now with sediment buildup in the soil and mud.[31]

Many other cases of fertilizer and pesticide runoff from banana plantations—one form of nonpoint pollution—have been evidenced in Costa Rica. In 1992, for example, toxic nematicides from plantations near Tortuguero in Limón province were linked to a massive fish kill. A lagoon near Tortuguero was, as one newspaper proclaimed, "white with dead fish" floating in it. Even so, the minister of natural resources at the time, Hernán Bravo, claimed it was difficult to trace the exact origin since it was nonpoint contamination.[32]

Likewise, waste generated by the banana industry has been cause for concern. The Mata and Mata study found that 3.5 million tons of waste were produced annually by the plantations. An IUCN report claimed that 2.14 tons of waste, three-fourths of which is nonbiodegradable, are produced for every ton of bananas. Part of the mess has been due to the blue plastic bags used to protect bananas from the damaging rays of the sun. The bags were typically removed in the field, tossed into streams or canals, and carried off to the sea, adding to ocean pollution and endangering giant turtles and other marine life.[33] In 1992, under heavy pressure from local and international environmental groups that were threatening worldwide banana boycotts, a consortium of banana growers agreed to construct a recycling plant for the plastic bags (to be Costa Rica's largest recycling center), formed a Banana Ecology Commission, and started a "zero plastic" program. According to reporter Michelle Sheaff, it appeared as if the banana companies were "turning green." Corporación Bananera Nacional, for example, appointed prominent environmental activist Alexander Bonilla to its board of directors to oversee a reforestation plan in phased-out banana plantations. More important, the Rainforest Alliance and Fundación Ambio of Costa Rica joined together to develop the "ECO-O.K. Banana Project," which helps fruit growers meet a code of environmental conduct. The standards deal with how growers should avoid clearing rainforest for plantations, establish greenways of native vegetation along roads and rivers, control the use and storage of pesticides, and manage organic and plastic wastes. It's a voluntary program, but those who meet the standards are rewarded with an "ECO-O.K." seal of approval and can apply stickers directly to the certified bananas to promote their more ecologically friendly produce. One study found that Chiquita, the industry leader, has been "especially vigorous" in investing in "broad, costly changes . . . to benefit the environment." It concluded that the program is "an example of what biologists and conservationists can accomplish by venturing into what was once considered enemy territory—in this case banana company boardrooms." And Jorge Cortés noted that the problem with blue bag pollution has definitely improved.[34]

The dilemma with Costa Rica's banana industry is both environmental and social. Some plantation owners say they are working to reforest their lands. Cortés claims none have done so. The owners claim to bring in thousands of jobs to the country, but bringing more people in can be part of the problem. Luis Fournier notes that importing seasonal workers is a huge "demographic problem" and is Costa Rica's foremost environmental challenge for the twenty-first century. He cites as evidence the large influx of Nicaraguan laborers seeking work on banana plantations and the pressures on the environment and public services that have resulted.[35]

Not all conservationists agree. Alexander Bonilla claims that workers have to have employment and a place to live before they can ever begin to think about conserving resources, although he adds that they should be encouraged to learn sustainable agricultural methods. Likewise, environmental attorney Roxana Salazar believes that the banana workers do not represent "an ecological problem" and notes that recent immigration legislation is working to address the problem.[36] The immigrant workforce is in part due to the fact that most Costa Ricans refuse to do that kind of hard work for such low pay.

But perhaps the problem has a wider base. Hardly limiting the blame to the government of Costa Rica or the large corporate plantations, John Vandermeer and Ivette Perfecto assert that the "same biologists, ecologists, and eco-tourists who love the rain forest when they're in Costa Rica also love to slice bananas on their cereal in the morning." They suggest that with the "penchant for viewing the world in isolated little disconnected fragments, it is apparently difficult for us all to see the connection between the knife that slices the banana in our cereal and the chainsaw that slices tree trunks onto the rain forest floor."[37]

And while cattle production at one point seemed to offer economic salvation, it instead added to Costa Rica's agricultural dilemma. It lowered the per-acre output of production, eliminated other crops, and increased the amount of food to be imported for local consumption. An estimated 96,000 to 192,000 acres are taken out of crop use annually for the cattle industry. Most of the conversion has been for short-term value and has had heavy environmental consequences—part of Costa Rica's struggle to confront an economic reality. When farmlands became ranchlands, displaced peasants were not absorbed into the cattle workforce. Coffee production requires 130 working days per hectare per year (rice sixty and beans thirty-seven), but cattle require only six. Advances in agricultural technology also translated into less need for field hands. With so little work to be found in the country (and what work there was paid poorly), thousands of *precaristas* had no other choice than to return to San José or other cities—the completion of the colonization cycle. Twenty-five percent of the rural population of 150,000 became classified as "landless workers/farmers"—the highest percentage in Central America. Hence, a development contradiction emerged in the late

1970s when 90.3 percent of all land in production (reduced to 82 percent by 1985) for the cattle industry was accounting for only 12 percent of total agricultural exports and a small percentage of the GNP.[38]

Those kinds of statistics prompted geographers and economists to conclude that the beef boom was actually "underdeveloping" the Costa Rican economy, increasing tensions among the people, and creating social and economic problems. They pointed out how the cattle industry had displaced a sustainable harvest of timber—resulting in a $4.68 million net loss in the economy from potentially marketable hardwood trees. The cattle industry had become a "drag on the economy" instead of its greatest motor and had concentrated the wealth into "landed elite" by squeezing out many small farmers.[39]

Agriculture, in general, cannot be ignored in Costa Rica. It is the nation's leading industry, and agricultural lands cover one-half of the country. Two-thirds of the national economy revolves around agriculture, with bananas as the top crop (occupying nearly 100,000 acres of lowlands and still controlled by foreign corporations), followed by coffee, sugar, and beef. Cacao is still an export crop but is raised primarily on small farms. Food crops like rice, corn, beans (the principal source of protein for most Costa Ricans), fruits (especially pineapples), vegetables, and palm oils are other secondary, but important, products. There are many small subsistence farms, but about three-fifths of all Costa Rican farms are either of medium size or *minifundias*—farms that grow subsistence crops and some export products. Large estates make up only 3 percent of Costa Rican agriculture. Cattle ranchers tend to take too much land out of more useful, sustainable production and, as one study notes, employ "few and enrich even fewer." Costa Rica has had limited success with land reform, but it has often not been compatible with the government's emphasis on agricultural development.[40]

Hopes to stimulate the economy in the 1970s and 1980s by producing more internationally marketable products—an economic theory known as "comparative advantage"—prompted more land to be cultivated. Thousands of acres were turned into citrus groves and ornamental plant fields. Visions of high yields necessitated the introduction of great quantities of chemical fertilizers and pesticides that the crops required. To cope with the debt crisis of the early 1980s, Costa Rica further accelerated these measures. The International Monetary Fund (IMF) insisted that Costa Rica produce more nontraditional crops like pineapples, flowers, and ornamental plants. These could be sold in an ever-growing world market to generate capital flow to help satisfy creditors. By the late 1980s the nontraditional crops accounted for 30 percent of all Costa Rican agro-exports.[41]

While international lending organizations considered this a success, Costa Rica was experiencing difficulties with comparative advantage. Major multinational corporations (e.g., Del Monte, United Brands, and Philip Morris) were controlling the growth of export products while not enough beans, rice, and corn were being planted to feed the nation. *"Frijoles sí, flores no"* ("Beans yes, flowers no") became the rallying cry for a 1987 *campesino* protest of these policies, led by farmer-activist Carlos Campos. Warning against an agrochemical "dependency," Campos wrote that "the reality is that we Costa Ricans are now dying, that we are destroying our soil, and from now on we should begin to demonstrate that, as farmers, it is necessary to present alternatives."[42]

From 1950 to the 1980s, then, Costa Rica sustained vast environmental damage from its agricultural development. It has been suggested that "Costa Rica was rapidly becoming a runaway train on a steep and curvy downhill grade" before policies started to change to preserve what environment was left.[43] Deforestation became a significant rallying call in the conservationist community, urging the government of Costa Rica to legislate against forest abuse. In the late 1960s the Ministry of Agriculture appointed a committee to study the problem and draft a bill that would enable the government to limit deforestation. The result was the Ley Forestal (Forestry Law) of 1969, which, in many ways, became the turning point in Costa Rican conservation history. The law (discussed further in Chapters 3 and 8) established a system to designate and administer protected areas, such as national parks and monuments, that would be off-limits to forestry and agriculture. It also established the General Forestry Directorate to regulate the timber industry and discourage unwise forestry practices.

The Forestry Law of 1969, however, hardly slowed deforestation outside protected areas. In the decade following the law's passage, Costa Rica experienced a 29 percent total forest loss.[44] Several authorities have tried to pinpoint how this could have happened. Luis Fournier blamed the lack of long-range planning, despite increased awareness of conservation needs. Carolyn Hall explained how the law was not actively enforced and how the permitting process was ineffective. Permits were to have been obtained by forest users from the DGF before any timber could be cut from private or public lands, but the new forestry agency lacked "the funds and trained personnel to enforce the law." While the DGF was supposed to have complete control over all timber cuts, it has been reported that by 1989 roughly one-half of all trees felled lacked the proper permits.[45]

Likewise, many thousands of trees were harvested in banned areas. Deforestation occurred in parks and on the perimeters of protected areas, which affected their overall environmental integrity. Because funds were scarce, as Bill Weinberg reported, insufficient vigilance near protected zones opened the way for "ranching, slash-and-burn *campesino* farming, high-pesticide corporate agriculture (such as banana plantations), or timber exploitation" on the borders of the parks and often extended into them. In 1971, only two years after the Forestry Law was enacted, forestry biologist Joseph Tosi of the Tropical Science Center issued what became a famous warning—that by 1985 there would be virtually no natural forests left in Costa Rica if the deforestation rates of the time continued. Luckily Tosi's predictions for forest loss did not completely materialize, but by 1987 Costa Rica was still losing 120,000 acres of forest a year.[46]

The bleakness of the above scenario has certainly tested Costa Rica's image as a "green republic." Fortunately, the scenario is being offset by changes occurring in Costa Rica. Squatter colonization persists but has declined dramatically since the mid-1970s. In 1977 the Reforestation Law was passed, which was the government's first attempt to restore degraded forest lands. The government repealed the tax on uncultivated farmland and established tax incentives, loan assistance, and technological help for reforestation efforts. It has been an expensive project that has not yet been totally successful on a nationwide basis, but it has great economic potential for providing a sustainable wood-products industry. One project near Turrialba called Programa de Diversificación has been successful in repopulating trees and employs the services of local small-scale foresters.[47]

Reforestation has many logical advantages. Lands that were formerly banana plantations, however, are especially slow to reforest or to produce much of anything else. Likewise, there are many thousands of reforested acres that have become plantations of single-tree species and therefore, as Hall relates, "insignificant in relation to the magnitude of the ecological problem they are intended to solve."[48] The most common plantation

Figure 5.   Hillside Deforestation near Turrialba

tree crop in Costa Rica is teakwood. Teak trees (*Tectona grandis*) are tall Asian timber trees that are an introduced species in Central America and thrive in Costa Rica's lowland tropical areas, especially on the Pacific Coast. Teakwood is a hard yellowish wood that in the past was often used in shipbuilding. It now enjoys a healthy world market for other wood products, especially in the increasingly wood-starved Far East. The problem is that thousands of acres of deforested land are being proclaimed "reforested" by the teak industry. Advertisements across the country hail such benefits as erosion control, soil conservation, and wildlife cover that teak plantations supposedly offer.

The plantations, however, are a far cry from the original forest cover. Teak trees are planted in symmetrical rows, grow at even heights, have weeded and well-groomed rows between them, and are felled at the same time when mature. The reforested plantations "help the soil for a while," forestry botanist Luis Fournier recently explained, "but eventually the soil deteriorates with more cuttings." The industry advertisements, he asserted, do not give the complete picture and are used to get more people (often foreigners) to invest.[49]

As powerful a problem as deforestation is in Costa Rica, in many ways it did help wake up a nation to its environmental responsibilities. The voices of many started to become louder for the more rational conservation of natural resources. Lobbying became intensive for the designation of more and more national parks and protected areas. Part of that solution meant that the government would have to take a more active position in legislating protection and funding enforcement. Recent steps have been taken to crack down on wilderness exploitation. The Rural Guard conducts spot checks for illegally cut logs (often hidden in produce trucks). At the urging of the DGF (and despite a great uproar from the timber industry), the government declared a state of emergency concerning the deforestation crisis in the late 1980s. Agencies can now suspend permits to cut trees outside of private plantations and can prohibit the export of unfinished wood products. Likewise, funds have been earmarked specifically for the enforcement of these measures.

None of these successes occurred spontaneously. Environmental reforms, reforestation, national park development, and ecological education did not evolve in Costa Rica without the will and determination of many Costa Ricans. The result can be seen in the history of Costa Rican conservation, as will be discussed in subsequent chapters.

3 *The Conservationist Response*

The national parks belong to all Costa Ricans equally, and therefore
they have the right to enjoy them . . . but also the duty to
protect them.

Mario Boza, *Guía de los parques nacionales de Costa Rica*

Early "Parks" and Conservation Laws

As in most countries, conservation policies in Costa Rica were a mid- to
late-twentieth-century phenomenon. While there were no actual national parks in Costa Rica until 1970, some earlier measures had attempted to deal with preserving parts of the nation's natural heritage.
One concept of protecting areas goes back to 1863. It was then that the
government set aside a tract of forest on both sides of the Camino del
Norte to be excluded from cuts. In 1906 the Legislative Assembly passed
Law No. 36, which obligated the executive branch of government to
recommend a general forest policy to the Assembly. While this law
prompted some initiatives and orders, it was vague and no national policy was created.

An influential person in early conservation policy making was Enrique
Jiménez Núñez. Jiménez earned his graduate degree in engineering in
Belgium but returned to Costa Rica where, according to Luis Fournier, he
"started to form an awareness for environmental problems."[1] Appointed
to the office of state secretary of development and agriculture, Jiménez

promoted a plan to diminish the burning of forests, which resulted in the Ley de Quemas (the Fire Law) of 1909. The law established guidelines for the use of fire to clear forested land. Jiménez understood the connection between forest cover and water supply and wrote that burning mountainsides "destroys many of the principal sources of the public wealth, it disfavorably modifies the normal rates of rainfall . . . [and] has transformed the most prosperous and rich countries into deserts."[2] Unfortunately, the Fire Law lacked any strong enforcement measures and did little to prevent deforestation in the decades to come. Jiménez also advocated a project that would have nationalized all of Costa Rica's water systems in 1910 (which did not culminate into law) and devised a plan to eliminate the dumping of coffee plantation by-product waste into rivers in 1914.

Other conservation policies were enacted in the early decades of the twentieth century. In 1913, for example, the government classified Poás Volcano as "protected" but provided no authority or enforcement to monitor the mountain. In the same year, the government declared a 600-foot swath of forest inland from Costa Rica's coasts, and an 800-foot swath along river banks, to become the first "national forests." Again, there was a lack of clarifying language and authority to enforce any protective measures. Two laws were passed in 1923 aimed at preserving water. The first, Law No. 52, prohibited the dumping of waste products from sewers, dairies, and slaughterhouses into the nation's rivers; the second, Law No. 68, was for the protection of watershed systems.

The 1930s witnessed additional, albeit nominal, initiatives to protect the nation's forests. In 1930 a regulation was decreed to establish a system of forest guards (*guardabosques*) to ensure the conservation and rational use of the forests. The enforcement of the act was placed in the office of the "forestry chief" of the national agricultural department in 1933.[3] Law No. 13 of January 1939 went a bit further to establish "preserves" around Poás and Irazú volcanoes and in the forests on both sides of the Cordillera Central. The law, however, was really more like a philosophical resolution because it included no exact delineations or enforcement clauses. Called the General Law on Vacant Lands, this measure declared that all vacant lands "that have no legitimate title for private owners, have not been registered with the Public Register, [and] are not occupied by a public service" would belong to the state. The law also established the government's right to eminent domain.[4]

There was limited interest in conservation measures in the 1940s as well. Recognizing the international aspect of preserving nature, Costa Rican delegates signed the Convention on Nature Protection and Wildlife Preservation in the Western Hemisphere in Washington, D.C., in 1940 (although it was not ratified in the Legislative Assembly until 1966). In 1943, when Costa Rica's segment of the Pan American Highway was constructed, biologists Charles Lankester and Mariano Montealegre proposed the idea of protecting as a "national park" a region on both sides of the road that they discovered was home to what they believed were the world's largest oak trees. Law No. 197 of 1945 designated 6,000 feet on both sides of the highway as a "national park" (the first time such a term was used in Costa Rican legislation) and stipulated that no forest exploitation would occur in the area. Unfortunately, the law was never really put into effect, placed no one in charge of its administration, and therefore left the oak forests open for timber cutting. The law was abrogated in 1973, as former park service attorney Ana María Tato explained, "because there was nothing left to protect."[5]

In 1948 a political upheaval ended in the revolution of National Liberation that thrust José Figueres Ferrer into the presidency of the Junta Fundadora of the "Second Republic" (1948–1949). The revolution, however, did not disrupt plans for a Costa Rican delegation to attend and participate in the Inter-American Conference for the Conservation of Renewable Natural Resources that was held in September of 1948 in Denver, Colorado. The conference, promulgated at the Third Inter-American Agricultural Conference in Caracas three years earlier, was a forum designed to share ideas from the countries in the Western Hemisphere and to promote regional cooperation on conservation concerns. One of the Costa Rican participants presented a paper on the growing interest in forest protection in his country and how the state should be actively involved in overseeing conservation to guarantee "a land with resources for the future."[6]

José Figueres and the government of the Second Republic placed emphasis on education and social services, abolished the military (an act that Costa Ricans often cite as vital for freeing government funds for such things as higher education and, later, conservation), and established the Instituto Costarricense de Electricidad (ICE)—the country's public utility corporation that supplies electricity. Understanding the importance of forest cover for ensuring the hydrologic needs of the ICE, the Figueres administration issued a decree in 1949 to establish a Forest Council to inventory forest resources and to protect forested watersheds from diseases and fires. Although noble in theory, Luis Fournier later lamented that "in practice, this entity was never put into action."[7] It was eliminated four years later. Also in 1949, however, the Ministry of Agriculture and Livestock (MAG) added a Forestry Section division to its responsibilities. This proved to be a decisive move because the nation's forests remained under MAG jurisdiction until the mid-1990s.

The administration of president Otilio Ulate (1949–1953) supported other conservation-minded ideas. In 1950 the government established the National Week for the Conservation of Natural Resources. The event was organized by an interdisciplinary amalgam of government agencies (including the ministries of public health, agriculture, industries, and education) and was designed to remind the citizens of Costa Rica of their duty to conserve soil and water for the long-range benefit of the country. The commemorative week, always held in June, has been observed with celebrations, symposia, and special events every year since its inception.

In 1953 the National School of Agriculture initiated legislation that resulted in the passage of the Soil and Water Conservation Law, signed by President Ulate. Spearheaded by agricultural engineer Alvaro Rojas Espinoza, the law required that soil studies be conducted on agricultural areas to determine the rational use of the land. But it also contained language that authorized MAG to earmark areas to be protected as "reserves, parks or national forests . . . for common use." Despite the fact that MAG never took advantage of this opportunity, the law helped fuel a growing conservation awareness in the nation and, as Luis Fournier notes, was "perhaps the most important [legislative] event of the time period."[8]

Other efforts that assisted conservation marked the second (noncontiguous) term of President José Figueres (1953–1958). In late 1953, for example, Figueres named a study commission to develop legislation for the creation of a national tourism council. Commission members visited Peru, Mexico, Argentina, and the United States to seek ways to develop a park system in Costa Rica. Their work culminated in the passage of Law No. 1917, which created the Instituto Costarricense de Turismo (ICT) in 1955. Part of ICT's mission was to designate a 1.2-mile radius around each volcano crater in the nation as a "national park." But "without technical criteria for national park objectives at this time," reminisced a former park service official, "economic and ecological reasons impeded the execution of that dimension of the law."[9] In 1958 an ICT study addressed where other national parks should be established, further emphasizing volcanoes and oak forests, but economic considerations once again thwarted implementation of the plan.

Costa Rica's first wildlife legislation was also a product of the mid-1950s. The Wildlife Conservation Law of 1956 (revised in 1961) defined wildlife as "those animals that are not domesticated or domesticated animals that have turned wild" and went on to state that all such creatures were "the property of the State." It declared that the wildlife were part of the "renewable natural resources of the country" and that the "conservation, restoration, and propagation of all wildlife useful to man" was of "fundamental interest" to the public. The law also spelled out hunting and fishing regulations but stated that they did "not apply to farmers who [could] kill wild animals on their property because they were threatening to destroy their crops."[10]

To oversee such policies, the law established a wildlife office within MAG. It also created a five-member National Wildlife Protector Committee that would make recommendations to MAG, study MAG's abilities to regulate wildlife, and serve as a general advisory board. The committee, however, seemed lopsided and padded; three members represented hunting and fishing organizations, one was a government fiscal agent, and only one was a biologist from the University of Costa Rica.[11]

As could be expected, the law prompted intensive lobbying and spirited debate on both sides of the issue. Hunting and sporting organizations argued for its support, and humane society members lobbied against the law when it was being considered by the Legislative Assembly in 1961. Opponents argued that the Protector Committee was too much like the fox guarding the henhouse.[12] Nonetheless, the bill became law and changed very little even with revisions in 1970.

Other attention was given to wildlife issues in the 1970s when the Costa Rican legislature endorsed international treaties regarding threatened or endangered species. In 1974 it ratified the Convention on International Trade in Endangered Species (CITES), which established a system of trade sanctions and a worldwide reporting network to reduce the traffic in threatened wildlife. And two years later on a more regional level the Legislative Assembly ratified the Convention for the Protection of

Flora, Fauna, and Places of Natural Scenic Beauty in the Countries of the Americas. That convention specifically outlined how national parks and reserves should be established and guarded for wildlife protection.[13]

To evaluate the country's policies for the protection of native flora and fauna and eventually to recommend changes in the Wildlife Conservation Law, the government sponsored a week-long wildlife symposium in 1980. Called the First National Congress on Wildlife Conservation, the event was organized by the Biological Studies Department of MAG and the National Wildlife Protector Committee. Presiding over the congress were Hernán Fonseca (MAG), Gerardo Budowski (CATIE), and Augustín Rodríguez (ICE). Participating organizations included the hunting and sporting clubs, CITES authorities from Costa Rica's U.N. office, the Association of Costa Rican Biologists, CATIE, several colleges and universities, the tourism council (ICT), and two environmental groups. President Rodrigo Carazo gave one of the opening addresses, and speakers and presenters represented a virtual "who's who" in national conservation activism. Participants included Alexander Skutch, Gary Stiles, Archie Carr, Joseph Tosi, Mario Boza, and Alfonso Mata. Many of the presenters were leading proponents in the development of Costa Rica's national park system, including Alexander Bonilla, Roger Morales, José María Rodríguez, Sergio Salas, Carlos Valerio, Murray Silberman, Christopher Vaughan, and many other biologists and conservation leaders.[14]

One of the outcomes of the symposium was the revised Wildlife Conservation Law of 1983 (further revised in 1990 and in 1992). The new policy eliminated much of the "public utility" language of wildlife as a natural resource and concentrated more on protecting threatened species. Gone was the language allowing farmers to hunt at will, and in its place were stronger hunting regulations. The National Wildlife Protector Committee was also modified to include only two representatives from sportsman organizations. And, most important, provisions were built into the law to establish certain national wildlife refuges.[15]

Many conservationists in Costa Rica had come to understand all too well that protecting the nation's wildlife meant protecting habitat and ecosystems. In the late 1950s, for example, forest ecologists Luis Fournier and Gerardo Budowski had begun reforestation research projects in the central Pacific and Atlantic regions of the country. Their aim was to recuperate the tropical forest ecosystems by ways of natural regeneration.

But at the same time, the forests were being increasingly threatened with the influx of squatter farmers and their families seeking new lands to clear and farm. Changes in land ownership and rises in population meant that thousands of rural Costa Ricans sought out *tierras baldías* (vacant lands) that were owned by the state. Aware that the problem was getting out of hand as far back as 1942, the Legislative Assembly passed the Squatter Law (Ley de Parásitos or Ley de Poseedores en Precario), which sought to halt squatter settlements on government land.

But the solution became part of the problem and actually exacerbated the exploitation of public lands. James Rowles, an authority on Costa Rican agrarian reform, notes that corruption and abuses of the Squatter Law resulted when large landholders "exchanged lands occupied by squatters (whom they often incited to invade) for virgin state lands." The corruption illustrates how squatters were really more of a symptom of the larger problem of inequitable land distribution—a concern that did not go unnoticed by José Figueres and the revolutionary movement of the Second Republic. In fact, as Rowles points out, Squatter Law abuses "had a great deal to do with the desire [of the Figueres junta] to reform existing agrarian legislation," and they became part of "the political ideology that guided the dominant Partido Nacional de Liberación (PLN) since the Revolution." [16] A key member of the early PLN was the junta's minister of agriculture, Bruce Masís, a strong proponent of agrarian reform and conservation. Masís led the efforts to eliminate the Squatter Law and to replace it with a land reform bill. The junta thus named a commission to study the problem and to draft a new agrarian code.

But reform legislation was slow in the making. José Figueres never made it a priority during the junta years (1948–1949) and the special commission never even met. Reform plans moved slowly through the legislative process during the Otilio Ulate administration (1949–1953), with a special commission again appointed to study the issue. Called the Committee on Agriculture and Colonies, it finally drafted reform legislation in 1953—only to be interrupted by the national election that gave José Figueres a landslide victory and a second term (1953–1958). Figueres had promised that the government would create a special institute to deal with lands and colonizations and named yet another committee to draft such a law.

By 1955, and only because of Bruce Masís' perseverance, the commission's proposal to establish a government institute for lands and colonizations finally made it to a committee of the Legislative Assembly. Political maneuvering by the opposition party, however, prevented its passage in the mid-1950s and delayed the law until 1961. But finally, after years of executive commissions and legislative committees, the Law of Lands and Colonizations was approved by the Assembly and signed by President Mario Echandi. It has been amended and revised eight times since, but its purpose has remained the same: to administer agricultural colonization through its administrative agency, the Institute of Lands and Colonizations (ITCO).

Whether ITCO's goal has been successfully achieved remains to be seen. In its first ten years of implementation (1962–1972), 3.7 percent of rural families ($n = 7{,}174$) received ITCO benefits—mainly in the form of attaining the legal rights to land they had already been occupying. Only 1,525 families benefited from the redistribution of 98,400 acres of land. Likewise, ITCO was able to resolve only 43 percent of the squatter conflicts (involving 75,600 acres) presented to it during that decade. And in the 1970s and 1980s the incidence of squatting (or *precarismo*) accelerated beyond the point that ITCO could properly keep up with it.[17]

The law and its results are important to consider here for the effects they have had on conservation efforts in Costa Rica. First, the law was designed to "contribute to the more just distribution of wealth" in Costa Rica by "avoiding the concentration of national lands in the hands of those who would use them for specialization against the general interests of the nation." More important, the law delineated which areas of the country were *not* open for agricultural colonization. It established the authority "to determine what land should not be exploited by agricultural workers" and crystallized government policy to acquire and expropriate "those lands that were not fulfilling any social function" (i.e., not being used for agriculture). Oddly, the bill named these lands "State Agricultural Properties" even though they consisted primarily of volcanoes and other lands unsuitable for cultivation. Later amendments to the law added riverways, islands, and watersheds vital for the nation's hydrologic needs. None of these "national reserves" could be colonized, fenced, or plowed, used for any construction, or used to cut wood. And the law made very clear that any and all lands not under title of private ownership legally belonged to the state.[18]

ITCO, whose name was later changed to the IDA (Instituto de Desarrollo Agrario [Institute of Agrarian Development]), monitored the regulation and enforcement of colonization policies. As a benefit to conservation efforts, the agency was staffed with personnel from MAG's Lands and Forestry Department, including four engineers trained in forestry from CATIE. Likewise, it was entrusted with the designation and development of nature reserves.

The first such reserve to be created was in 1965 at Cabo Blanco on the southernmost end of the Nicoya Peninsula in northwestern Costa Rica. But instead of being initiated by ITCO, Cabo Blanco was the unlikely result of the efforts of a Scandinavian couple who resided in the area. Olof Wessberg, a retired officer in the Swedish Air Force, and his Danish wife, Karen Mogensen, had moved to the peninsula in 1955 to live a simpler life and raise organic fruit. Acting on a life-long dream to leave the cold of northern Europe and to live in tropical America, Wessberg and Mogensen left Sweden to work on a farm in Ecuador. They later moved to Guatemala, California, and Mexico but never felt that those places satisfactorily suited them. Then, based largely on a dream Mogensen had one night, they decided to move to Costa Rica. After visiting several parts of the country, they settled at Montezuma at the southern end of Nicoya, bought land overlooking the gulf, and spent the next ten years raising over thirty varieties of fruits and coming to know intimately the flora and fauna of the region. Bill Weinberg, a journalist who became acquainted with Mogensen in the late 1980s, wrote that the couple "lived a life of vegetarianism and [had] a reverence for nature that bordered on the mystical, taking great joy in the company of monkeys and coatimundis."[19] The idyllic little world of Wessberg and Mogensen started to change very rapidly in the late 1950s, however, when larger and larger patches of cleared areas started to appear in the forests across the peninsula. They watched as hundreds of squatters moved into the region, cleared land for crops, and then sold out to lumber and cattle companies when the tropical rains eroded the cropland. Worried that the last remnant of forest habitat of their beloved wildlife would completely disappear, Wessberg contacted some wealthy acquaintances in California and requested that they purchase the land as a wildlife refuge. The friends declined but told Wessberg that he should contact international conservation organizations that might take up the cause. Acting on a late-night impulse, then, Wessberg wrote an appeal and sent it to various groups. He related how jaguars and tapirs were already extinct in the area and that rapid habitat loss was endangering the populations of ocelots, pumas, deer, peccaries, agoutis, coatimundis, and several species of monkeys on the peninsula. "When we settled here six years ago the mountain was always green," Wessberg lamented in his appeal, "today it has great brown patches, and in March and April it is shrouded in smoke, much of it on fire. . . . Two years more, and the mountain will be dead."[20] In 1961 his appeal appeared in the magazine of the World League against Vivisection and for the Protection of Animals.

Donations for the purchase of Cabo Blanco soon materialized. The British World League against Vivisection contributed 51 percent of the funds needed, and other monies came from the Sierra Club, the Nature Conservancy, the Friends of Nature, and the Philadelphia Conservation League. The environmental groups, however, preferred to give their contributions to a government agency responsible for the conservation of the area. But the only Costa Rican agency empowered to expropriate land for such purposes at this time was ITCO, which had no experience in managing preserves. ITCO "was interested in helping farmers to get more land to clear—the opposite of what we wanted," complained Mogensen in a later interview, "they never did understand what it was all about." Three years later and after over twenty trips made by Wessberg to San José to deal with government officials who would not answer his letters, ITCO finally expropriated the land at Cabo Blanco and created an "absolute biological reserve"—the country's first nature reserve. During that time, however, more colonizers had moved into the area, and, upon hearing that the land might be expropriated, cut down more trees to "improve" the land by making it more suitable for crops. Mogensen recalled that "a lot of people here really didn't understand what the land was being expropriated for."[21]

The next problem that Wessberg had to confront was in guarding Cabo Blanco. ITCO hired only one warden to monitor the entire reserve, who, according to Mogensen, was a big drinker. He also attempted to make a little extra money on the side by killing the last ten grey spider monkeys—found nowhere else in the world—for the oil in their fat that supposedly had medicinal qualities. Wessberg had him fired. Another warden felled trees inside the reserve to plant crops. After a few more journeys to San José to complain about these problems, the government allowed Wessberg to develop his own questionnaire to screen prospective wardens. The system he used proved so helpful that by the early 1970s, when a national park service had been established, officials offered him an agency position there. He declined on the grounds that he had no desire to move to San José.[22]

Wessberg's last campaign for conservation on the Nicoya Peninsula came in the early 1970s when he lobbied for establishing an additional reserve around the town of Montezuma. He solicited $500,000 from the International Union for the Conservation of Nature (IUCN) in Switzerland. Gerardo Budowski of Costa Rica was the director general of IUCN in those years but was forced to refuse Wessberg's request because it asked for "way too much money." He urged Wessberg to seek government approval and to have the University of Costa Rica and the OTS conduct feasibility studies of the project before the IUCN could consider such a request.[23] The project never materialized.

While Cabo Blanco became Costa Rica's first nature reserve in 1965, the next year marked the creation of the first national monument. The purpose in creating Santa Rosa National Monument, located on the Santa Elena Peninsula in the far northwestern corner of the country in Guanacaste province, however, was more as a means to preserve and tout the historical value of the area than as a measure to protect the tropical dry forest in which it was located. Santa Rosa had been a large working cattle ranch, but it was also the place where a volunteer Costa Rican brigade had defeated William Walker and his invading band of American filibusters in 1856. Walker, who entertained grandiose notions of establishing his own personal empire in Central America, complete with slavery (which had been abolished in the region) and English as the official language, was pushed back into Nicaragua, never to set foot on Costa Rican soil again. Thus the Battle of Santa Rosa had become a source of national identity and pride (as well as an important national holiday) for many Costa Ricans, especially for Guanacastecans. La Casona, the large hacienda near the battle site, survived as a monument to this important historic event (see Figure 6).

But Santa Rosa was "invaded" again in the 1930s when Nicaraguan strongman Anastasio Somoza García bought the hacienda as a personal ranch and investment. Never popular with democratic Costa Ricans, Somoza's presence outraged Ticos who over the years pressured the government to oust the dictator from the area. Not until 1966, however,

Figure 6.   La Casona at Santa Rosa National Park (*source:* National Archives of Costa Rica, Servicio de Parques Nacionales series, file 19)

did the Legislative Assembly finally vote to expropriate 3,000 acres of Somoza's land surrounding La Casona. It then directed ICT to manage Santa Rosa as a national monument.

Seeing the historic and touristic value in preserving this part of Costa Rica's national heritage, ICT welcomed the opportunity and hired Kenton Miller, a CATIE parks planning specialist, as a consultant for the project. But Miller recognized that the tropical dry forest in which Santa Rosa was located (among the very last remnants of this ecosystem anywhere in the world) was being threatened by slash and burn agriculture and the expansion of livestock pastures. Thus the chance to extend protection over a larger area loomed very large for Miller, and he recommended that the government buy 30,000 acres of the fragile environment to be developed into a park. ICT backed the plan and the government eventually paid Somoza roughly $500,000 for the land. In 1971 the status of Santa Rosa changed from national monument to national park—making it one of Costa Rica's first such designated areas.[24] National park status, however, was made possible only by the passage of the Forestry Law of 1969, the history of which is vital for understanding the subsequent history of conservation in Costa Rica.

Legislating Protection: The Ley Forestal

Participants in, and students of, Costa Rican environmental policy making agree that the Forestry Law of 1969 was the key to future conservation successes. Called the "principal milestone," the "transcendental step," and the "turning point" in the country's conservation history, the Forestry Law's impact on the rational use of forest resources cannot be underestimated.[25] Yet missing in the literature is any explanation of the history and career of the law, the mechanics behind its enactment, public reaction to its passage, and the changes it has undergone in the late twentieth century.

With the creation of Cabo Blanco Nature Reserve and Santa Rosa National Monument in the mid-1960s, concern developed in certain sectors of the government regarding the lack of comprehensive guidelines to administer protected areas and to conserve other forest resources. One official who was keenly aware of the problem and who worried about the impact of unregulated deforestation was Guillermo Yglesias, minister of agriculture and livestock in the administration of President José Joaquín Trejos (1966–1970). In 1967 Yglesias named an interdisciplinary committee to research the problem and to prepare a draft forestry legislation proposal. Heading the commission was stalwart conservationist Alvaro Rojas Espinoza, who had had successful experience in organizing and seeing to fruition the 1953 Soil and Water Conservation Law and the 1961 Law of Lands and Colonizations. Representing government agencies on the commission were members from the Ministry of Industry and Commerce, the National Committee for the Conservation of Natural Resources (dominated by the hunting and fishing organizations), the electricity institute (ICE), and the Institute of Lands and Colonizations (ITCO). From the private sector were representatives from the Agriculture and Stockgrowers Association and from the Wood Industries Association. And representing the University of Costa Rica was forest ecologist Luis Fournier, who, Yglesias stated, had "an enormous understanding of forestry management." Professor Fournier later remembered, however, that he felt like "un golondrino solo" (a lone swallow) on the commission because of his more active position for environmental protection.[26]

The special commission worked for nearly a year on the proposal. During that time the members consulted the forestry laws of Venezuela, Mexico, and the United States and hired forestry consultant Nestor Altuve to help draft the legislation. Altuve was a Venezuelan forestry specialist who had helped pass protective legislation in his home country, had been chief of the Venezuelan forestry service, and at this time was employed as a sylviculturist with the UN's Food and Agriculture Organization (FAO) in Rome. On 14 June 1968 Guillermo Yglesias sent the commission's proposal to the Legislative Assembly. In an accompanying letter, Yglesias explained that the proposed legislation was "for the defense, conservation, and safer exploitation of our renewable natural resources." He asserted that the country had "been waiting over seventy years" for such a policy and that ever since Law No. 36 of 1906 (which authorized the executive branch to create national forestry guidelines), there had been many initiatives and orders but nothing that had ever become a concrete national law.[27]

What the commission's proposal called for, then, was the legal sanction for the state "to ensure the protection, conservation . . . and development of the country's forest resources." To that end, the law would establish a General Forestry Directorate (DGF) within the MAG to "administer the forest patrimony" and "to provide technical support to the wood products industry." Additional MAG duties would include creating protector zones, working to conserve wildlife, combatting soil erosion, controlling forest exploitation, and providing forestry education. To advise on such issues, the law would create a Forestry Council with members selected from the various government agencies involved with land and resource issues. The law would outline regulations for the felling, transporting, and marketing of timber from the country's forests and would establish penalties (stiff fines and jail terms) for policy infractions. It mandated that there be no livestock grazing on public lands without the written approval of the DGF. And, vital for the more organized designation and management of protected areas, the law would define and provide for the creation of a system of national parks to be administered by the DGF. Lands defined as national parks, forest reserves, and protector zones would be off-limits for agricultural colonizations.[28]

In trying to sell such a proposal to members of the Legislative Assembly, Yglesias stressed the economic benefits that would accrue from the bill's approval. After all, much of the bill's intent was directed toward the concept of "multiple use" and was similar in many ways to the public lands management language of U.S. conservation policy. Article One, for example, suggested that the law would be for protecting and conserving the forests, but also for their "exploitation . . . and development . . . in accordance with the principle of multiple use of renewable natural resources." Yglesias noted that the law would "assure the best exploitation of the forests for the benefit of a more dynamic economic development of the agricultural sector." He argued that because of Costa Rica's high rainfall and mountainous topography, protecting the forests, and therefore the soils, would be "one of the most promising economic activities" that the nation could undertake.[29]

In accord with Costa Rican legislative procedure, the proposed law was sent to committee before being debated in the Assembly as a whole. It went to the Permanent Commission on Government and Administration, where proceedings opened on 19 August 1968. Guillermo Yglesias was called on to introduce the proposal. "There has been a general anxiety among Costa Ricans," he began, "about putting order and regulation to the irrational exploitation that our forests are undergoing at this time." He then asserted that "in reality, if we continue in the steps we are now taking, within a few short years Costa Rica will not have any wood, we will not have any forests to exploit." Yglesias stressed that supplying guards in the forests (a strong FAO recommendation) was one method to start counteracting abusive forest practices. When one commission member asked him why the Executive Office could not just authorize the appointment of forest guards without going through the legislative process, Yglesias responded that this was impossible without the legal authority of a law on the books. "I expect enormous reaction from the woodcutters," he admitted, "and from the people who are taking advantage of the forests . . . [and] are making lots of money from it, because this law will end that."[30]

When the legislative commission next met to consider the Forestry Law, the members heard from Luis Fournier and others on the proposal team. Fournier minced no words: "You're becoming more aware of irrational forest exploitation. . . . [Even] a superficial land analysis of Costa Rica shows that only fifty percent [of the country] remains in forest." And he stressed how the inconsistent and rivalrous nature of having five or six government agencies involved with different aspects of land management was leading to the "atomization" and "anarchy" of conservation policy. He noted that there would be "good incentives" and "stimulants like tax relief" to encourage landowners to cooperate. In terms of enforcement, he related how the committee estimated that 300 forest guards and twenty-five support staff would be needed.[31]

In order to gauge regional reaction to the proposed bill, the legislative commission solicited responses from municipalities around the country. Many municipal leaders and town councils mailed or wired in straw

votes taken on the bill and most were favorable in nature. Typical of
many was the response from the municipality of San Pablo Turrubares,
stating that the law would give nothing but benefits for future generations. "It is an injection of fresh air in the continual fight for a better and
more fertile Costa Rica. . . . The natural resources are a source of incalcu-
lable value . . . [and] an immense treasure."[32]

Statements of support also came in from the minister of industry and
commerce and from international experts in the conservation field. But
much of the support came in the form of backing the proposal for its
economic benefits. Dr. Herster Barres, a forestry official with the FAO,
testified that Costa Rica's population was estimated to double by 1988 (it
nearly did) and that well-managed forests would mean that more paper
products and books would be available for the people. He also stressed
that Costa Rica's economy would benefit from such paper-hungry giants
as Europe and Japan, as their demand for pulp would increase over the
years.[33]

Likewise, there was strong opposition to the proposal. Conflict developed around the duties of the colonization institute (ITCO) and the tourism council (ICT) in distributing or managing government lands. The
problem was in the identification and designation of "lands not suitable
for agriculture," which ITCO was often in the habit of distributing and
which conservationists believed should be protected. Under the new forestry law, such lands could fall into preservation categories that officials
at ITCO believed should only be in their jurisdiction to determine and
officials at ICT believed should only be in theirs. ICT director Richard
Castro argued that the law that created his agency in the mid-1950s "authorized [it] to declare which zones [would become] national parks" and
that Santa Rosa National Monument was in its "custody" and being managed just fine. Opposition also came from certain private sectors that
stood to lose from the law. The Costa Rican Construction Association, for
example, lobbied against the proposal.[34]

Opposition notwithstanding, the Permanent Commission on Government and Administration unanimously approved the proposed forestry law and sent it to the Legislative Assembly on 29 April 1969. It
had been in committee for ten months and lasted in the Assembly as a
whole for seven more. During that time the legislature received an unprecedented outpouring of petitions, letters, and telegrams from various
sectors of the country in support of a national conservation policy. A

twenty-two-page petition, for example, was sent from students of the Coto Brus and Osa Agricultural College in southern Costa Rica urging members of the legislature to pass the law. The students declared that they "could not continue celebrating the National Week for Natural Resources if the forests, waters, soils, wildlife, and places of scenic beauty continue to be subjected to increasingly more intensive destruction." And the president of the prestigious Association of Biologists (Colegio de Biólogos) of Costa Rica sent notice to the Assembly that his organization was in complete support of the measure.

Schoolchildren across the country also sent many letters and telegrams to the Legislative Assembly urging members to vote for the proposal to protect forests and natural resources. Indicative of many was a telegram from the high school students of the Liceo Rodrigo Facio stating, "We desire a better future for us via a forestry law that will also improve the economy of our beloved Costa Rica." Others wrote supporting the law as a means to preserve the woods, the animals, and the birds that represented the country's natural heritage.[35]

The media had a less active role in supporting the cause, but *La Prensa Libre* openly campaigned for its approval. In a long editorial published on the day the bill was to come up for a vote (25 November 1969), the paper endorsed the law and urged Assembly members to support it. It praised the measure as "an important legal instrument . . . to stop the axe from continuing its destructive work" and the only hope to "save [our] natural resources for future generations."[36]

Opponents were against the law for a variety of reasons. ITCO sent word to the Assembly members that more time was needed for its attorneys to study the proposal and how it would affect land colonization efforts. Private citizens wrote that the government had no business setting aside certain areas of land. Representative of these individuals was Rodrigo Salas Retana from Guadalupe, who noted that "it's not like Costa Rica is a big country like the United States. We do not have that much private land; we are not big enough for this, even though [many people] just see San José and think we're huge."[37] But the opposition was the minority opinion. On 25 November 1969 the plenary session of the Legislative Assembly passed Law No. 4465, the Ley Forestal.

Public reaction to the creation of the framework that would protect Costa Rica's forests and establish national parks was modest at best. The Forestry Law came to a vote when the Assembly found itself, as one newspaper put it, "in the biggest of squeezes"—when it had "never been in such a tight spot with so much pending legislation."[38] Perhaps that was part of the reason that the country's largest newspaper, *La Nación,* did not report the law at all on the day it passed and waited two days before ever mentioning it with a small article on page 44. The paper's "capitol hill"–style legislation column never did mention the Forestry Law. Bigger legislative news was the debate in the Assembly to finance a sport center in San José. Part of the reason also lies with the breaking news stories of the day with which the new conservation policy had to compete. Newspapers logically gave far more coverage to such national headline events as the tropical storm and flooding that caused a great deal of destruction in southern Costa Rica and to the José Figueres presidential campaign.

Likewise the media gave more attention to such international topics as the successful landing of Apollo XII, the unraveling of the tragic events surrounding Lieutenant William Calley and the My Lai massacre in Vietnam, antiwar protests and hippies in the United States, the continuing saga of violence between Honduras and El Salvador, and a deal between Anastasio Somoza and Aristotle Onassis regarding the "canalization" of Nicaragua. Ironically, on the days surrounding the creation of a law to protect forests, *La Nación* ran large display ads for Steyr Tractors that could "conquer the Costa Rican countryside" and for Volvo logging trucks (called *madereros*), which were supposedly superior to their competitors for hauling huge logs in the rough mountainous terrain. And even campaign ads for José Figueres promised "land for everyone" and acknowledged that "the demand for land exists" and that the government had "only started to satisfy it." The only newspaper to report on the Forestry Law on the day of its approval by the Legislative Assembly was *La República* in a short article on page 13. *La Nación* ran an article concerning the law two days later and quoted President Trejos at the signing ceremony. "The step that has been taken with this law," he began, "is transcendental for the progress of Costa Rica . . . [and] means a great deal for the rational exploitation of forest resources."[39]

"Rational" is not always the word that can describe forest use since the passage of the Forestry Law in 1969. Deforestation has left its ugly mark on the Costa Rican landscape—much of which has occurred since the law went into effect. *Precarista* squatting increased in the 1980s and only recently has slowed to some degree. Logging continues in restricted areas that are inadequately patrolled, and the nation's forestry policies are still enforced with insufficient funds and fewer personnel than needed. A green ethic does not yet pervade the business community and is especially absent in the forest extractive industries.

Yet one must bear in mind the alternative and ask what directions land use might have followed without the Forestry Law. In that light, then, it becomes easier to see how the law can be viewed as a success in other dimensions of conservation. That it provided the vehicle to set aside areas as national parks and biological reserves has been its most successful benchmark. It is to that dimension that we must turn next. But in understanding the career of the law—and it indeed has been a long and multifaceted one with revisions and reforms groaning through the legislative process in 1977, 1980, 1986, 1990, and 1996 (the last of which will be discussed in Chapter 8)—it is clear that it was the initial and most important step of the conservationist response to the environmental problems so besieging the nation by the end of the 1960s.

4 The Development of National Parks and Other Protected Areas

The Costa Rican national park system gives some hope that the marvellously diverse communities of tropical organisms will be preserved for future generations to enjoy and for future scientists to study.
L. D. Gómez and J. M. Savage, "Searchers on That Rich Coast"

"A Thousand and One Tricks"

The capstone of Costa Rican conservation policy and, indeed, the dimension of conservation most known to both Ticos and foreigners is the country's system of national parks and other protected areas. The 1969 Forestry Law outlined that "national parks" would be created not only for the conservation of flora and fauna (as had been the case with earlier park experiments), but also to offer opportunities for recreation, tourism, and scientific research. Interestingly enough, the decision to designate such areas was granted to the president of the country upon the advice of a National Forestry Council, made up of delegates from several different government agencies and the University of Costa Rica. But while many important parks were created this way, executive decree would be a proviso tainted with political undertones during some administrations.

The Forestry Law was also the instrument that provided for the establishment of a National Parks Department within the General Forestry Directorate (DGF), a division of the Ministry of Agriculture and Livestock (MAG). Funding for the DGF and its park service came via the Forestry

Fund, which the law established to generate budgets and to channel donations to the proper agencies. The law stipulated that additional oper-
ating funds would be derived from the Costa Rican general revenue.

To head the new National Parks Department, the DGF hired Mario A.
Boza—a graduate of the University of Costa Rica's School of Agron-
omy and recent recipient of a master's degree in forestry from the Inter-
American Institute (later called CATIE) in Turrialba. Boza, who had studied under Gerardo Budowski and Kenton R. Miller and had written his
M.A. thesis on a development and management plan for a proposed Poás
Volcano National Park, was already working in the planning office of
MAG when the Forestry Law created the National Parks Department. The
background on why and how Boza became so actively involved in conservation issues, and his enthusiasm for national park development,
made him the logical candidate to take charge of the new parks department.

The origin of Boza's conservationism was his enrollment in Dr. Miller's
national parks course in Turrialba. He was directed there by Professor
Budowski, who had sensed that Boza's initial interest in teakwood production was being superseded by an increasing personal commitment to
biological preservation. Boza gained from Miller's course and especially
from a field trip the class took to visit conservation areas in the United
States in 1967. Miller took his students to Florida and Tennessee to visit
U.S. national forests and parks, and when they arrived at the Great
Smoky Mountains National Park, according to one source who met Boza
shortly thereafter, "it was love at first sight; he devoted every waking moment to learning about parks." Reminiscing about this baptismal experience later, Boza told another interviewer, "The first time I saw a whole
park working was in the Smokies." "I saw the people going back and
forth, using the facilities," he recalled, and on seeing "all the things that
had grown up around the park because it was there . . . I thought Costa
Rica was ready for that." Miller remembers the effect the visit had on
Boza: "On a free day just outside Great Smoky Mountains National Park,
I asked if anyone wanted to go back into the park. . . . Boza did, and that
evening he turned to me and said 'Is there a possibility that I could
change my thesis and study how to develop a real national park for my
country?'"[1]

In 1968 Boza attended a one-month international training course in
national parks management in Aspen, Colorado. The seminar, entitled

"International Short Course on the Administration of National Parks and Equivalent Reserves," was jointly sponsored by the University of Michigan's School of Natural Resources, the U.S. National Park Service (USNPS), and the Washington, D.C.–based Conservation Foundation. That experience further accelerated his interest in seeing parks established in Costa Rica and assisted him in creating ideas for his thesis. On Dr. Miller's recommendation, Boza wrote a master plan for Poás Volcano just north of San José. This was a logical place to start thinking about accessible national parks (the Cabo Blanco Nature Reserve had restricted public access) since it was close to a major city and had an all-year road to the rim of the volcano. Likewise, it was an ideal location for protecting the spectacular cloud forest that surrounded the volcano and that was prime habitat for the resplendent quetzal—an ever-threatened species due to regional deforestation. Boza's plan called for facilities similar to ones he had seen in U.S. national parks, including a visitor center, nature trails, interpretive signs, and access to view the crater.[2]

Boza also visited different parts of Costa Rica to become better acquainted with areas that could be considered for conservation. In 1969 he traveled with a group of interested people to Tortuguero to view the marine turtle nesting areas that Archie Carr and his family had been working to protect since the mid-1950s. Tortuguero, on the Caribbean coast of northeastern Costa Rica, is surrounded by lush tropical lowlands and is difficult to get to, even today; thus the group journeyed by bus, train, boat, mule, and foot, having plenty of time to visit and become acquainted with each other in the process. This was an important experience for Boza since among those in the party were former president José Figueres and his family. Figueres was running for an unprecedented (nonconsecutive) third presidential term. (He won later that year and served in office from 1970 to 1974.) His wife, Karen Olsen de Figueres, was deeply interested in conservation issues and especially in national park development for Costa Rica. Also on the trip were Kenton Miller, Gerardo Budowski, and a UCR biology student and avid outdoors enthusiast named Alvaro Ugalde. Ugalde later returned to Tortuguero with the couple's son, José María Figueres (who twenty-five years later, in 1994, was elected president of Costa Rica) to spend a month tagging green turtles with the Carrs. Needless to say, the connections forged on the Tortuguero trip were of the utmost importance for all concerned.[3]

With a master's degree in hand and his position in planning secured at MAG, Boza next set out to generate public support for the benefits of national park development. In 1969 he wrote editorials to San José newspapers, extolling the economic value that tourism to national parks could offer and citing the boon tourism had been to East Africa's economy. Then when the Forestry Law was passed later that year and Boza was named chief of the new National Parks Department in 1970, the opportunity opened up to put into action many of the dreams and ideas he had been advocating. Understanding the gravity of his new work, he stated that it was the dangerous environmental brink at which Costa Rica had arrived that spurred the need to act quickly and decisively: "A series of environmental problems like deforestation, poaching, erosion and pollution seriously threatened the conservation of the cultural and natural heritage of the nation." The creation of the national parks system, he explained, was "to preserve at least representations of this heritage."[4]

Boza's next step was to fortify his department by training others in park planning and management. He definitely needed the help. "The new department was given responsibility for all of Costa Rica's volcanoes, a nature reserve [Cabo Blanco], and the Santa Rosa National Monument," Boza later recalled. "The problem was that it had no budget and only one employee—me." Thus he contacted Alvaro Ugalde (still a student at UCR) and urged him to attend the one-month national parks training course in the United States. Via funds from Archie Carr's Caribbean Conservation Corporation, Ugalde attended the seminar and ended up staying an extra two months at a different training course held at Grand Canyon National Park in Arizona. When he returned to Costa Rica in 1970, Boza placed him in charge of Santa Rosa National Monument and then left to complete the training course himself.[5]

Ugalde recalled that those early years were slim for the new department and that "the Park Service didn't have the money to hire me." Santa Rosa had been "pretty much abandoned by ICT [the tourism institute] because the Forestry Law said it was to be managed by the park system, and Cabo Blanco was still being managed by the Wessbergs, and that was it." He and Boza were confronted with a variety of needs—guards, construction materials, maintenance supplies, political support for their programs, and so on—and had very few means to attain them. Thus, they learned to be clever. Boza explained how "the idea was to seize any favorable opportunities or circumstances that came up, even unexpectedly, to invent a thousand and one tricks to get what we needed." [6]

One of the tricks that worked the best was to capitalize on the connections they had made. One individual in particular was the most influential for park support: the First Lady of Costa Rica, Karen Olsen de Figueres. Similar to many first ladies in the United States, Doña Karen (as she is affectionately known in Costa Rica) took on a special cause or avocation during her husband's term. The cause she chose was preserving the environment and establishing national parks. Allen Young, an American naturalist who spent a great deal of time in Costa Rica during the embryonic stages of its park development, goes so far as to say that the national park system was "rooted" in the efforts of Figueres. Mario Boza has referred to her as "our fairy godmother of conservation." [7] In a presentation he gave at the 1972 World Conference on National Parks in Jackson, Wyoming, Boza spoke at length regarding Doña Karen's important role:

> First Lady Señora Karen de Figueres has not only given her full support to the theme of conserving the natural patrimony of the country, but has gone much further by proposing a large scale program . . . for establishing and funding a system . . . that would comprise no less than sixteen new parks.
>
> . . . Through the president, she can get proposals for new legislation, . . . she can ensure the support of the agency heads and legislators belonging to her party, seek certain kinds of international aid which can only be obtained by approach at the presidential level, etc. In short, it was only after Doña Karen began to help us directly that our park program began to make rapid progress. [8]

Likewise, she joined environmental groups and served as a member of several conservation commissions.

What is rarely discussed, however, is *why* Figueres became so personally involved. In a 1992 interview, Doña Karen explained that she became motivated to work on environmental issues out of a religious, "conscience-oriented" calling. "Helping people become conscious of what God has given us, of what brotherhood means . . . and of our responsibility as stewards of the land," she remarked, was "so essential to me." Continuing, she stated, "each person's value and responsibility [toward the land] brings unity and balance . . . and instills a consciousness of who we are in Costa Rica." She also mentioned that her interest in the environment was an extension of her educational and professional background as a sociologist. This discipline had helped her understand how the "development [of a country] is not logical without considering long-range values." "Too much thinking today," she explained, "is short-term or for right now." Born in Denmark, raised in the United States, but "one thousand percent Costa Rican" most of her adult life, as she explains it, Doña Karen viewed her role as First Lady as being a catalyst for national park protection.[9]

Other people also offered valuable assistance. Arthur "Tex" Hawkins, for example, volunteered much of his time to help Alvaro Ugalde in Santa Rosa. Hawkins, a U.S. wildlife biologist-journalist who had been a Peace Corps volunteer with Costa Rica's Fish and Wildlife Office, and Ugalde were aware that problems had started to mount in Santa Rosa while Boza was out of the country completing his training with the USNPS. They were concerned that forty families of squatters had moved into the Playa Naranjo area of Santa Rosa, had started to clear it of forest, and had proceeded to set up farms. Likewise, as Ugalde recollects, "one of the rancher neighbors up on the dry forest area of the volcanic plateau had stolen sixty hectares [approximately 150 acres]—just moved his fences sixty hectares into the park." The park had but one workman at the time (and he and other forestry officials were turning a blind eye to the damage), and so, as Ugalde relates, "Tex and I decided to fight for Santa Rosa as volunteers. . . . *We* were the park service, and neither of us worked for it. It got very heated."[10] They also alerted Boza to the problems. When he returned to San José, he wrote the MAG minister about the destruction and sent copies of his letter to various newspapers to arouse public support. With headlines such as "Santa Rosa in Flames; National Park Being Burned" (although it was not yet officially a national park), the government got the message and proceeded to remove the ranchers and to relocate the squatters. The job fell on Ugalde (still an unpaid volunteer), who worked hard to create good relations with the *precaristas*. He ensured that the government pay them for their improvements and assist them with their move to different lands.[11]

But while the government issued bonds to buy out the squatters and to help finance future park development at Santa Rosa, the troubles did not end when the squatters left. On the very day that the last family had been successfully removed, Boza and Ugalde learned that there was a bill in the Legislative Assembly aimed at taking Santa Rosa away from the new National Parks Department and returning it to ICT. The bill was sponsored by the president of the Assembly, Daniel Oduber, who was a powerful cattle rancher from Guanacaste and a friend of the Santa Rosa–area rancher who had been illegally running livestock in the park. Oduber's bill, supported by ICT personnel who had opposed the Forestry Law that transferred Santa Rosa out of their domain, would have opened up the park to more grazing by other area ranchers.

At that point Boza and Ugalde started a campaign against Oduber's proposal. Noticing that the funding clause for the bill levied a new tax on liquor, the two men actively engaged the business community to lobby against the proposal. They also enlisted the support of the Costa Rican Biologists' Association (Colegio de Biólogos), whose members wrote letters in defense of the parks department and lobbied against the bill. But most important, as Boza put it, "we called on our fairy godmother."[12]

When told of the situation, Karen Olsen de Figueres talked with or wrote every member of the Legislative Assembly and outlined why Oduber's bill should be rejected. According to Boza, she also wrote a personal letter to Oduber asking him to withdraw the proposal. As the story goes, she showed "considerable political artistry . . . [and] asked her husband—without telling him the contents of the letter—if he would deliver it himself to Oduber." President Figueres handed him the message, but Oduber refused to relent. Nonetheless, when the Assembly voted, not one *diputado* supported the measure. Its unanimous failure represented a victory for Boza and Ugalde as well as for the future of the national parks program. It also illustrated the significance of Doña Karen's attention to conservation concerns and was a hallmark for her continued involvement in national park causes. Santa Rosa was officially changed to national park status in March of 1971 and Ugalde was appointed its first salaried administrator two months later. "So the Park Service now had two people," he stated, "or three, if you count Mario's secretary."[13]

A "Towering Responsibility": The Early Years of Park Development

The first task facing Mario Boza and the National Parks Department was, as Boza put it, to decide "what type of parks . . . [to] create first." He decided to steer a practical course—to concentrate on one or two areas and

to make them models for future park development. He related how the
idea was "to create parks in areas of stunning beauty, on historic sites
commemorating heroic exploits of the past, and in areas of demonstrated importance for conservation." The goal was "to merge historical,
scenic, and natural values so that no one could object, making it easy to
sell the public on the idea of conservation"—no easy task in 1970. Besides "intensive deforestation to open new lands for agriculture and
cattle raising," he explained, there was also an "active trade in wild animal products, very weak environmental education, [and] total indifference to environmental problems on the part of the general public and
decisions makers." Working without a model, without any experience,
without much funding, and with only "five guards and a vehicle," then,
became a daunting task. "We found ourselves faced with the towering
responsibility of developing a system of national parks and equivalent
reserves," Boza remembered, and "we realized immediately how much
we needed: staff for administration, protection, and tourist and visitor
services; funds to purchase land, buildings, equipment, supplies, uniforms, medicine, and fuel; training for staff; and published materials for
interpretation." [14]

But parks they did create. The first area officially to be protected under
the new guidelines of the Forestry Law was Cahuita National Monument
in September of 1970. Cahuita, which was changed to a national park in
1980, is located on Costa Rica's extreme southeastern Caribbean coast
and includes tropical forest, miles of pristine beaches, and a 1,500-acre
coral reef that is the only well-preserved reef on Costa Rica's Caribbean
coast. That same month a small part of what would in 1975 become
Tortuguero National Park (up the coast from Cahuita) was declared protected for marine turtle nesting grounds. In January of 1971, Poás Volcano was declared a "pilot national park," and many parts of Boza's master plan that had been his M.A. thesis were converted into the working
management plan for the park. Poás Volcano—a mountain that had
been discussed, designated, and labeled with different forms of conservation tags and had been "managed" by several different government
agencies since 1939—finally became Costa Rica's first official national
park. Two months later, in March of 1971, which happened to be the
115th anniversary of the battle against William Walker and the filibusters, Santa Rosa's status was changed from "national monument" to "na-

tional park" to become Costa Rica's second official national park. The executive decree to create the park was signed by President José Figueres. (See Figure 2 for exact locations of these parks.)

To celebrate the inauguration of Santa Rosa National Park and to honor the anniversary of the Filibuster War, the parks department decided to host an on-site ribbon-cutting ceremony on 20 March 1971— the same date as the famous battle in 1856. According to newspaper accounts, 8,000 people attended the event, including a variety of government dignitaries, local officials, and schoolchildren from around Guanacaste province. MAG minister Fernando Batalla signed the national park proclamation on the steps of the famous Casona. Vice Minister Alvaro Rojas Espinoza (who had been so instrumental in passing conservation legislation in the 1950s and 1960s) read the first articles of the decree to the audience. President Figueres was unable to attend, but the First Lady assisted with the ribbon cutting and gave a brief speech. After requesting a moment of silence for the Costa Ricans who had lost their lives in the 1856 battle, Doña Karen asserted that Santa Rosa represented a "symbol for the homeland, a symbol for the future development of Guanacaste, and a symbol for the integration of the entire Costa Rican family because it is here that one finds the past, the present, and the future."[15]

Daniel Oduber, the president of the Legislative Assembly who had unsuccessfully tried to remove Santa Rosa from the parks department a year earlier, was also on hand to deliver a speech. Making an abrupt about-face, Oduber now spoke glowingly about Santa Rosa and directed his remarks to the schoolchildren in the audience. He exhorted them to preserve Santa Rosa against "contemporary filibusters." "To you we hand over a united and peaceful country," he began, "assured of the fact that you will defend this sacred land, tree for tree and palm for palm." He also challenged them "to show the world that here in Costa Rica we defend natural resources and the beauty of nature, and that we know how to respect religiously . . . the nature that God has given us." In attendance were officials from the United States. Statements were read by representatives from the offices of President Richard Nixon and Secretary of Interior Rogers C. B. Morton, congratulating the government of Costa Rica for establishing the park. "The great battle of 1856," began Morton's message, could be compared with "the great battle of our days—the conservation of the environment and of the national heritage."[16] And also at the gathering was Kenton Miller (then at FAO)—assuredly gratified at the conservation successes of his former student, Mario Boza.

But while the creation of these initial national parks can be seen as a success, Boza's first year as Parks Department chief was filled with challenges and setbacks. Early in his tenure he wrote Gerardo Budowski (then a director at the IUCN) that "I have hundreds of problems that I would like to discuss with you." At Cahuita, for example, land acquisition had been a problem. A former park service attorney explained that "the legal mandate to acquire lands could not be carried out because the Cahuiteños were very obstinate in those days . . . and the community viewed the creation of the park with distrust." "The government," she continued, finally "reached an agreement with the residents of Cahuita saying that the State would not proceed with any land expropriations until they were satisfied" with the arrangements.[17]

Trouble was also brewing once again in politically besieged Santa Rosa. Official park designation, the act of having a full-time administrator (Alvaro Ugalde) on site, and a dignitary-laden inauguration ceremony could not prevent a third scandal from hitting the newly created park. In June of 1971, just three months after the grand opening ceremony, the National Youth Movement and the Biologists' Association complained to San José newspapers that Santa Rosa was being overrun by livestock. Trails and picnic areas that the youth organization had helped to build were being severely damaged by cattle grazing in the park. The Colegio de Biólogos estimated that several thousand head of cattle in Santa Rosa had converted the national park into "a virtual ranch."[18]

Worse, it soon became known that the minister of MAG himself (who also was over the National Parks Department) was involved in running cattle in Santa Rosa and had abetted fellow ranchers in the region to graze their cattle there. Complicating matters was the fact that Mario Boza and Alvaro Ugalde knew that their boss was the policy violator and that they were frustrated about not knowing how to handle the scandal. Nongovernmental conservation activists like Alexander Bonilla also knew what was going on and were equally perplexed. Just whom does one approach to report the agency head's misdeeds?[19]

Enter once again Karen Olsen de Figueres. "This incensed me!" Doña Karen recalled, adding that it became the turning point for her to get involved in this and other environmental causes. "It gave me the green light" to try to make a difference, she stated, and hopefully "gave the green light to like-minded people to get involved." The problem was that MAG director Fernando Batalla was appointed by her husband and claimed that the scandal was the work of a biased, liberal press. He argued (mistakenly) that grazing cattle was part of the management plan of the park. It was not; in fact, it was a direct violation of Article 81 of the Forestry Law. Thus, she lobbied her husband to act on the violation and worked to expose the problem, even though, as she admitted, "I was conscious it would bring trouble at home."[20]

The courts eventually had the violators remove the livestock. Some of the cattle, however, had to be killed by park employees who distributed the meat to hospitals. When asked about the political ramifications of denouncing this scandal, Figueres replied that she "was born to serve . . . [and that] political positions do not belong to us, they are only loaned— they are not fulfilled just by getting votes." From that time on, Doña Karen lobbied for national parks, funding, and international assistance on ecological issues. In 1972, for example, she used her position to solicit funds from UNESCO on behalf of the National Parks Department and the Caribbean Conservation Corporation for the on-going marine turtle protection program at Tortuguero.[21]

Twenty years later, Karen Olsen de Figueres was still involved in environmental issues. Her husband's death in 1990 did not deter her from running for an at-large seat in the Legislative Assembly (which she won), where she continued to be active in environmental policy making. She identified her work there as an effort to attain "consistent" government attention to rational and sustainable use of the country's natural resources. Legislation she was working to pass in 1992 concerned preventing Isla del Coco (off the Pacific Coast) from tarnishing its national park status by becoming a casino island for which many people with "right now" attitudes and "short-term economic hopes" were pushing. She introduced legislation banning the importation of foreign toxic waste to be dumped in Costa Rica, supported the idea of a Western Hemisphere "green belt" corridor to run from Canada to Chile (which would "cause a political and environmental unity" across the Americas), and advocated that San Lucas Island become a marine research station for the University of Costa Rica. In the administration of her son, President José María Figueres (1994–1998), Doña Karen retained the office of "itinerant ambassador and counselor" to the president. She remains involved in a variety of social, environmental, and international issues.[22]

Mario Boza and Alvaro Ugalde did not enter the political fray that rocked Santa Rosa with the 1971 cattle crisis and in which Karen Olsen de Figueres was so personally involved. Since one of the perpetrators was their supervisor, they logically stayed their distance. Not so, however, when the fourth scandal hit Santa Rosa one year later. Because a severe drought was adversely affecting agriculture in Guanacaste in the late spring of 1972, the director of MAG decided to allow area farmers and ranchers to cut hay in the park's savanna grasslands. The area had been protected from fires and hunters for two years by the fledgling park staff and Peace Corps volunteers who were enraged at the ministry's decision.

Harvesting in the park was more than Santa Rosa administrator Ugalde could take, and this time he decided to oppose very actively the agriculture minister's decision. The result was that the minister was going to fire Ugalde from Santa Rosa. But Boza did not give him the chance; he transferred Ugalde to Poás Volcano and moved the director of that national park, Vernon Cruz, to Santa Rosa. The switch seemed to mollify the ministry because Cruz was not as vociferous against the government as Ugalde. The hay-cutting experiment did not turn out to be very successful and the ministry never tried it again.[23]

Larger problems loomed, however, in funding the national parks once they were created. Boza recalled, "The biggest challenge we faced was breaking out of the vicious cycle between the need to develop a system of national parks and the lack of resources for doing so." The Forestry Law outlined how the DGF and its parks department would be funded from both regular and special budget allocations from the Legislative Assembly. Boza remembered, however, that "it was always a terrible fight to have our funding needs included in the general budget, because we had to compete with programs for building highways, schools, airports, and other public works, and even with other departments in the same ministry. Those were very hard times; our arguments were weak because we lacked experience, and we did not have public opinion on our side. We survived more by luck and determination than anything else."[24]

Much of Boza's determination and hard work was directed at looking for funds outside of government sources. He started to make appeals to international assistance agencies and to conservation foundations. The

World Wildlife Fund was the first organization to respond in December of 1971 with a check for $5,000 to help with the protection of Tortuguero.[25] Boza undertook a far more ambitious fundraising project the same year. He wrote a "project proposal" entitled "Pilot Study of Potential Park Sites and Reserve Areas throughout Costa Rica" and sent it to his friend and mentor Gerardo Budowski at the IUCN in Switzerland. He noted that a Tropical Science Center (TSC) team of experts "with intimate familiarity with natural areas throughout Costa Rica . . . and recognition in the field of natural resource conservation" had offered to conduct the "badly-needed pilot study of potential park site(s)" if funding could be obtained. Personnel on the team included such conservation-minded stalwarts as Alexander Skutch, Leslie Holdridge, Joseph Tosi, Robert Wilson, and Olof Wessberg. Steve Harrel, a specialist in forest recreation planning, would lead the team and prepare the final program for the IUCN's consideration.[26]

Boza also wrote Myron Sutton, at the Division of International Affairs of the USNPS, to solicit his help in making some contacts at the offices of international conservation organizations and to help him plan a fundraising visit to the United States. Sutton obliged and helped Boza to arrange interviews at the Conservation Foundation, the National Geographic Society, the Nature Conservancy, and the Ford Foundation.[27] Boza traveled to the United States in the summer of 1971 and was successful in marketing his country's conservation needs to the different organizations. The trip was the start of a long and warm relationship between the administration of the Costa Rican park system and the international philanthropic community.

One of the areas for which funding was so desperately needed and what became one of Boza's greatest challenges was in staffing the new national parks. As one National Parks Department report put it, "Getting professional personnel—guides, guards, laborers, cooks, and others— [was] one of the major problems of the park service" and was a "principal preoccupation of [its] director" in those early years. Starting with the original five guards (who were paid seventy-five dollars a month) and a small office staff, Boza learned to be creative in accomplishing goals and paying for projects. He used funds donated by international organizations to pay overtime wages to staff members from other government agencies, especially from the Ministry of Public Works, to construct roads and firebreaks in conservation areas. He procured labor and guard duty from different local branches of the Rural and Civil Guards (Costa Rica's national police force). He utilized volunteers from the National Youth Movement (estimated by one report to be worth $8,000 in free labor), the Costa Rican Boy Scouts, and a variety of different local groups to help construct paths and maintain other park services.[28]

In 1971 Boza wanted to send two other promising conservationists to study in the parks program in the United States. He contacted Myron Sutton again at USNPS to see about the possibility of arranging courses and park visits for Sergio Salas and Ernesto Crawford. But this time Boza wanted the Costa Ricans to observe how park programs functioned in tropical settings. He sent Salas and Crawford to the Caribbean National Forest in Puerto Rico, to a national park in the U.S. Virgin Islands, and to Everglades National Park in Florida. They also attended the ten-week "Introduction to Park Operations" course that the USNPS held at its facility in Harper's Ferry, West Virginia. Crawford returned home, but Salas extended his trip to include visits to national parks in the American West and, upon Sutton's suggestion, even to Hawaii Volcanoes National Park. He returned to Costa Rica via stops at protected areas in Mexico and Guatemala to further enrich his understanding of tropical conservation.[29]

Boza also relied on other people to help with various national parks projects. He received the able assistance of scientists at the Organization of Tropical Studies (OTS), TSC, and CATIE to help with the research and planning of different national parks. Another individual, Tex Hawkins, who had helped Alvaro Ugalde during the Santa Rosa crises, offered his journalism skills to Boza to help develop a public relations program for the new parks department. Boza obviously had few funds with which to pay Hawkins, so he solicited help from IUCN.[30]

Hawkins, originally a Peace Corps volunteer, paved the way for many other workers from that organization to help with conservation efforts in Costa Rica. In 1971 the Peace Corps decided to send twenty volunteers to Costa Rica, but increased the number when many of its workers were expelled from Bolivia due to a political crisis there. One hundred of those volunteers (not all in the field of conservation or ecological sciences) were diverted to Costa Rica—a move supported by President José Figueres and the U.S. ambassador to Costa Rica, Walter Ploeser. For Boza and the parks department, the assistance came at an opportune time—when funding and experience were scarce and needs were great. According to an agency report, the Peace Corps "was one of the most important sources for bringing in workers who could complete a diverse range of tasks—technical as well as administrative." So great was their assistance, Boza later wrote, that "at one point we had eighteen Peace Corps volunteers and only twelve national staff."[31]

Peace Corps workers were put to work in a variety of different positions. Alan Moore, for example, helped in park administration and was instrumental in developing plans for the conservation and management of volcanic areas. He solicited ideas from the director of Hawaii Volcanoes National Park, who was only too glad to send letters and photographs of ideas that worked well for signs and other visitor services. Steve Cornelius was a herpetologist who not only assisted in the study of marine turtles but was also used by Boza to help draft legislation for the protection of the giant reptiles. And Christopher Vaughan was a wildlife biologist among whose early duties in Costa Rica was to research the trade in endangered species.[32] Vaughan, like Hawkins, stayed a long time after his two-year stint in the Peace Corps. He ended up making Costa Rica his home, wrote the management plan for Corcovado National Park, and today is a professor at the National University.

Vaughan's project on the marketing of Costa Rican threatened species is indicative of the emphasis Boza placed on creating parks for their importance in protecting biological diversity—even at the relatively early date of 1971. In a grant request to the IUCN for his project, Vaughan explained that he would be investigating the "volume and diversity of wildlife which leave this country annually bound for international markets." He related how quetzals, "innumerable" parrots, sloths, ocelots, tanagers ("shipped sixty in a box"), and green turtles (for their meat and shells) all commanded high dollars on the black market. To illustrate the size of the problem, Boza wrote the U.S. Fish and Wildlife Service explaining how an American company was killing one hundred of the giant marine turtles *daily* and shipping the meat to U.S. markets. Part of Vaughan's mission was to use wildlife photography exhibits and other media to produce "educational programs aimed to 'turn people on' to the treasures they possess and stress the necessity of preserving it."[33]

Boza took full advantage of this type of public relations opportunity that the Peace Corps workers provided. He used them to write newspaper press releases to keep the media up to date with conservation news and park developments. Jaime Socash was a Corps volunteer in graphic arts who was put to work to design pamphlets, exhibits, signs, and color schemes for the National Parks Department. Kirk Koepsel was a volunteer in Costa Rica in the early 1980s who, along with trail construction, maintenance, and staff-training duties, also had essential public relations responsibilities. He lobbied for support and organized trips into protected areas for residents who lived near them as a way to acquaint the people with the benefits of conservation.[34]

Many Peace Corps units have worked on conservation issues in Costa Rica since those first years of national park development. By the early 1980s the parks department came to rely on these volunteers but became more selective in choosing who would be accepted. The service now expected workers to have degrees in mechanical engineering, hydrology, natural resource management, marine or aquatic biology, forestry, range management, zoology, and wildlife conservation among other degrees in those respective fields. Course work on "recovery of damaged ecosystems" or "forest regeneration" as well as field experience were highly recommended. As needs continued and the department became more professional, these criteria reflected the trend to develop more sophisticated conservation policy.[35]

Boza also had to tackle other administrative and conservation concerns. Night poaching in protected areas was an ongoing problem. Acquiring equipment, supplies, machinery, and construction materials for the parks became a difficult and expensive chore. Again Boza had to rely on international contributions for many of the day-to-day equipment needs of the parks. He had to find funding and materials to restore the Casona and other buildings in Santa Rosa. And he had to work on keeping a proposed jetport *out* of Santa Rosa. He again solicited help from Gerardo Budowski on this matter and asked him to send President Figueres a letter explaining why an airport in Santa Rosa would be harmful to the park. Budowski sent the letter; the jetport was not constructed.[36]

Setbacks and challenges, however, were matched by conservation successes. Costa Rica's first two national parks, Poás Volcano and Santa Rosa, were functioning well and gaining in popularity in the early 1970s. Between 1971 and 1972, 70,000 people visited Poás Volcano and 15,000 visitors went to Santa Rosa. The first foreign tourists to Santa Rosa, Californians traveling south down the Pan American Highway in two pickup trucks in January 1971, found the park by accident and were pleasantly surprised with all the monkeys and other wildlife they were able to observe.[37]

Boza actively sought public support for national parks by preparing materials on their historical value for magazines and newspapers, and he wrote his own brochures that appealed to the patriotism of the readers. His pamphlet on Santa Rosa, for example, was entitled *Santa Rosa: Cuña de nuestra soberanía* (Cradle of Our Sovereignty). He made sure one was sent to every member of the Legislative Assembly. He also personally invited every Assembly member to the opening ceremony of the new visitor center at Poás Volcano National Park in August 1972. Many attended. Boza also persuaded high schools to include national park information in their science curriculum and sponsored student trips to the parks. The National Youth Movement also hosted weekend trips and work camps to the parks. Community development associations, local Rotary and Lions clubs, and even the Folklore Dancing Club all became active supporters of the national parks cause. The strategy was applauded by Luis Fournier, who wrote that "it resulted . . . in having a double function: to protect the cultural and natural heritage of the nation as well as to provide public recreational services."[38]

These early successes did not go unnoticed by the international conservationist community. IUCN invited Boza to speak at its Second World Conference on National Parks in 1972. The conference was to be held near Yellowstone—the world's first national park—and was to be part of the 100th anniversary of that park's creation. Boza responded that "it was a great honor to be invited to write a paper" for the conference and that he would accept "with great enthusiasm" the chance to attend the event. He wondered, however, if such a new program as that of Costa Rica's— only two years old at the time—could be of much service or example to international conservationist delegates. Frank Nicholls, the deputy director general of IUCN, replied that Costa Rica's new parks program and recent successes made for an even better reason to have Boza speak and would serve as a stimulus for other small, developing nations.[39]

In his presentation, "Costa Rica: A Case Study of Strategy in the Setting Up of National Parks in a Developing Country," Boza told fellow delegates at the conference about his plans for establishing and managing Poás Volcano and Santa Rosa. "The common feature of these two parks," he began, "is that they are attractive both to the people of the country and to visitors from abroad, are of easy access, and have great national significance, conditions which made their establishment possible without opposition from anyone." While this optimism obviously downplayed the opposition of local stockgrowers in and around Santa Rosa, it did represent prevailing sentiment for park creation in those years. One newspaper reporter related how Boza, "in his quiet, studious manner," told of how Costa Rica's park development did not have "the explorer's drama that surrounded the start of America's national parks at Yellowstone a century ago," but how it was "an idea whose seed must be carefully planted and nurtured to obtain public support that will allow it to compete with the nation's other demands." [40]

The support came. Other national parks and reserves were created in the early 1970s: Manuel Antonio National Park on the Pacific Coast (1972); Rincón de la Vieja National Park—an active volcano in Guanacaste that is home to hot springs, fumaroles, hidden waterfalls, and mixed dry and evergreen forests (1973); Guayabo and Negritos Biological Reserve—rocky islands in the Gulf of Nicoya that are a haven for shorebird rookeries and tropical dry forests (1973); Guayabo National Monument (coincidentally with the same name as the island reserve but actually inland near Turrialba)—Costa Rica's largest archaeological zone with pre-Columbian Indian ruins dating back to A.D. 800 (1973); and Barra Honda National Park—a series of steep caverns on the Nicoya Peninsula that were not "discovered" until 1967 (1974).

Each of these new parks has its own story on how it was selected, planned, and eventually designated and managed by the National Parks Department. Newspaper articles gave attention to each area and advocated their protection. Manuel Antonio National Park (named after a Spanish conquistador who is buried there), however, was an area not originally sought after by Boza and the parks department. That park was the product of local initiative—a drive by residents there who, so unlike locals near other areas such as Cahuita and Santa Rosa, actively campaigned to conserve the area as a national park.

The Manuel Antonio site had at one time been owned by the United Fruit Company as a result of a land trade by the government of Costa Rica. Due to its terrain, however, the firm never cleared it for banana production and thus later sold it to other private interests. Boza, who had never been to the Manuel Antonio beaches and forests on the Pacific Coast and who was busy dealing with crises in other parks, was reluctant to take on another project in late 1971 and early 1972. Vernon Cruz, the one-time director of Poás Volcano and Santa Rosa parks, however, urged that he look into the possibility. Cruz had spent personal time at Manuel Antonio and was familiar with why residents of Quepos (a town near the park area) and others were fighting to save the land: not just for the beauty of the mixed tropical forest that meets the Pacific with pristine white-sand beaches, but also because they were opposed to the foreign capitalist developers who were trying to build luxury resorts there. Quepos had a history of avid syndicalist activity since the 1930s and had elected Communist Party members to the Legislative Assembly. The people there were just not ready to have outside capitalists come in with disregard to local feelings. A variety of groups, including a small farmers' association, the high school student council, a chapter of the local National Youth Movement, and a prominent leftist family all became involved in working to keep the developers out. Some people even resorted to "monkeywrenching" tactics like cutting down fences and threatening to bomb the gate of a construction site. Thus, Cruz convinced Boza of the bright opportunity that existed for park expansion, and the two of them, along with Peace Corps volunteer Christopher Vaughan, flew to the area and surveyed it as a potential park site.[41]

Boza must have been impressed with what he saw. When he returned to San José, he drafted a bill to declare Manuel Antonio a national park and got a Quepos *diputado* to sponsor it in the Legislative Assembly. A delegation from the Assembly toured the area, saw the destruction started by the construction firm, and rallied for the bill's approval. President Figueres signed it into law, and a bond was levied to buy back the property and to pay for its development as a protected area. Today Manuel Antonio is the smallest but one of the most visited of Costa Rica's national parks—averaging about 200,000 visitors a year.[42]

Manuel Antonio and the other new parks were designated during the 1970–1974 administration of President José Figueres. While it was Figueres' pen that signed the parks into law, their creation and successful operation did not come without the determination, hard work, and support of various individuals inside and outside of the government. Mario Boza spearheaded the work, but he had the welcome support of many fellow biologists, geographers, and social scientists at Costa Rican universities. According to Alexander Bonilla, one such avid supporter, professional associations as well as mountain-climbing and caving clubs, environmental groups, garden societies, and youth groups all "played very important roles in the development of these wild areas." International organizations like IUCN, World Wildlife Fund, Nature Conservancy, Sierra Club, and various European environmental groups all continued their financial and technical assistance. And people like French conservationist Jean-Paul Harray, Prince Bernard of the Netherlands, Prince Philip of England, and others involved with international environmental concerns were people Boza remembers as being "very pleased to lend themselves to our cause."[43]

One organization that was extremely helpful in technical assistance and moral support was the U.S. National Park Service. Boza cultivated his friendship with Myron Sutton and Julio Marrero (of the USNPS in Puerto Rico) and often corresponded with them on matters of tropical conservation. Sutton sent Douglas Cuillard, a naturalist at Everglades National Park, to Costa Rica several times to consult on various projects. One that Cuillard assisted in was helping to develop a network of paths that would survive the high rainfall and moist conditions at Poás Volcano. Cuillard sought the advice of the director of Olympic National Park in Washington State, who was used to similar weather patterns, and found out from him that a gravel and wood-chip combination withstood the Pacific Northwest's rainy conditions better than other path-building materials. Othello Wallis from the USNPS regional office in San Francisco provided advice on developing marine national parks, and Arthur Hewitt, the acting superintendent of Hawaii Volcanoes National Park, was consulted on protecting volcanic areas.[44]

Boza and his small staff also received assistance and moral support from international agencies. John Milton, the director of international programs for the Conservation Foundation in Washington, D.C., took special interest in Costa Rica's early parks and got his organization to help fund projects. The Costa Rican government applied for and received a $1.8 million loan from the Central American Development Bank for the development of Poás Volcano National Park. And the Peace Corps, the British Volunteer Services Organisation, and the Caribbean Conservation Corporation continued to send much-needed volunteer workers throughout the seventies and eighties.[45]

The early years of the development of national parks in Costa Rica bear the very heavy imprint of Mario Boza and Alvaro Ugalde. Indeed, Boza has written that he and Ugalde and others "launched the conservation movement in Costa Rica."[46] While this is not too much of an overstatement, other scientists and activists were closely involved. One of the most important of these in the early years was Vernon Cruz. After his stints as director of Poás Volcano and Santa Rosa, Boza created an administrative job for him back at park headquarters in San José. He became a "floating administrator" to visit potential park sites, to present slide programs regarding the park system, and to visit with communities that might be affected by park development. He remembers very well how hard he, Boza, and Ugalde worked in those early years and why they kept it up: "Sometimes we'd work through the night at Boza's house. He was always working all the time with lots of projects. He kept us busy with all his ideas. It wasn't really working. We *liked* the problems, the feeling of responsibility for the nation's resources. . . . [A]ll anybody thought about was how fantastic nature was, and how important it was to protect it for everybody."[47]

Interestingly, as much as Boza and Ugalde worked together, they have been described as having quite opposite personalities. The "reticent, scholarly" Boza and the "outgoing, combative" Ugalde seemed to balance each other out. Likewise, they were members of rival political parties—Boza, the more conservative Christian Unity Party (dominated by the Calderón family), Ugalde, the more liberal National Liberation Party (of the Figueres legacy). One article in the 1970s reported that "some people surmise that the two friends maintain affiliations with opposing parties so that no matter which side wins an election, the parks will have an advocate with connections."[48]

Connections or not, Boza learned that he was going to be transferred out of his position in 1974. José Figueres' presidential term had expired and the winner of that year's election was none other than Guanacaste rancher/lawyer and president of the Legislative Assembly, Daniel Oduber Quirós. Although Boza was not of Figueres' political party (the PLN), he nonetheless had retained his position as head of the National Parks Department. Oduber was also of the PLN but replaced Figueres' minister of MAG with Rodolfo Quirós, who was over the parks department and evidently wanted political unity within his ministry. Boza left to help develop a school of environmental sciences at Universidad Estatal a Distancia (National Open University) but cleverly maneuvered to get Ugalde (who was in the PLN) appointed his successor at the parks department.[49]

Thus, a new chapter of Costa Rica's conservation history opens with

Alvaro Ugalde as director of national parks. Mario Boza remained active in conservation efforts throughout the next decade, albeit in different venues of the private and public sectors. Most important, a system was now in place to conserve the nation's natural heritage, it was functioning with responsible personnel, and conservation in general was gaining in popularity with Costa Ricans. The system was soon to be tested by the challenges that lay ahead.

CHAPTER 2

5 *Conservation Continued*

THE ODUBER YEARS

I believe nature's beauty is for everyone to enjoy, not just a few. . . .
[T]his small country . . . has a diversity of climates and species that
makes it important from the scientific point of view. That's why we
want to keep as much of our territory as possible in a condition to be
studied and enjoyed by people.

Daniel Oduber Quirós, interview with
Andrew Reding, "Voices from Costa Rica"

"The Greatest Friend the National Parks Ever Had"

After Alvaro Ugalde's transfer from Santa Rosa to Poás Volcano and after
he had worked as director of that park for about a year, he decided it was
time to consider getting a master's of science degree. He took a one-
year leave from the parks department in 1973 to study at the University
of Michigan's School of Natural Resources on an OAS (Organization of
American States) scholarship. Upon his return to San José in 1974, he
learned that he had been appointed director of the National Parks Department in the new administration of President Daniel Oduber.

That Ugalde and Oduber were of the same political affiliation and that
Mario Boza had assisted in the nomination process were assuredly factors
in Ugalde's appointment. But the move was surprising in some ways
since Ugalde had locked horns with Oduber on the Santa Rosa controversy of 1970. Several years later Ugalde mentioned in an interview that
he tried to stay out of Oduber's sight the first few months he was in office:
"But one day I ran plunk into the President coming out a building.
'Ugalde! Where are you now?' the President asked. 'In the parks depart-

ment,' I replied. 'Come see me,' he said. My heart sank. But I was surprised. Instead of Oduber being revengeful, he became the greatest friend the national parks ever had." [1]

President Oduber's interest in national parks stemmed largely from his belief that the parks could be an economic boon for tourism. This was actually an insightful stance since the term "ecotourism" was hardly in use in the mid-1970s and Central America was hardly a popular destination for foreign tourists. But Oduber saw the value of national parks for use by local Costa Ricans as well. Early in his term he proposed spending $3.5 million to create a series of small urban parks within a half-hour's drive of San José in second-growth forest and farmlands of the Central Valley. This "great recreational reserve" idea never materialized, but Oduber was successful in dramatically increasing the size of the Costa Rican park system, which did open the door to thousands of Tico and foreign tourists. In their book on Costa Rican national parks, Mario Boza and Rolando Mendoza wrote that Oduber and Rodolfo Quirós, the new director of the Ministry of Agriculture (MAG), gave priority to programs dedicated "to the conservation of nature and renewable resources as a way of contributing to the country's socio-economic development." [2]

For tourism or conservation, then, expansion of the national park system continued at a rapid pace during Oduber's term in office (1974–1978). More important, conservation successes occurred without the controversies that had marked the earlier years of park development. "Fights during the Oduber administration were almost non-existent," Alvaro Ugalde later recalled, "the president was supporting everything." Naturalist Allen Young, who conducted research in Costa Rican national parks during this time period, wrote that Oduber "nurtured and developed" the park system. [3]

The praise is well deserved. By presidential decree Oduber created the large national parks of Tortuguero (previously protected as a nature reserve), Corcovado (a remote tropical wet forest on the Osa Peninsula in southwestern Costa Rica—one of the most species-rich areas in the entire country), Chirripó (Costa Rica's highest mountain at 12,500 feet and home to one of the only Andean *páramo* life zones in all of Central America), and Braulio Carrillo (a tropical wilderness area of steep, forested mountains just north of San José). He also approved measures to amplify Santa Rosa National Park, to provide more developed services at Rincón de la Vieja National Park, and to establish the Dr. Rafael Lucas

Rodríguez and Palo Verde national wildlife refuges and the Isla del Caño, Hitoy-Cerere, and Carara biological reserves (see Figure 2).

All totaled, national park and equivalent reserve acreage nearly doubled during the Oduber presidency. The country's percentage of territory designated as protected jumped from 2.5 percent in 1974 to 4.5 percent in 1978.[4] Likewise, the creation of each of the new parks or reserves reflected a growing conservation ethic in Costa Rica in the mid- to late 1970s. And like the earlier parks, each of the protected areas had its own particular genesis story. The origins of Chirripó, Corcovado, and Braulio Carrillo especially exemplify the links between a nascent but growing environmental movement and the development of national parks and protected areas.

Chirripó (sometimes referred to as Macizo del Chirripó or Cerro del Chirripó) in the Talamanca range in south-central Costa Rica was promoted by the mountain-climbing club of the University of Costa Rica. Club members had started lobbying for the mountain's protection and designation as a national park in 1972; their efforts finally paid off when President Oduber declared it as such in August 1975. But leaders in the club valued the peak for more than just climbing and hiking; they understood how conservation would help to preserve the mountain's variety of ecosystems. The park is approximately 109,000 acres and includes not only Chirripó's peak, *páramo* grasses and shrublands, and glaciated valleys, but also thousands of acres of rare high-altitude oak forests that originally were to have been protected (but never really were) in the 1940s along the Pan American Highway. These forests are a vital part of a network of watersheds providing hydrological power to generate electricity for tens of thousands of Costa Ricans. The benefit of conserving Chirripó and its environs for its ability to produce electrical power, then, helped the mountain climbers sell the idea of converting the area into a national park.[5] And the park is testimony to the work and success of Costa Rica's budding conservation movement. UCR mountain-climbing club members Adelaida Chaverri, Alfonso Mata, Jorge Moya, and others who led the lobbying effort for Chirripó became active participants in the Costa Rican environmentalist community.

The history of Corcovado National Park—100,000 acres of rare and endangered Pacific Coast rainforest—also begins with individuals within the scientific community who lobbied for its protection. The reason so many people were concerned is that the forests of the Osa Peninsula represent a unique ecosystem in Central America that was quickly being threatened. Christopher Vaughan, the Peace Corps volunteer who wrote the management plan for the park, asserts that Corcovado is the only remaining Pacific Coast tropical wet rainforest in the region and possibly in all of Latin America. Tropical botanist Gary Hartshorn has written that Corcovado's forests are "the most exuberant in Central America" and that they are "just as impressive as the best forests . . . in the Amazon Basin or . . . Malaysia and Indonesia."[6] Such a place also represents the home to the largest populations of jaguars and Baird's tapirs in all of Central America and is habitat for hundreds of bird, reptile, and amphibian species.

The problem was that such an impressive forest was drawing the attention of logging companies, and the rivers and hills of the Osa Peninsula were attracting mineral prospectors. Unbeknownst to colonial conquistadors or explorers, the peninsula was laden with gold. Prospectors did not start mining there until the 1930s, but more and more people had trickled into the area by the 1960s. Timber companies cut trees, speculators sold land, and squatters followed to set up farms on cleared land or commenced panning for gold. To obtain legal title, the *precaristas* needed only to occupy the land for three years. Many aggressively defended their territory with guns, creating a truly violent mid-twentieth-century "frontier" atmosphere on the Osa Peninsula.

By 1972 the situation was dire enough to draw the attention of biologists and conservationists. Some environmental studies had previously been conducted on the peninsula, but none had recommended creating a national park. Forest ecologists Leslie Holdridge and Joseph Tosi from the Tropical Science Center (TSC), for example, had been hired by a large timber firm in the mid-1950s to develop forest management plans for the area. While they did not specifically recommend protected status for the Corcovado region at the time (there was no forestry law or national park service in existence yet), they did see the area's value for tropical research. They opened a TSC biological field station on land leased from the timber company in 1964 and shared the facility with students from the Organization for Tropical Studies (OTS).

Others continued investigating Osa's tropical forests. On the recommendation of Christopher Vaughan, Mario Boza and Alvaro Ugalde from the parks department flew over the peninsula to consider it for park status. Ugalde supported the idea, but Boza was not in favor due to the

population of *precaristas* living in the region. But as time went on, economic interest in Corcovado's trees and land increased. A Japanese firm
was looking into logging the area and a U.S. firm was interested in converting the subsequently clear land into citrus groves. Many letters from
conservationists around the country in support of making Corcovado a
nationally protected area started pouring in to the national parks office.
When Ugalde assumed the directorship of the parks department in the
Oduber administration, he rekindled the idea of a national park on the
Osa Peninsula. He sent Olof Wessberg (the Swedish orchard farmer who
had worked so hard to establish the Cabo Blanco Absolute Nature Reserve) on an initial park feasibility study.[7]

Wessberg and his wife, Karen Mogensen, had been intrigued with the
Osa Peninsula by the reports they had heard of its tapir population and
exotic plant species. Mogensen first visited Corcovado in June of 1975
and related how beautiful and pristine it was. Her husband went later the
next month, as Mogensen recalled later, overtly to look for a different
species of avocado tree to add to his orchard at home in the Nicoya Peninsula. However, she admitted that Wessberg was actually on a mission
from the parks department to survey the area. Either way, Wessberg never
returned. He was killed by a machete blow to the head by a local man
who accompanied him into the rainforest. The murder was shrouded in
mystery; the man admitted to the killing, then recanted and blamed his
father, then later admitted it was he who was the murderer. Was it a con-
spiracy? Mogensen, crushed by the news, raced to Corcovado to search
for the body and found it. She later told an interviewer that the police
investigation was inadequate and that she believed the murderer was
paid to commit the crime. The suspect was later convicted. Mogensen
continues to live in her modest home in Montezuma near Cabo Blanco
where she can commune with the monkeys and coatimundis who she
believes "are so much happier than we are . . . [and] are much more in-
telligent." "They can live on the land for thousands of years and leave it
beautiful," she philosophized. "We humans come in and in twenty years
it is destroyed."[8]

Less than a month after Wessberg's assassination, President Oduber
announced his decision to support the creation of a Corcovado National
Park. "The foreigner who died to defend natural resources deserves a
monument," Oduber told a *La República* newspaper reporter. He compared the crime to the violence in the Middle East but suggested that

"here we kill people for defending a tree, an animal, a plant . . . [t]his is very serious." Two months later, to the dismay and disgust of some of his cabinet members, President Oduber declared Corcovado a national park. Most of the land was government property and the rest was acquired from a timber company through a land swap. Oduber promised full support and funding for the park's development and operation and offered a start-up grant of over $100,000 from his presidential discretionary fund. The parks department also received $10,000 from both the World Wildlife Fund and the Rare Animal Relief Effort to be used for Corcovado. Nine guard positions were created and eleven members of the Rural Guard were posted in the newly designated park.[9]

The problem was that Alvaro Ugalde had estimated that only forty-five families would need to be removed from the park and that the total cost involved, including the park start-up expenses, would be around $175,000. He soon learned, however, that there were more than 1,500 *precaristas* with hundreds of head of livestock. Some families had been living in the area for over twenty-five years, and all squatters, by Costa Rican law, had to be reimbursed for "improvements" to the land. And because there were no roads into the park, all families and livestock would have to be moved by boat or airplane—further increasing the cost of the relocation effort.[10]

Ugalde had to approach President Oduber with the new information that the cost would be more like $1.2 million. "I was sure I'd be fired the day I had to tell the news to the President," Ugalde said in an interview with two U.S. reporters, "but he took it calmly, telling me: 'It may cost ten million colones now, but how much more would it cost fifty years from now? We will do it.'" Ugalde was delighted. "Corcovado has been a real exciting experience," he wrote a friend at the U.S. National Park Service a few months after the park was declared. "With the president backing us, we have been able to get from the government two million dollars in six months and the old dream is now a reality. . . . I am as optimistic as ever."[11]

Braulio Carrillo National Park in the Cordillera Central north of San José was also the result of a spirited lobbying campaign by members of Costa Rica's scientific and conservationist community. The park was named after the country's third president from the 1830s who worked to create national unity and dreamed of uniting the Caribbean and Pacific ports by roads with the population centers in the Central Valley. His efforts eventually resulted in a road from San José to Puntarenas on the Pacific Coast, but the steep, densely forested mountains of the Cordillera Central that separate San José from the Caribbean lowlands prevented much of a road from ever being built. Transportation for nearly one hundred years was limited to a railroad that had been constructed in 1882 by a division of the United Fruit Company or an extremely slow, curvy road going south from San José to the port town of Limón via Cartago and Turrialba.

For over a century, then, the need had been great to construct an improved road from the capital to the Caribbean. It was not until 1973, however, that serious plans and financing materialized for the project. As part of an effort to bring modernized transportation and communications to Costa Rica to assist in its economic development in the early to mid-1970s, the World Bank agreed to finance a modern highway that would run north out of San José and then over the tropical mountain range to connect with the town of Guápiles in the Caribbean lowlands. But when the bank hired the Tropical Science Center to conduct an environmental impact study on the project's feasibility in 1975, it learned that a modern road through the mountains could open the area to agricultural colonization, cause massive deforestation, and severely threaten the variety of ecosystems that are found in the region. The study was conducted by Leslie Holdridge and Joseph Tosi. They found that massive deforestation in the Cordillera Central would result in heavy flooding with disastrous effects on the people and their economy in the Caribbean lowlands and would destroy the very highway being built. The TSC study approved the highway project only on the condition that a conservation unit be declared to protect the forest surrounding the proposed road.

With Alvaro Ugalde as its director in those years, the park service lobbied to declare a region far greater than just the area surrounding the highway to become what is today Braulio Carrillo National Park. Ugalde and his department received the welcome support of conservation groups around the country. One of the groups that was the most active on the issue, and that worked to make sure conservation measures were implemented during the road's construction, was the Colegio de Biólogos (Biologists' Association). UCR biologist Pedro León, a member of that organization who was particularly involved in the cause, claimed that Braulio Carrillo was "a classic example" of a successful "compromise." He wrote letters to government officials on behalf of the association saying that "unless a park was created along the road, there wasn't going to be a road—that erosion would destroy it." President Daniel Oduber agreed and signed an executive decree to declare the area a national park in 1977. The Legislative Assembly approved the measure a year later (with some modifications), thus creating an 80,000-acre park, most of which is inaccessible wilderness. Gerardo Budowski once said that "Braulio Carrillo may be one of the most interesting parks in the world, totally unknown even though a half hour away from a big city." The park had nearly 4,000 visitors its first year of operation. The San José–Guápiles Highway was completed in 1987—nine years after the park declaration.[12]

The president assisted conservation efforts in other ways also. He declared 1977 as the "Year of Natural Resources." He issued decrees providing legal protection to many endangered species, including quetzals, macaws, manatees, tapirs, jaguars, ocelots, and other felids, birds, and reptiles. And he worked to increase the parks department budget from $600,000 in 1976 to $1.75 million in 1978. The department's staff tripled (it doubled in 1977 alone) and included 400 employees by the end of Oduber's term. And he was instrumental in helping to acquire international financial assistance to support new parks and staff. The U.S. Agency for International Development (AID), for example, loaned the government of Costa Rica $1.2 million for a five-year management plan for Braulio Carrillo National Park. Smaller amounts came in from Philadelphia Conservationists, Inc. (which had Theodore Roosevelt III as an influential board member), the Nature Conservancy, the Natural Resources Defense Council (NRDC), and the Rockefeller Foundation. The NRDC's funds were to be used specifically for researching sustainable development and deforestation issues. The University of Michigan School of Natural Resources donated money to the National Parks Fund, and the London-based World Pheasant Association sent donations to help protect curassow and chachalaca habitat in Corcovado.[13]

Alvaro Ugalde learned that not all of the international conservation groups' funds came easily. The Nature Conservancy's international office, for example, sent a representative to Costa Rica in 1977 who expected five-star service. In a letter to Ugalde after her visit, Sandee Garihan wrote that "there should have been a well-organized itinerary for me to see most of the country as possible." She went on to complain that she had to find evening entertainment and the theater by herself in San José. And she advocated keeping an airstrip in Corcovado (a decision that Ugalde and the parks department had been struggling with) so that people like her on tight international schedules could enjoy a visit to even the remotest of areas.

In a most telling letter of response, Ugalde not only addressed Garihan's concerns but provided a rare glimpse into his insights that were compounded by the hectic schedule he was forced to keep. He opened the letter by apologizing for the delay of his response—"due to the amount of work and lack of help"—and continued: "lately I have had hardly any time of my own. . . . Sometimes I feel very tired, but unless I have been brainwashed, I believe we don't have much time in this mad race against destruction. There are not many more individuals in Costa Rica working in this field, therefore I cannot just simply send everything to hell. . . . Although we make a lot of mistakes, I just hope that what I am doing is the right thing and not just a waste of time." Several months later Garihan replied to Ugalde's heartfelt message, apologizing that it took her so long to write; she said that she had had to take a one-week vacation in Tampa (where she "loved the theatre") to recuperate from Costa Rica and that she had just returned from "a six-week jaunt on the French-Italian Riviera." [14]

The Servicio de Parques Nacionales

One of the most important changes that occurred during the Oduber years was in the status of the National Parks Department. First, in 1975 the department within the General Forestry Directorate (DGF) was elevated from "subdirectorate" to "general directorate" with greater individual autonomy. Then in 1977, with the Legislative Assembly's approval of the National Parks Act, it was completely separated from the DGF and became the National Parks Service—Servicio de Parques Nacionales (SPN)—its own division within the Ministry of Agriculture. The change of status was more than just bureaucratic shuffling; it established the legal framework for the SPN's work and provided the freedom for the SPN to expropriate land for parks. The act specifically made it illegal for any part of a national park to be removed from park status except by legislative decree. It allowed the SPN to set entrance fees, to make recommendations for new parks, to define park regulations, and generally to expand its services with fewer hierarchical hurdles. It was a change that

Mario Boza and Alvaro Ugalde (who retained his job as head of the newly named SPN) had been advocating for over five years and one that took a great deal of hard work to pass.

Lobbying for a more autonomous parks department within MAG began in 1972 when Mario Boza sent a draft proposal to the Legislative Assembly. It outlined how a separate parks service with its own budget could better promote recreation and tourism, the conservation of nature, scientific research, public education, the preservation of historic and archaeological areas, and the protection of watersheds and indigenous reserves. The proposal was sent to committee, specifically to the Commission on Social Affairs, where it was batted around until 1977.[15]

Lobbying both for and against the proposal occurred during the early 1970s when the bill was in committee. The Association of Costa Rican Industries opposed the measure, explaining in a letter to the commission that a separate national parks division would be "too ambitious for Costa Rica" and would be too expensive. Members of that organization saw the proposal as a new way to levy unnecessary taxes on businesses and considered Costa Rica's ratification of the International Convention for the Protection of Flora and Fauna to be sufficient for wildlife conservation. Groups in support of the measure included the Association of Biology Students, which wrote urging the commission to approve the bill and send it to the Assembly as a whole. "The richness of our wildlife," one letter from the organization began, "is converting itself into a myth." It went on to suggest that a more powerful parks division would be able to conserve the country's natural resources more efficiently.[16]

One of the most important proponents of the National Parks Act was none other than Karen Olsen de Figueres, whose husband was still president of Costa Rica when the bill was first under consideration. In fact, as Mario Boza explained in testimony to the commission in November of 1973, it was Figueres who was one of the project's originators. She had supported Boza and his proposal from the beginning and worked to lobby various *diputados* for its approval. Boza also explained that such problems as night poaching and an insufficient number of park guards were reasons that Doña Karen and others saw the need for granting the parks service more legal authority and funds with which to protect the parks and reserves.[17]

The legal authority of the new act, according to former park service attorney Ana María Tato, was essential. The act made very clear fifteen prohibitions for visitors and property owners in and around the parks that would serve as the legal base for park acquisition and land expropriations. All of the property and expropriation guidelines, she explained, advance the "national park objectives" and represent a legal "necessity" as opposed to "arbitrary decisions [made by different] administrations."[18]

After three more years of changes and reconsiderations, the Legislative Assembly approved the bill and in August of 1977 President Oduber signed it into law. The new SPN seemed to function better on its own accord within MAG and lasted there for nine years. In 1986 it was transferred to a newly created Ministry of Natural Resources (MIRENEM) but retained its "directorate" status. In 1994 MIRENEM was changed to the Ministry of Environment and Energy (MINAE) and the SPN was dissolved. In its place is the National System of Conservation Areas (SINAC), which manages national forests, parks, monuments, and biological reserves.

Designating new parks and having the active support of the president for a more independent and better-financed park service, however, did not solve all of Ugalde's problems. In 1975, for example, trouble brewed when the parks department announced plans to expand Cahuita National Monument on Costa Rica's southernmost Caribbean coast. Residents there were upset to learn that the government was planning to expropriate more land in the area to develop Cahuita into a national park. They thought that "national park" designation would convert their small town into an Acapulco-style beach resort and hotel complex and bring with it the attendant social problems caused by tourist zones. Local farmers and fishermen opposed the plan, fearing it would infringe on their livelihood.[19]

Opposition to the parks department culminated at a public hearing held in the town of Cahuita. Ugalde attended the meeting to represent his department and argue for the development of the national park, but, as he later related to reporters, "it seemed like I was the only defender." Because residents of this part of Costa Rica are mainly black, English-speaking *caribeños,* however, Ugalde switched to English during his presentation, which greatly aided his cause. "After I explained to [the] Cahuitans that the real threat came from the land developers and wealthy people from San José who wanted beach-front vacation homes or land for speculation," Ugalde recalled, "the local people realized that the park would give the best protection to their way of life." When the people at the town meeting voted, the result was a near unanimous decision to support the park.[20]

News of Costa Rica's park creations and expansions started attracting foreign visitors in the mid- to late 1970s. In 1978, President Oduber's last year in office, over 34,000 foreigners visited the national parks and reserves. While that figure represents only slightly less than 10 percent of the total park visitation numbers (357,000), it does signal the start of a trend. Many foreigners, especially those from the United States, wrote directly to park service chief Alvaro Ugalde to request information and maps of different protected areas. Most of the letters began with comments like "I have recently read (or heard) that . . ." and some type of request for information. Many even asked what type of gear they should bring for certain areas of the country for different times of the year. Ugalde responded to every request.[21]

Mario Boza, Alvaro Ugalde, President Oduber, and other park proponents were of course pushing tourism as an economic benefit of national park development, but sometimes foreigners got the wrong idea about conservation in Costa Rica. An article in the *Washingtonian* in early 1977, for example, praised Costa Rica as "a great escape to go hunting." When Ugalde saw a copy of the article, he was enraged. He penned a no-nonsense, strongly worded letter to the paper's editor-in-chief explaining how the SPN was having enough trouble as it was with poaching and trying to restore populations of endangered species without the paper blabbing that the country was a haven for hunters. He related how conservation areas in Costa Rica were intended for the free transfer of biological properties and were to be used for scientific research or to be enjoyed for their scenic and natural values.[22]

In fact, other relations with the United States started to sour somewhat in the mid-1970s. Although Mario Boza had enjoyed a strong working relationship with the U.S. National Park Service's Division of International Affairs during his time as parks chief, Ugalde's experience with the USNPS was less productive. Again, without mincing words, Ugalde wrote one staff member of that division in the spring of 1976 that "it would be important to see some more interest in Latin America from the U.S. National Park Service; up to now, relations have been rather cool." He did not specify exactly what he wanted from the USNPS in that particular letter, but three months later he reiterated his concern directly to the head of the Division of International Affairs, Robert C. Milne, saying, "I look forward to warmer relation between us."[23]

Ugalde was frustrated in those years because, despite the designation of more national parks in Costa Rica, deforestation in unprotected areas was causing grave environmental dangers. In a report to the Legislative Assembly in early 1976, he warned that the "situation is extremely critical"—that Costa Rica was in a "state of true ecological catastrophe." He explained that "enormous clear-cuts" were damaging "important watersheds" and that extensive forest fires were occurring on a daily basis. He pointed out that although forest destruction threatened the survival of wildlife, it also created severe problems for humans by decreasing hydropower potential. To stem this tide, the government conducted studies to establish more forest reserves (apart from national parks). Although 225,000 were set aside as forest reserves, the majority, as Luis Fournier has written, "in reality were not legal or physically consolidated" and thus were not protected from cuts by loggers or farmers. Mario Boza explained that the problem was that the forest reserves were managed by different guidelines. "It's a big mistake to try to manage a forest that doesn't belong to you," he said. "Parks have worked because we [SPN] own them, and because the Park Service has a clear mandate to protect land, while the Forest Service [DGF] has a lot of other responsibilities."[24]

In another attempt to address the forestry crisis, Costa Rica hosted a variety of conferences and symposia during the Oduber years (three in 1974 alone). Some were national and others were regional for Central America. Many of Costa Rica's conservationist leaders—like Luis Fournier, Sergio Salas, Adelaida Chaverri, Rodrigo Zeledón, Rolando Mendoza, Pedro León, and Mario Boza—were participants and guest speakers at the conferences who evaluated the successes and dilemmas of the Costa Rican conservation experience.

In 1976 the government established the Consultative Commission on Natural Resources to formulate a long-range plan of action for Costa Rica's forests. Composed of Alvaro Ugalde (who took a six-month leave of absence from SPN to be its technical coordinator), Mario Boza, Oscar Arias, and others, the commission proposed establishing a national institute for natural resources and environmental conservation (INDERENA). The new agency would have the power to formulate national policy to arrest the "galloping deforestation" that the nation was experiencing. The institute would replace the DGF, since, as Ugalde explained in his usual manner of not beating around the bush, it lacked the "resources, organization, and power" and was too "small [an] organization for [such] a large task."[25]

But despite President Oduber's endorsement, the Legislative Assembly refused to support INDERENA. Finances, disagreement on the necessity of establishing a new agency, and perhaps the *diputados'* underestimation of the gravity of deforestation at the time defeated the proposal. Ugalde returned to his post at SPN to fight for Corcovado and to deal with other park concerns. Forest reserves (or national forests) remained in the domain of the DGF until the agency reorganizations of the mid-1990s created SINAC.

For his part in vitally assisting conservation efforts and specifically for his determination to decree Corcovado National Park in the face of so many odds, President Daniel Oduber received the coveted Albert Schweitzer Award from the World Wildlife Fund in 1976. He was also the recipient of the New York Botanical Garden's 1977 Green World Award for his "outstanding leadership in preservation and protection of the natural environment." In presenting the award to him, Howard Irwin, president of that organization, said that Oduber had "displayed great courage" in working to create Corcovado National Park and that "his bold action is not only to the credit of Costa Rica, but should serve to inspire leaders of other countries to follow suit." While in New York accepting the honor, Oduber also addressed the United Nations and spoke against international military spending, the absence of which in Costa Rica helped to ensure funds for conservation and social programs.[26]

Nine new protected areas (nearly 350,000 acres of land) were added to the Costa Rican national park system during Oduber's term in office. In a 1986 interview, the former president reminisced about his role in conservation: "I have emphasized conservation in order to afford future generations of Costa Ricans the pleasure of enjoying the nature I enjoyed as a child and adolescent. . . . It is of global interest to defend all the treasures we have. . . . We're very small, but we can be an example . . . of a society that struggles for peace, justice, and beauty."[27]

When Oduber's term of office was over in 1978, many people wondered if harmony between conservationists and the office of the president would be a thing of the past. The new president, Rodrigo Carazo Odio, who represented a coalition of opposition political parties, survived a vicious election campaign and was soon to face an economic cri-

Figure 7.   Vista at Braulio Carrillo National Park

sis that would test conservation policy and other social services to their very core. But, as we shall see, environmentalists' worries about his administration would be ill conceived. How in fact conservation measures dramatically *increased* during a time of severe economic crisis during the Carazo years warrants attention here.

6 Conservation through Crisis

CARAZO AND THE ECONOMY

No la vimos como una tragedia; la vimos como un desafío.
Alvaro Ugalde, personal interview, 25 June 1992

(We didn't see it as a tragedy; we saw it as a challenge.)

"Obstacles Became Opportunities"

The Costa Rican national park system was in its first decade of existence when it faced serious cutbacks and restrictions due to the severe economic crisis that hit the country in 1979. Characteristic of most of the Latin American world, Costa Rica went into deep financial debt as a result of overextended loans from international banks. Unable to service the notes, Costa Rica soon became one of the seventeen most highly indebted nations of the world and had the highest per capita debt in Latin America. Much of the problem had to do with factors outside of Costa Rica due to the international economic recession of 1979 that was partially a result of dramatic increases in oil prices. The recession spurred high interest rates in the world capital market and a decrease in prices for traditional products that Costa Rica had to offer. The wars in Nicaragua and El Salvador during this same time period weakened the Central American Common Market, which further hurt Costa Rican trade.

By 1985 the external debt amounted to $3.8 billion (equal to $1,500 per person in Costa Rica) and was the largest per capita debt in the developing world. For Costa Ricans this translated into spiraling inflation (hovering around 48 percent in 1980–1982), a doubling of unemployment (from 4.3 percent in 1979 to 8.7 percent in 1982), austerity measures, and federal spending cuts. Especially hard hit were the budgets of environmental management agencies like the General Forestry Directorate (DGF) and the National Park Service (SPN).[1]

Despite budget cutbacks, however, these years were also marked by a significant increase in conservation efforts and national park and equivalent reserve designations. From 1978 to 1982, the years of the administration of President Rodrigo Carazo, the amount of land protected by law in Costa Rica increased by nearly 583,000 acres, or 4.7 percent. At the beginning of Carazo's term there were approximately 451,000 acres of land designated as conservation areas (or 3.5 percent of the country's land mass); by the end of the term there were approximately 1,033,000 acres (or 8.3 percent of the country). Some of the new areas included Palo Verde, Isla del Coco, and La Amistad national parks and Isla Bolaños National Wildlife Refuge. Significant expansions of Guayabo, Corcovado, Manuel Antonio, Santa Rosa, Tortuguero, and Braulio Carrillo national parks were also decreed by President Carazo.[2]

"Keeping a clear vision . . . and a conception of priorities" was how the former president described his role in conservation through crisis. The priorities originated early in his life—he had spent much of his childhood in a rural, agricultural setting in the mountainous area near Turrialba. It was there that Carazo gained an early appreciation for the land and nature. As he has written in his memoirs, "The rural environment shaped my vocation, my love for family, for the Homeland, and for a great interest in the values of that Costa Rica . . . for all of my life." Likewise he has maintained a religious belief in the proper stewardship of the land: "Insofar as our faith teaches us that man was made in the image and likeness of God, we know that the Creator gave us an important responsibility: to take care of that environment so wisely prepared as our home."[3]

In his term as president during the economic crisis, Carazo acted on the values he had learned earlier in life. "I had the fortune that my childhood and youth took place in an environment of hard work, poverty, and austerity," he reflected in his memoirs, conditions that "forged habits in my years as a child that I still appreciate and want to conserve." He also claimed that his interest in conserving forests stemmed from an Arbor

Day experience he had as a college student at the University of Costa Rica. For Carazo, saving as many of Costa Rica's natural resources as possible was a means to promote a long-range economic savings for the country. Thus, dealing with the economy (he was an economist by profession) but continuing the government's active commitment to conservation (by then only a ten-year-old program) meant taking strong leadership in promoting new parks and making thoughtful appointments to key conservation positions. To the surprise and delight of those who wondered if Carazo would continue the conservation momentum of the Oduber administration, Carazo named Mario Boza as his advisor on natural resources and retained Alvaro Ugalde as head of the National Park Service. He also appointed Hernán Fonseca as minister of agriculture, in general a supporter of the parks program. Promoting conservation during the economic crisis also meant working closely with private conservation organizations ("the environmental groups greatly aided my work") and recruiting financial assistance.[4]

Finances in Costa Rica were definitely short. Carazo was the first Latin American president to suspend payments on international loans. The International Monetary Fund (IMF) thereupon imposed strict austerity measures on Costa Rica and urged quick development of nontraditional crops to market abroad. Choosing "to defend the honor of Costa Rica" and not wanting to impoverish the citizens of his country, as one former staffer put it, Carazo kicked the IMF out of Costa Rica and promised not to devaluate the *colón*. Holding out for more than a year, he was forced to devaluate in 1980. In his own words, Carazo emphasized that "there is no internal problem or crisis that should serve as an excuse for a government to submit to impositions made from abroad . . . [and] for this we broke with the IMF and decided to stop all payments on interests and amortizations of the external debt." Fighting for "the respect of our national sovereignty," Carazo was the only president to boot the IMF out of a country.[5] But although exports were higher during the Carazo years than those of his predecessor (Daniel Oduber)—accounted for by such new crops as pineapples, which enjoyed robust external demand—and personal savings, exports, and GNP were all higher than during the years of his successor (Luis Alberto Monge), the country did suffer from a weak economy. Internationally renowned tropical biologist Thomas Lovejoy (who worked with Costa Rican conservationists during the crisis), however, compared this period to the Great Depression in the United States, not only for its financial stress, but also for "recognizing the urgency of conservation projects."[6]

The national park system had its work cut out for it. James Barborak, a national parks planning consultant from the United States who was hired by the SPN to work in Costa Rica in the late 1970s and early 1980s, posited that the country's economic crisis presented the SPN's greatest challenge to date: "justifying before the public and legislative powers that more expenses were necessary for acquiring, managing, and administering the areas in its care." José Rafael Mora, the director of the National Parks Foundation, which was created to help raise and distribute conservation funds, agreed and wrote in a letter to one potential donor that "effective management of existing areas is sometimes as tough a problem as the creation of new ones." And Alvaro Ugalde mentioned that it was fortunate that many parks were already in existence before the crisis, but to manage them and create new ones during this period was to "transform crisis into opportunity."[7]

The Carazo government did what it could to continue funding the parks program. But while the administration's "enthusiastic support for financing the SPN" was immeasurably helpful, as Luis Fournier noted, inflation reduced the purchasing power of the already cut budgets. One park official recalled that "we lost eighty percent of the buying power of the rest of the budget between 1980 and 1986."[8]

The opportunity that came, then, according to Ugalde, was "to look for money in other places." A fundraising campaign the likes of which the Costa Rican conservationist community had never before witnessed was launched. Nationally, members of Costa Rican environmental groups solicited contributions, donated time, and did volunteer work in the parks. Internationally, many different governmental and nongovernmental organizations were tapped for funds and support. A 1979 loan for $5.5 million from U.S. AID, for example, was an instrumental source of funds targeted for environmental education, soil conservation, reforestation projects, and for forestry and other natural resources management. Similar aid programs in other countries—e.g., CIDA in Canada, SIDA in Sweden, FINNIDA in Finland, DANIDA in Denmark, NORAD in Norway, GTZ in Germany, and ODA in Great Britain—started working with Costa Rica and made loans earmarked for conservation causes.[9]

Responses to grant requests from nongovernmental organizations were equally successful and helpful. Twenty-six organizations from around the world helped with financial and technical assistance. Groups such as the Sierra Club, Rare Animal Relief Effort (RARE), Caribbean Conservation Corporation, New York Zoological Society, Philadelphia Conservationists Inc., World Wildlife Fund, International Union for the Conservation of Nature (IUCN), the Nature Conservancy, and others all financially supported the parks program in Costa Rica during the crisis years. And grant supporting organizations like the Tinker Foundation and the Rockefeller Brothers Fund made generous contributions.

As a legal way to monitor these loans and contributions, Mario Boza, soon into his new position as presidential advisor on natural resources, believed that a nonprofit organization was needed. With the help of government attorneys, he established the National Parks Foundation (Fundación de Parques Nacionales, FPN) in 1979 as a quasi-governmental body. It set out to seek grants and to solicit and channel major contributions (corporate or private) for specific conservation causes. Its first board of trustees included Boza (president), Alvaro Ugalde, SPN assistant director José María Rodríguez, and UCR biologists Luis Diego Gómez and Pedro León. The board hired José Rafael "Rafa" Mora as its first executive director and, by 1982, four other employees. The first donation came in 1981 from the Caribbean Conservation Corporation for 300,000 *colones* (approximately $6,200).[10]

The FPN board members learned to be quite creative, direct, and specific in their fundraising appeals. The Animal Research and Conservation Center of the Bronx Zoo, for example, contributed $30,000 to help the FPN purchase photographic equipment for an environmental education project in early 1982. A letter from that organization mentioned that "we had quite a visit with Mario [Boza] last week. . . . [He's] quite an ambassador." In an FPN report in June of the same year, Rafa Mora reported that the World Wildlife Fund had donated over $1,100 for the construction of a new guard station on the east side of Corcovado National Park, the Caribbean Conservation Corporation had given $9,000 for Santa Rosa National Park, a private donor had sent $4,125 for vehicle restoration and various projects at Tortuguero, and even the Minnesota Nature Conservancy had contributed $150 for miscellaneous equipment.[11]

The FPN board implemented other innovative ideas to raise funds. It sold brochures, books, and T-shirts at national park visitor centers. It created an "Honorary Members" category for the FPN to honor individuals who had played a strong role of support. People on the list included Daniel Oduber, Karen Olsen de Figueres, Gerardo Budowski, Kenton Miller, and prominent international conservationists like Jacques Cousteau. Funds that were raised went toward maintaining, upgrading, and expanding of national parks. President Carazo had made clear that "one of the objectives" of his administration was the "completion and consolidation of the wilderness areas of Costa Rica." [12]

Carazo's first move as president to accomplish such goals was to decree Isla del Coco National Park in June 1978. The park consists of the entire 6,000-acre Isla del Coco—an isolated volcanic island in the Pacific Ocean 300 miles off the country's west coast. Often called "Costa Rica's Galapagos," Isla del Coco is home to 140 endemic species of flora and fauna that evolved in isolation, is noted for its rather tame animal life due to an absence of natural predators, and is difficult and expensive to get to. It is characterized by lush pre-montane rainforests and palm groves—home to the Roosevelt palm (*Rooseveltia frankliniana*), which was named after the U.S. president who visited the island four times between 1934 and 1940. Coral reefs grace its shores.

Carazo was particularly happy to have been able to assist in the island's protection. He and eighty dignitaries made the long trip to Isla del Coco in an old tuna boat to dedicate it as a park, becoming the first Costa Rican president to visit a national park while in office. There was reason to rejoice in its designation; the island has not been without its fair share of troubles over the years. First referred to on a map in 1541, Isla del Coco became a haven for pirates in the eighteenth and nineteenth centuries. By 1973 pirates had introduced pigs and other domesticated animals to run loose on the island. Its supply of fresh water, coconuts, and meat (pigs that thrived there for centuries) made it a favorite stopover for whalers and pirates who are thought to have hidden valuable treasures in its forests. Mario Boza has written that "it is believed that more pirate treasures have been buried on this island than anywhere else in the entire world." The government of Costa Rica claimed Isla del Coco in 1832 after it authorized the rescue of shipwrecked Chileans from the area. [13]

A century and a half later, evidence of environmental degradation from these past experiences still exists. Joseph Franke writes that "pigs, cats, goats, and white-tailed deer have all done considerable damage." Pigs, "probably the worst offenders," he explains, "loosen so much soil in the process of rooting for food that they have been implicated in causing the death of coral on some of the reefs" (due to erosive runoff). Cats are also a problem ("they kill and eat anything that moves"), and introduced flora such as coffee plants and guava trees "replace the less aggressive native understory plants." Likewise, trumped-up stories of hidden riches brought in treasure hunters from different parts of the world, which further threatened the overall ecological integrity of the island. According to Boza, over 500 such treasure hunts have been conducted— meeting with very little success; "only a few doubloons have been found to date."[14]

Not long after the park was declared, ASCONA (Asociación para la Conservación de la Naturaleza), Costa Rica's largest environmental group in the 1970s and 1980s, recommended that only "a very controlled and limited number of visitors" be permitted to visit the island in order to maintain its pristine environment. The SPN agreed and created such guidelines, but budget cuts forced the government to replace its park guards on the island with public security guards (paid out of a different budget). The change did not go over well with the country's leading tourism company (Adventures in Costa Rica), which ran well-regulated, guided tour experiences of the island. Its president, Michael Kaye, wrote directly to President Carazo complaining that the new guards were "dirty, inattentive, unwelcoming, and uncaring"—conditions that made him wonder if they were fit to enforce the island regulations. Carazo turned the matter over to the ministers of agriculture and public security to resolve the problem through improved training. The FPN's Luis Diego Gómez later wrote Carazo thanking him for the way he had handled "the delicate situation." And Carazo was obliged to turn an earlier Isla del Coco concern over to SPN when he received a request from an elderly European man (nationality unknown) to live his final days and die on the island. The park service denied the request, citing statutes that disallowed such park uses.[15]

The question of treasure hunting, however, has not been as easy to dismiss. In the summer of 1982, SPN received an especially convincing request for a "retroexcavatory" expedition from a San José businessman. The letter stated that the project would be conducted "conforming to all requirements and controls . . . [to] protect the area's ecological conditions." As per civil code, the treasure hunter promised to fork over 50 percent of what he found to the government and, rather obsequiously, offered to donate 5 percent to SPN because "without a doubt the national parks constitute the future of the country." He swore that he was "completely sure of the location of the treasure from which the nation and the [Park] Service will derive enormous economic benefits."[16] He, like all the others, found no treasure.

Despite that fact, ten years later a wealthy American treasure hunter received permission to proceed with a multimillion-dollar search using sonar and ultralight aircraft. He agreed not to cut down a single tree or to incur any other disturbances on the island or coral reef. From the start, however, the expedition was shrouded in controversy. The problem lay in the fact that the treasure-hunting concession was supported by Hernán Bravo, chief of SPN's parent agency, the Ministry of Natural Resources (MIRENEM). According to UCR marine biologist Jorge Cortés, who became involved in the affair, there was internal conflict within the ministry and Bravo wanted the approval process expedited. He sent SPN director Alvaro Ugalde to meet directly with the Americans at Isla del Coco. Amazed and flustered by Bravo's temerity, Ugalde called on Cortés, whose specialty is in coral reefs, to look over the proposal and assess its environmental impact. Cortés recalled that the meeting he had with the Americans "was like meeting with the Mafia." "These big guys in suits came out," he said, "and literally asked me 'How much do you want?'" Cortés opposed the plan, but because the enterprise was to have paid $100,000 for the concession, MIRENEM granted the permission anyway. Cortés never believed the amount was paid, despite what Bravo claimed in a television appearance in which he answered questions about the scandal. The Americans never found any treasure.[17]

As if that were not enough controversy for one little island in one year, there was a proposal for Isla del Coco to become more of a developed tourist attraction in 1992. Plans were for a large casino complex to open on the island, which would include hotels, swimming pools, and beaches. Karen Olsen de Figueres vigorously opposed such a proposal when she was a *diputada* in the Legislative Assembly and sponsored legislation against it. She was opposed to the "right-now attitude" to get rich quick that was behind the plan and questioned "how much it [would] cost in the long term." The casino plan failed and access to the island today remains very limited (there is no air service). Camping is not allowed; overnight visitors are required to stay on their boat. Thus, Isla del Coco is a remote, pristine national park that Rodrigo Carazo said he was glad to have had a hand in protecting as a "gift to mankind."[18]

Carazo also had a personal interest in designating another piece of land—the El Murciélago ranch in northwestern Guanacaste province. By presidential decree on 13 September 1978 he declared a 28,600-acre ranch to be an extension of Santa Rosa National Park. El Murciélago (The Bat) had been the vacation hacienda of Nicaraguan dictator Anastasio Somoza Debayle, who would be ousted from his country in the 1979 revolution. The land, near where Somoza's father had owned land before it was expropriated in 1966 to become Santa Rosa National Park, was a sore point for many anti-*somocista* Costa Ricans, including President Carazo, who sided with the Sandinistas in the Nicaraguan conflict. Thus, many legislators, newspaper editors, and other Ticos applauded Carazo's move to expropriate the Somoza hacienda.

In his words, Carazo explained that he and many other Costa Ricans had resented Somoza's "growing investments" in their country and had worried that it could lead to an armed invasion from a base at El Murciélago. They had reason to worry. Earlier in 1978 Somoza's troops had crossed into Costa Rica to raid Nicaraguan guerrilla camps and had killed several Costa Ricans in the melee. At that, Carazo broke relations with Nicaragua and called Somoza a "disgrace to Central America." He also upped the number of police patrolling the border to 6,000 members and borrowed 500 Venezuelan rifles, as the *Washington Post* reported, "to fend off Nicaraguan incursions."[19] Likewise, Somoza had already been using his ranch for "periodic vacations," Carazo wrote in his memoirs, "and had been traveling there by air from Nicaragua . . . without completing any form of official immigration authorization." Thus he continued, "I decided to expropriate his ranch and surrounding lands . . . he didn't deserve to be an owner of one square centimeter of our soil." In May of 1979 the Legislative Assembly approved the takeover and later that year, with Carazo's blessing, divided the El Murciélago sector into two parts: a majority of the area would become part of Santa Rosa, and an adjoining part would be directed by ITCO (the land colonization authority) for the benefit of small farmers to settle. Regarding the Santa Rosa extension, Carazo wrote that El Murciélago would "contribute in a great way to the country's conservation of ecological riches for Humanity, and at the same time protect resources for an ever closer future."[20]

Some inherent problems lurked in this official park extension. For one, as José Rafael Mora at FPN pointed out, it was "physically separated from the main body of the park." And while he lauded it as an area that "protects the superb northern coast of the Santa Elena Peninsula, . . . [t]ransportation for park patrols [was] extremely difficult." Likewise, Alvaro Ugalde and others at the SPN believed that Carazo's expropriation had a hidden agenda outside of conservation. They maintained that El Murciélago actually had been divided up *three* ways—with the third, smallest part to be utilized by the Ministry of Public Security as a training base for Nicaraguan Sandinistas.[21]

Actually, this scenario fueled growing discomfort for Ugalde as head of the Park Service in the new Carazo administration. Relations had not started well very early into the term. First, the previous administration had assigned the SPN a new responsibility toward the end of Daniel Oduber's term in office that ended up causing Ugalde a great deal of grief: management of the National Zoo—which, but for a few exceptions, is designed to showcase Costa Rican fauna and is located in the historic Amón district of San José. The problem was that a free-roaming population of white-tailed deer got a bit out of control and began grazing on rare plants cultivated by botanists who were planning to move a botanical garden into the park. Ugalde was ordered to do something about the problem; when trapping the deer failed, he ordered them shot. Zoo workers killed fourteen deer just days after Carazo was elected. The press sensationalized the story, some animal-rights attorneys took the Park Service to court, and Ugalde was indicted for destruction of government property. But while the jury in the trial found Ugalde not guilty, the zoo case boded badly for starting work with a new administration.[22]

Second, and more significant, the public security forces training Sandinistas on part of the old El Murciélago grounds had crossed into Santa Rosa National Park. Ugalde strongly disapproved. "They were using park fences and trees as targets for practice with heavy weapons," he recalled later. "I got the feeling we were losing the park." Frustrated that it would prove to be a bad precedent and that the situation was growing worse, Ugalde wired the public security minister with a typically succinct message: "Your soldiers are destroying Santa Rosa National Park. The area is under the responsibility of the National Park Service and I ask that you get them out of the park."[23]

The telegram caused rockets to fly at President Carazo's cabinet meeting that, unbeknownst to Ugalde, took place that very afternoon. "I was later informed that I was accused of being unpatriotic, or some sort of traitor, and that I should be fired from the Park Service," Ugalde told an interviewer in 1981. "What saved my skin was that . . . the minister of agriculture, was very supportive of his staff." Fortunately for Santa Rosa, the public security personnel and the Sandinistas left the park, but it was at the expense of frayed relations between Ugalde and Carazo.[24] And once again, Santa Rosa was at the heart of controversial policy making, the fifth in a series of scandals (see Appendix 3). The turmoil was enough to make Ugalde think it was time for a change. Soon thereafter, he took leave of his position to begin doctoral studies at the University of Michigan. The new acting director of SPN was the very capable José María Rodríguez de la Guardia, an architect by profession who had been the assistant director of SPN for two years under Ugalde. Around the time he left, Ugalde voiced his frustrations in a letter to a friend at the Nature Conservancy, lamenting that "it seems not much could be accomplished during this administration."[25]

For the record, quite a bit continued to be accomplished on the conservation front in the next two years of Carazo's term. The year 1980, for example, marked the tenth anniversary of the Costa Rican parks program. To commemorate the occasion, on February 5, Carazo hosted an anniversary ceremony at the Casa Presidencial. It included an executive decree that expanded Guayabo, Manuel Antonio, Corcovado, and Tortuguero national parks—adding approximately 37,000 acres to the park system. Each expansion added vital wildlife habitat, fragile ecosystems, and important watersheds to be protected under national park guidelines.[26]

Toward the end of his term in office, Carazo also signed a proclamation that would greatly increase the size of Braulio Carrillo National Park. With the San José–Guápiles road project under way through the mountains of Braulio Carrillo, some conservationists were dissatisfied with the amount of land that was to be protected and began lobbying for its expansion. The Organization for Tropical Studies (OTS) entered the campaign as a way to create a biological corridor from Braulio Carrillo to its La Selva research station just north of the park. To do this, the government would have to buy out several landholders' properties. But with few funds readily available and with the urgency of protecting the area as quickly as possible looming over him, Carazo used a different approach to achieve the end result.

Recognizing the need "out of an intimate sympathy with the cause," as a Carazo staffer later put it, the president declared the area in question a *zona protectora* (a temporary legal status protecting the area against any property changes or development schemes) until the OTS could start a fundraising drive for the corridor. The OTS had been working with UNESCO to designate the region a World Biosphere Reserve and, as Carazo explained in a note to his minister of agriculture, Hernán Fonseca, the *zona protectora* status would freeze the area until those details and finances were worked out. He also solicited the assistance of his minister of justice, Elizabeth Odio Benito. "Given the urgency for immediately and adequately protecting this important zone that has a treasure of natural resources," he wrote in a memorandum to her, "I'm asking for your maximum cooperation in preparing all of the legal documents necessary."[27]

The MacArthur Foundation came up with a one million dollar matching grant that was met by a combination of sources that included the OTS, World Wildlife Fund, Fundación de Parques Nacionales, the Nature Conservancy, and the Costa Rican government. By the last six months of Carazo's term, the challenge had been met and the expansion of Braulio Carrillo was made possible. David Clark, the director of OTS, hailed the campaign as the "largest international conservation program in Costa Rica up to that date."[28]

In June of 1980 Carazo designated 23,400 acres of lowlands along the Tempisque River in southern Guanacaste as Palo Verde National Park. Abutting the Rafael Lucas Rodríguez National Wildlife Refuge, which had been declared by President Oduber, Palo Verde was a unique park in Costa Rica because it represented the largest and most threatened system of seasonal wetlands in the country. It is home to over 250 species of birds, has one of the highest concentrations of wintering waterfowl in the region, and supports populations of rare storks, ibises, and spoonbills. In his decree protecting the area, Carazo cited how Palo Verde would preserve "a place of particular importance for the conservation of migratory and resident birds . . . one of the richest areas of avifauna in the country."[29]

By the end of Carazo's term, Palo Verde National Park was to be clouded in a regrettable presidential controversy, as will be discussed in detail below. But before his term expired, the president worked to leave a final conservation hallmark of his administration: the creation of the International Park of Friendship, La Amistad. The expansion of existing parks and the creation of new parks like Palo Verde, important as they are for their significance in working to protect vital ecosystems, pale in comparison with the size and importance of Carazo's last park project. The creation of La Amistad, approximately 500,000 acres of tropical wilderness in the Talamanca range of south-central Costa Rica (see Figure 2), nearly doubled the size of the entire national park system. It was established in April 1982 as an "international park" with Panama, on whose border it adjoins. It was the first such park in Central America and the first area to be declared a World Biosphere Reserve by UNESCO (Man and the Biosphere Program) in the Central American and Caribbean region. The Biosphere unit includes La Amistad and all of its surrounding conservation areas (e.g., Chirripó National Park, two biological reserves, five indigenous reserves, one wildlife refuge, one national forest, and the Wilson Botanical Garden). Calling La Amistad the "pride of the nation," Carazo was pleased to play a role in this historic undertaking and remarked in his memoirs that "Costa Rica had brought forward, with great effort, a fundamental wealth for preserving the planet and humanity."[30]

La Amistad's official designation was a long time in the making. The idea of having a World Biosphere Reserve in Costa Rica originated in 1974 when a representative of UNESCO visited the country and met with a committee made up of Luis Fournier, Mario Boza, Rodrigo Zeledón, Gerardo Budowski, and others to consider the proposal. The plan continued to evolve with the idea of making it a binational friendship park later that year at the Central American Meeting on the Management of Cultural and Natural Resources. For the next four years, however, the plan lay dormant.

In late 1978 President Carazo met with a water-user association in southern Costa Rica to discuss ways of protecting the Talamancas' important watersheds. While there, he rekindled the idea of creating an international park as a way to help accomplish that goal. Soon he was meeting with various officials from the Republic of Panama to start hammering out the details. Undeterred by a series of coups and changes of governments in Panama, in March 1979 Carazo and Panamanian president Aristides Royo signed the final agreement. It proclaimed La Amistad Park to be "a symbolic gesture of the excellent relations of friendship and fraternity between the two people's governments, of the high scientific and ecological value of the region, and the necessity of conserving and preserving the [area's] flora and fauna."[31]

The next step was to organize a series of meetings and workshops to develop a scheme for the development of the park. Mario Boza, as President Carazo's natural resources advisor, was a key figure involved. He met with officials from the SPN and OFIPLAN (Oficina de Planificación, the government's financial planning office) and with representatives of the Panamanian president's office and the Panamanian Institute of Natural Renewable Resources. Next the TSC was tapped to survey park boundaries and to conduct research on the flora, fauna, and ecosystems of the entire regions. CATIE was contracted to study the planning of park services and installations. The TSC and CATIE studies were completed by September 1981 and were financed by OFIPLAN. However, because of the economic crisis and the devaluation of the *colón* at the time this research was performed, OFIPLAN had only about one-fifth of the funds that originally were to have gone toward the La Amistad project. But once again, the problem was seen as a challenge. It opened an opportunity for university students to help with the work that needed to be done and to earn college credit for it.[32]

They could not have chosen a better place for a hands-on ecological experience. The Talamanca Mountains embody eight of the twelve Holdridge life zones. They are home to 215 species of mammals, 250 species of amphibians and reptiles, 115 species of fishes, and 560 species of birds. They represent one of the most species-diverse and species-rich places in Central America for vascular plants.[33] What the area is not good for, however, is any form of crop cultivation. There are just too many steep slopes and too much inadequate soil to support agriculture—facts readily advanced by park proponents and planners.

Another component of the research on both sides of the border concerned the indigenous peoples who lived in that part of the Talamancas. The mountainous area is where Costa Rica's largest number of native peoples live and work—over 10,000 Guaymís, Brunkas, Cabécares, and Bribris—many still in traditional ways. Subsistence agriculture, hunting, and gathering are mixed with small farming ventures in the lowlands outside of the mountains by the majority of these Indians. Keeping these points in mind, the research team worked with the indigenous groups to recommend the creation of a series of reserves around the perimeter of La Amistad. The government agreed and established the reserves.

The end product of all the research was a forty-nine-page inventory of La Amistad's natural and cultural resources, socioeconomic characteristics, and a proposed management and development plan to make the area into a national park. A host of different Costa Rican and Panamanian government agencies all had a hand in finalizing the study.[34] Part of the responsibility for seeking funds for the park again fell on FPN since government money was really not available. A letter to the World Wildlife Fund from FPN director José Rafael Mora illustrates the degree of need: "Since there are now no facilities, everything from tents and sleeping bags to medicines and horses will be needed. The rangers will have to build lodging, cut trails, and literally create the park from the ground up."[35]

Finally, on 4 April 1982, President Carazo signed the executive decree that officially inaugurated La Amistad International Park (the section in Panama is simply called Amistad National Park). Carazo hosted a press conference to mark the occasion and had various dignitaries speak. Murray Silberman, who had replaced Mario Boza as the president's natural resources advisor, mentioned that the park had been "expropriated at no cost to Costa Ricans" and that it could be "a tourist draw on a par with Kenya." But the fact that it overlapped into Panama caused reporters to question the president more on the political situation of their neighbor to the south than they did on conservation in the Talamancas. Gerardo Budowski recalled that Carazo ended the press conference "by begging them to ask him something about [La Amistad] after a half hour of answering questions about [Panamanian strongman] Manuel Noriega."[36]

Soon thereafter, Carazo and a bevy of officials and reporters made a trip to La Amistad to visit the area and, similar to the presidential visit to Isla del Coco, conduct a brief on-site ceremony. Helicopters and jeeps were used to transport the roughly one hundred guests to the remote national park. While there, Carazo met with Guaymí *caciques* and viewed firsthand the terrain and landscape of the newly designated park.[37]

The international conservationist community rejoiced at the news of La Amistad's inauguration. Letters of congratulations poured into the Costa Rican government from all over the world. Michael S. Kaye wrote Carazo saying that "La Amistad, I am sure, will be recognized by the world as one of the most important protected areas on the planet." And in terms of what it meant for Costa Rica, as Murray Silberman wrote to a colleague in a similar position in New Zealand, because La Amistad "more than doubled the total area of national parks here, we are now, if not number one in the world in this regard, then pretty damn close!"[38]

And thus did La Amistad not only close out the term of Rodrigo Carazo but it also heralded the end of an era in Costa Rican conservation history.

Only a few national parks and reserves would be designated in what was left of the 1980s and in the 1990s. Mario Boza told the *Tico Times* that "we are moving out of the decade of declaration and into a period of consolidation and refined management of the parks."[39]

To help with these goals, Boza created an instruction manual for the management and administration of areas within the SPN's jurisdiction. In fact, it was also at this time that the whole way parks were being managed changed directions. Early parks were managed under the guidelines of a "master plan" but were criticized for seeming inflexible to the changing needs of the park. By the end of Carazo's term, then, the SPN required that a "management plan," an individual strategy or planning system, be written for each protected area. It had to include resource inventories, management programs for "integrated development," zoning and border delineations, mechanisms to evaluate and revise plans, and be printed and distributed for public access. Peace Corps volunteers and officials on loan from the FAO and UNESCO all wrote or assisted in the writing of various management plans during the low-budget and short-staff years of the economic crisis. SPN assistant director José Antonio Salazar further explained the benefits of the new system. In a memo labeled "'crazy ideas' for exploring new routes for protected areas under our care," Salazar urged that management plans be set up for "development stages." "In the specific case of Costa Rica where development conditions are so difficult," he continued, "slow but sure progress" worked better for park planning. The creation of the plans also produced the beneficial side advantage of getting the employees out into the field more so that they could better familiarize themselves with the area.[40]

In addition, the Carazo administration was characterized by a variety of other successful projects on the conservation front. In 1979 it backed legislation that provided tax incentives for planting trees and for not cutting timber on certain private lands as a way to discourage deforestation. In April of that year, Costa Rica hosted the two-week, fifty-nation Convention on International Trade in Endangered Flora and Fauna. Speaking there, World Wildlife Fund president Russell Train asserted that "Costa Rica has done more for conservation that any other Latin American country."[41]

President Carazo also became concerned that year about reports of pesticide-tainted runoff from banana plantations that was draining into the Caribbean at Cahuita and was starting to destroy the coral reefs.

He sent a letter to Standard Fruit requesting that the company reduce the runoff. But when the superintendent of Cahuita National Park approached the Standard Fruit manager to follow up on the president's letter, the manager is reported to have said, "Do you know what I think of this?" and, without waiting for a reply, tore up Carazo's letter.[42] It was then that marine biologist Jorge Cortés became involved with the coral reef issue, wrote his master's thesis about it, and worked to publicize Standard's poor stewardship and the ills of environmental contamination.

Also in 1979 Carazo took a personal interest in forming a network of biological research stations in the national parks and reserves. In a letter to his treasury minister, he outlined how the research stations could be used by Costa Rican university students and foreign researchers. They would also increase the country's prestige abroad among philanthropic organizations with the hope of attracting major conservation donations. According to Carazo, the stations would be "a form of non-extractive natural resource exportation." An important event that SPN sponsored that year was a research project on environmental education. The goal of the project was to form ways to use the national parks as tools in the "development of an environmental ethic" and "a better understanding of the relation between humans and the total environment and their responsibility in not degrading it."[43]

One of the events of 1979 that made national and international conservationists the happiest, however, was Carazo's veto of a proposed law that would have endangered marine turtles at Tortuguero. The law would have reduced the Caribbean's protective zone off the beaches from twelve miles to three. What this meant was that hunters would have been allowed to harvest turtles in unpatrolled waters in areas where the female reptiles rest during the day after ovipositing on shore. According to conservation writer George Reiger, people from around the world petitioned Carazo to veto the bill. And, as he continued, "whereas many other political leaders would have been inclined to sign the bill precisely because of all the outside (especially American) agitation, President Carazo recognized the dire ramifications of the legislation and vetoed it. Turtle aficionados sighed with relief."[44]

In 1980 the government sponsored the First Symposium on National Parks and Equivalent Reserves. The three-day conference was a way to bring together many of the people who had been involved with Costa Rican conservation issues and was used as a forum to assess the direction in which the national park program was headed. And in that same year, Carazo inaugurated the Center for Environmental Information and Documentation (CIDA), a joint project of the SPN and the National Open University. Its principal function is gathering and documenting information regarding Costa Rica's natural resources and the environment in general. It provides a data collecting and storing service that is used for environmental assessments, industrial planning, and research for educational projects.[45]

In 1981 Carazo and the director of OFIPLAN signed a declaration for the creation of a National Council for the Protection and Improvement of the Environment. The council would be a "coordinating and consultative organ" of the government and would be made up of representatives of various ministries and private organizations to "revise, integrate, and coordinate" national policy on the environment, make priorities, and analyze legislation.[46] Other programs that year included plans to increase cooperation between the SPN and DGF and for conservation departments to increase their involvement with Costa Rica's universities. And on a regional level Costa Rica hosted the Mesoamerican Workshop on Interpretation and Environmental Education. The three-week conference, organized by SPN and CATIE, was held at Manuel Antonio National Park and was designed to help conservationists from around Central America learn how to create national park management plans. It also served to promote ways of encouraging the development of environmental education and on-site interpretive facilities.[47]

Given the Carazo administration's record for national park designations and expansions and its emphasis on other conservation goals as listed here, it is surprising that Alvaro Ugalde said in an interview that "in the Carazo years, we [the SPN] didn't do much, we didn't get much political support, and we had a lot of trouble." Conversely, in 1981, Mario Boza and Rolando Mendoza wrote that "the National Park Service has very wide support from the government of the Republic [which] is demonstrated by many diverse programs, many of which are ideas of the very President, Rodrigo Carazo." They cited Carazo's attention to expanding the park system, increasing ground services, and creating CIDA as examples of his support.[48]

The Costa Rican national parks program not only survived but thrived during the debt crisis of the early 1980s. The crisis certainly challenged conservationists, but as Karen Olsen de Figueres put it when asked to describe those years, "Obstacles became opportunities." Surmising that "development is an attitude" and not merely governmental proposals, projects, and agendas, Doña Karen posited that the historical patterns of conservationist thought in Costa Rica led to its very ability to withstand the crisis. The vision of certain individuals was instrumental in channeling this course. Among those people, she related, was her late husband "Don Pepe"—who, by abolishing the Costa Rican armed forces in 1948, provided the means to fund other causes and who, again as president in 1970, designated the first national parks. She also listed people like Mario Boza, Alvaro Ugalde, and 1980s ASCONA leader Alexander Bonilla ("all of whom I love dearly")—who never wavered in their diligence to preserve Costa Rica's natural heritage, especially during the crisis.[49]

Both presidents Oduber and Carazo would have agreed with Figueres on the military versus conservation comparison. Oduber had stressed that very point when he delivered his address to the United Nations in October of 1977. And when asked by a *Washington Post* reporter what Costa Rica's secret was for a lack of some of the social problems that were affecting other Latin American nations, especially in view of the country's rapidly accelerating conservation program, President Carazo did not hesitate to answer. "The explanation is very simple," he stated, "we don't waste money on weapons, so we have resources for other things. The needs of our people come first."[50]

So opposed was Carazo to militarization that he believed Costa Rica would be the perfect host country for an international institute dedicated to the study of peace. His administration approached the United Nations in 1979 with such a proposal, and the General Assembly approved the University for Peace as an autonomous entity with partial U.N. support. While the school's mission is to teach students from all over the world the ways of nonmilitary conflict resolution, it also has an important environmental focus. Carazo explained that the school "concerns itself with everything that causes conflict in our time. We are, for example, enormously preoccupied with the destruction of the natural environment because that destruction is in turn causing serious outbreaks of violence in many parts of the world. What's more, the lack of resources for human survival is itself a source of violence."[51]

The university is located on land that was donated through an estate settlement near Ciudad Colón, twenty miles from San José on a wooded hillside with a vast view overlooking the Central Valley. The campus sits on 700 acres of forested land, 500 acres of which are to be preserved for their aesthetic value and scientific study. The current chancellor, Robert Muller (formerly of UNEP), is committed to a conservation curriculum that includes a master's program in ecology and peace. For his part in the school's creation, Carazo received the 1981 World Peace Prize from the International Association of University Presidents.[52]

Rodrigo Carazo, an economist by profession, advocated strong policies to help weather Costa Rica's debt crisis despite being severely criticized for his actions at the time and since. The facts are clear, not only on the more visible scale of increased acreage for protected areas, but also in terms of connecting conservation issues with solutions to social problems. The number of *precaristas* on public lands, for instance, was at an all-time high in the Oduber administration that preceded Carazo's term—despite a robust economy with low unemployment. *Precarismo* was more than halved, however, during the Carazo years, which unfortunately were characterized by the economic crisis and increased unemployment—conditions that usually result in greater population shifts to public lands.[53] Attention to housing concerns and other urban social issues helped to ease the brunt of the crisis, but standing firm against the IMF also played a significant role. He elaborated on this philosophy:

> The International Monetary Fund obeys the orders of its owners, the developed countries. . . . [I]t mainly focused on monetarist issues and not on social questions. . . . As for the World Bank, its representatives came to me with a suggestion. . . . In response to our foreign exchange problems in 1981, they told us we should stop eating meat, that we should export all we produce in order to obtain more foreign exchange. Had I taken them seriously, there would have been an uprising here. I would have had to tell the Costa Ricans, "Look, we can no longer eat meat. We're going to close all the butcher shops and all our meat will be eaten by the *señores* of the United States." How can the World Bank dare to suggest such a thing to a friendly country that has serious problems in this very difficult part of the world? But the policymakers in the Reagan administration don't have the slightest idea what they're doing because they simply don't know us. A very important U.S. official whom I met at a cocktail party said to me, "Someday I will have to come visit your beautiful island." I had to tell him that at that rate he would never make it.[54]

And, of course, producing more cattle for export would have accelerated pasture expansion and deforestation.

Concluding here, then, Rodrigo Carazo viewed conservation as a vital activity within his administration. "The national parks," he wrote, are "splendid natural laboratories which we offer to the international scientific community and also to the children, young people and adults who should not be denied the joy of direct contact with nature in its pristine state." And tying this belief to his concerns for world harmony, Carazo stated that his country's national parks "represent the contribution of the Costa Rican people to peace among men and good will among nations."[55]

The Palo Verde Controversy

There was little peace and less good will among conservationists toward President Rodrigo Carazo in the summer of 1981. One year (almost to the day) from when Carazo had designated Palo Verde National Park in southern Guanacaste, he indicated that he would be "segregating," or withdrawing, 9,900 acres from the park; he later upped it to 17,300 acres. The land, roughly three-fourths of the park's total acreage, had been, according to Carazo, expropriated improperly by the government—the landowners had not been paid the indemnity due them. The park's creation therefore had violated Article 45 of the Constitution of Costa Rica (regarding "inviolable private property") and Article 22 of the Ley Forestal, which concerned compensation for the acquisition of private lands.

Constitutionality notwithstanding, environmentalists inside and outside of the government were infuriated. The controversy dragged through the summer and into the fall of 1981 with some noteworthy twists and turns along the way. The issue itself reflects very well the deepening conservation conviction among Costa Ricans and their willingness to fight for a cause. The little that has been written on the subject, however, is polemical and imprecise. What merits attention here, then, is a review and analysis of the complete series of events to understand the controversy in its proper perspective.

At the heart of the matter was the fact that the Tempisque River Basin (where the park is located) is characterized by low marshy wetlands—

Figure 8. Scenic Overlook on the Tempisque River in Palo Verde National Park

Costa Rica's largest area for local and migratory waterfowl, but also prime real estate for the cultivation of rice. The land had been owned and operated by various agricultural conglomerates from Costa Rica, the United States, and Cuba, and with the recession in full swing, Costa Rica needed to produce as many agricultural crops as possible to increase its balance of trade. In July of 1981, when world prices for coffee continued to plummet, President Carazo announced a "new agricultural policy" that would promote increased production of other crops like beans, corn, and rice.[56]

News that Carazo was considering separating a part of Palo Verde known as "La Catalina" for rice farming reached the desk of his natural resources advisor, Mario Boza, as early as May of that year. Meeting with SPN director José María Rodríguez and SPN attorney Ana María Tato, Boza decided to mount a letter-writing appeal to Carazo with the hopes of swaying him against the decision. Tato's letter of May 25 listed a variety of reasons against splitting La Catalina from the park system, including the argument that if agriculture were permitted in the area, chemicals and pollution would pass through the national park and endanger the area's wildlife.[57]

Boza and Rodríguez wrote a longer letter to Carazo two days later outlining some of the legalities involved if Carazo segregated La Catalina.

Figure 9.   Park Warden in Palo Verde National Park

First, such a cut would be in violation of the Convention for the Protection of the Flora and Fauna that declared that national park boundaries could not be "altered." Second, it would be in opposition to the Ley Forestal, which stated very clearly, "Once a national park is created, no part can be segregated from it . . . without the approval of the Legislative Assembly." Finally, excising La Catalina would violate the National Parks Act that mandated that "the boundaries of the national parks could not be changed except by means of a new law." They went on to write how "the world [had] placed its eyes on Costa Rica" and that cutting the park "would represent a hard blow to the world conservation movement and a very dangerous precedent for our program."[58]

The next stop was the attorney general's office. Ana María Tato wrote Attorney General Manuel Freer Jiménez in June requesting his opinion on the legalities of the question, given both sides were now throwing different statutes and legal clauses back and forth at each other. In his "pronouncement" of June 24, Freer wrote that private in-holdings that the state "did not have the capacity to buy" could in fact be excluded from the park designation. Acquisition could only occur via funded expropriation, he wrote. Tato did not accept the decision. Two weeks later she petitioned Freer's office to restudy the case.[59]

Meanwhile, Carazo had decided to proceed with the park segregation plan. On July 2 he issued an executive decree reducing Palo Verde by 9,900 acres because "the State did not have available the economic means to complete the purchase of, nor the expropriation of, the farms."[60] Coincidentally, the decree came on the same day that Alexander Bonilla, conservation chairman of ASCONA, wrote a ten-page letter to Carazo urging him to change his mind. Bonilla was used to park controversies—he had been an SPN technician and a director of Santa Rosa and Poás Volcano national parks. He thus wrote with the authority of both knowledge of Palo Verde's ecology and of the interworkings of the Park Service and went more into detail on some of the scientific and legal points that had been expressed earlier by Tato, Boza, and Rodríguez. Carazo responded a month later with an eight-page letter explaining that the Convention for the Protection of Flora and Fauna was set up "to respect each nation's judicial laws under which the national parks were created." He again explained his position on the unconstitutionality of the La Catalina expropriations and assured Bonilla that "this administration has and will continue to work on conservation."[61]

Soon after the presidential decree, San José newspapers ran articles about Palo Verde. *La Nación* quoted agricultural minister Hernán Fonseca, who spelled out that the government simply did not have the funds to pay the landowners. It also quoted ASCONA's president, Oscar Hutt, who exaggeratedly proclaimed that Carazo was "trying to eliminate systematically, by one form or another, almost the entire system of reserves and national parks in Costa Rica."[62]

ASCONA stayed in the forefront of the Palo Verde matter and led the movement against the administration. By July it had announced that it would file suit against the government if the proposal did not go to the Legislative Assembly. A few days later the group announced it would send a draft bill to the Assembly requiring that body to ratify park creations—to reduce the authority of the president. On June 14 *La República* reported ASCONA's decisions with headlines indicating that "a battle" was brewing "to prevent the government from destroying parks."[63]

On the same day, ASCONA received the well-publicized support of a particularly prominent figure: former president Daniel Oduber. Oduber offered no political niceties when he announced his support for ASCONA. "The childish pretext that there is no money to pay for that part of the park," *La Nación* quoted him as saying, "is very poor and very doubtful." He went on to state that Carazo should have known that the park segregation would violate the Convention for the Protection of Flora and Fauna since he (Carazo) was president of the Legislative Assembly the year that body ratified it. He also suggested that the plan would decrease Costa Rica's international prestige and ended his press statement by urging people to ask who would "benefit the most" from the administration's plan.[64] Later that month, Oduber, an attorney, expressed interest in assisting ASCONA with its legal suit.

The Costa Rican economy also continued to decline as that summer moved slowly along in 1981. By July 15 the *colón* had been devalued by 74 percent. With that in mind, Carazo had a tough choice to make concerning the construction of a government-subsidized petroleum refinery (Refinadora Costarricense de Petróleo, or RECOPE). The president chose the politically rough, but fiscally sound, route and vetoed the proposal, which would mean the price of gasoline would increase. Carazo justified the move based on the belt-tightening austerity measures the country would have to endure to get through the crisis. On that same day, as further evidence the government had no money to spare, Carazo's minister of housing resigned, citing a shortage of funds with which to run his department properly.[65] The administration recited these examples as proof it had no funds with which to expropriate the La Catalina holdings.

But an even bigger bomb dropped the next day when *La Gaceta* (which prints the laws and decrees of the land once they have been made) printed President Carazo's executive decree segregating Palo Verde. The big surprise for everyone was that instead of the 9,900 acres he orally announced to be split from Palo Verde on July 2, there were 17,300 acres listed officially on July 16. As one can imagine, the outcry against this news was loud. A *La Nación* article stated that there was "severe opposition from conservationists" and that Ana María Tato had renewed her request for the attorney general to reconsider his earlier pronouncement. It quoted Alexander Bonilla's reaction on behalf of ASCONA and also said that the Organization of American States (OAS) and the United Nations had voiced opposition to the plan. It quoted Mario Boza asking of his employer, "What interests are moving behind this new illegality of our current government?" The paper did quote one person who sided with

Carazo, justice minister Elizabeth Odio Benito, who reiterated that the "confiscation" of the Palo Verde property without due payment was unconstitutional.[66]

The reduction of national park land was bad enough in and of itself, but conservationists' biggest fear was that the Palo Verde case would set a precedent for landowners around other protected areas to press for segregations also. The fears were well founded. Farmers near five other parks began clamoring for land to be released.[67] Two days later, SPN director José María Rodríguez explained to reporters that one petition called for cutting 260 acres from Cahuita National Park to be returned to farmland. At that point ASCONA officials wasted no more time and sent their National Parks Ratification Law proposal directly to the Legislative Assembly. A supportive *diputado* there, Miguel Angel Chaverría, demanded that agricultural minister Hernán Fonseca explain the Palo Verde decision in person to the Assembly. *La Nación* carried the news of these other possible park cuts on the front page—the first such coverage since the controversy unraveled. A few days later, the DGF received a petition to trim land off the La Carpintera (The Woodpecker) Protective Zone that was under its jurisdiction. DGF director Francisco Chacón did not allow it, a move that ASCONA was quick to applaud.[68]

Carazo's delayed revelation regarding the size of the cut at Palo Verde and news that landowners around other parks were petitioning for park reductions sent college students and others to protest in the streets. The day after the *La Gaceta* notice (July 18), a group of protesters in Ciudad Neilly near the Panama border blocked the road to the airport after Carazo had inaugurated a new stretch of paved road. His exit temporarily delayed, Carazo spoke to the protesters for over a half hour in a downpour of rain about the Palo Verde issue and other concerns. On July 28, a group of biology students from the University of Costa Rica and the National University staged a protest in front of the presidential mansion specifically because they opposed the Palo Verde cut. Displaying a banner that read "We Defend Our National Parks, STOP Segregation," the students met with an official of the presidency who listened to their concerns and promised to relay their message to Carazo. The group also had a round-table discussion with Mario Boza and Alexander Bonilla to plan what else they might be able to do.[69]

There was other public reaction. Numerous letters and signed petitions were sent from members of the Costa Rican Biologists' Association, labor unions, members of legislature, local school employee groups, enraged citizens, national and international conservation organizations, municipal leaders, sports clubs, and even a dance troupe. SPN employees also wrote letters of protest to their own ministry. One particularly stinging letter was sent by beekeeper Victoriano Hidalgo, who lambasted the government for altering the environment in a way that could adversely affect the production of honey. And someone even wrote a poem entitled "Requiem por un parque" (Requiem for a Park), lamenting the segregation and the precedent it set for other parks (see Appendix 4).[70]

There was not much official response to such public outcry. The administration did issue a press release on July 22 in which Carazo complained that many of the attacks on his decision were "unfounded . . . and did not deserve any special comment." The release also quoted Carazo responding to a letter written by Michael Wright of the World Wildlife Fund assuring that the administration was proud of its conservation record and would continue to do more. In fact, the administration directed the SPN to draw up a report to document Carazo's conservation record thus far into his term. The result was a paper entitled "The National Parks Program during the Carazo Administration," which listed new parks and reserves and compared the record to that of Oduber's term. (The report showed that Oduber had signed 316,758 new acres into the system while Carazo had approved 572,756.) Likewise, on July 28 the administration ran a half-page display advertisement in *La Nación* proclaiming in bold letters that "the State cannot take possession of private properties."[71]

One particularly enraged citizen was Mario Boza. Surely it must have been difficult to be the president's natural resources advisor during that summer of 1981 and be so opposed to the Palo Verde decision. But the notice about the additional acreage to be chopped from the national park was the coup de grâce. Boza tendered his resignation on July 22. Both major San José newspapers reported his departure, and *La República* printed his letter of resignation. In it he manifested his disgust about Palo Verde and his deep concern that the administration's decision was putting in jeopardy seven other parks. "Could you imagine a worse blow to the system of protected areas in the country," he asked in his letter to the president, "and could you imagine a more grave precedent against conservation of the country's natural resources?" He went on to assert that very few countries, and none in the developing world, had ever succeeded in completely paying property owners for lands dedicated to conservation. He also pointed out that the landholders in parts of Glacier and Everglades national parks in the United States had yet to be totally remunerated. Boza returned to his university post at that point.[72] Carazo named Murray Silberman to fill the position of advisor on natural resources.

Carazo was uncharacteristically reticent about Boza's departure. The only official response on record was in a letter he wrote to MAG minister Hernán Fonseca, which the president's office made public in the form of a press release. The letter did not directly address Boza's announcement, but it did allude to its cause and is important here to help decipher the whole situation. Carazo alerted Fonseca that he had "given the order to purchase" those 17,300 acres of Palo Verde for the coming fiscal year's budget (even though it would be of a different administration since the elections for a new president were close at hand). Thus, Carazo proved he did want to preserve Palo Verde—the money was simply not available in his budget. Accusations of ulterior motives—i.e., who or what was "getting to him"—were more in the imagination of his opponents than can be found in the historical record.[73]

Meanwhile, two other issues were pending in the Palo Verde situation: the National Parks Ratification bill in the Legislative Assembly (drafted to reduce the president's power to designate parks) and ASCONA's suit against the government. The Assembly took up debate on the ratification proposal in late July and early August. While the motion was eventually shuffled off to a committee, where it remained for over a year, discussion on the bill was telling. It represented the thoughts and opinions of people, many of whom agreed with Carazo, that did not receive media attention. Diputado Hubert Rojas Araya, for example, led the cause against the proposal because he felt the president should have the right to adjust conservation policies based on the needs of people. He stressed that such policies "affect thousands of Costa Ricans whose land is there one day and taken away the next" and that there had been "hundreds of injustices" of this sort.[74]

Diputado Rojas and others also spoke on what they perceived to be a dangerous direction in which the budding conservation movement was headed. Because ASCONA and the influence it was starting to have in affecting policy was a relatively new concept in Costa Rica, Rojas enjoined his fellow legislators to be cautious: "I'm not really against

ASCONA, but ASCONA wants to make Costa Rica into one big national park. Let's make national parks and biological reserves—but where's the money to pay Costa Ricans for their land? Or should all the land just be given over to ASCONA?"[75]

On the other side supporting the Ratification Law was Diputado Chaverría Méndez. He agreed with Rojas that thousands of people were "being evacuated from their lands . . . for the creation of national parks and reserves," but argued that it was not being conducted in an irresponsible manner. Most important, he hastened to call to the attention of his fellow *diputados* that often, like the case of Palo Verde, it was not poor *campesinos* whose land was being expropriated, but rather that of agricultural conglomerates—"millionaire businessmen"—who were often from abroad. Nevertheless, the proposal won approval and a year later made it out of committee and was approved by the Assembly.[76] The next president, Luis Monge, signed it into law.

ASCONA's lawsuit was ultimately not as successful as its legislative proposal. A lower court ruled in ASCONA's favor (based on the legalities of the Forestry Law and National Parks Act clauses) and invalidated the president's decree to segregate Palo Verde. At that, the administration quickly appealed to the Supreme Court, which reversed the lower court's decision and ruled in the government's favor (on the constitutionality question).[77]

Thus, the trimmed-off section of Palo Verde remained separate from the national park. But by as early as February of the next year, 1982, the government had agreed to purchase approximately 8,700 acres from the agribusiness corporations—slightly over half the amount of land that had been cut—for 21,162,000 *colones* (nearly $450,000). According to Alvaro Ugalde, whom newly elected President Luis Monge had reappointed as park service director, only seven million *colones* ($150,000) of that sum had been paid by this point, but the government was taking "formal steps" to pay the remainder.[78] But what started as a lengthy, drawn-out controversy ended in a quick and surprising way: the agribusiness landowners had donated the land back to SPN by the end of the decade. What the environmental groups, court cases, legislative action, citizens' protests, and international lobbying could not achieve, the rice growers made happen with one single move.[79]

What conclusions can be drawn from the Palo Verde experience? First, it is safe to admit that it was an unfortunate controversy that tainted the conservation record of Rodrigo Carazo. The words "Carazo" and "Palo Verde" seem inherently interconnected concerning conservation during the early 1980s. Most conservationists (both in and out of Costa Rica) link the two together when reminiscing about the early 1980s. However, keeping things in perspective was more of Mario Boza's role when approached on the subject. Obviously not fond of the memories of that summer in which he resigned from Carazo's service, Boza also admitted that the Carazo years witnessed valuable conservation advances. Likewise, he praised Carazo for his accomplishments on peace and other issues that have characterized his post-presidential years.[80]

Second, it is important to question the element of inevitability that seemed to characterize the controversy. The notion that it could have been avoided by either the president's refusal to be cowed by the agri-businessmen (as the record shows, there were other examples of as yet unpaid land acquisitions) or by the landowners' cooperation from the beginning (which would have saved many people a great deal of grief) is merely hypothetical, but nonetheless realistically possible. The problem, however, is that there is simply very little evidence to reconstruct the entire picture. Journalists of the day did little to investigate the root cause of the dilemma. Obviously, political reasons were not at the heart of the decision—Carazo, by all accounts, would have gained political popularity points had he backed off his decree. While the presidential campaigns were starting to rage that summer, it is interesting to note that neither Luis Alberto Monge (who won) nor Rafael Calderón (who lost) mentioned the Palo Verde affair in any newspaper advertisements or press releases. Perhaps it was just too much of a political liability either way it was addressed. Future political aspirations were moot anyhow since Costa Rican presidents may not be reelected to consecutive terms. And by Carazo's admission, he duly desired to see the area protected—he called for its budget allocation for the next fiscal term. Thus we are left with few choices on the decree's motivations and, given the overwhelming preponderance of economic evidence of the timeframe, must consider that the government simply was broke. Making tough, unpopular economic policy decisions like expelling the IMF, vetoing RECOPE, and excising part of Palo Verde, then, must all be lumped together.

Finally, the controversy represents a significant step in the evolution of the Costa Rican environmental movement. It became a rallying point for conservationists and biologists to band together to work for effecting change—experience that would be to their advantage in the not so distant future with other environmental crises. Moreover, it represents a genuine sincerity toward an ecological cause. People were not fighting to preserve their favorite lake to go boating on or some other popular recreational destination; they were fighting to save the country's most important system of wetlands, home to nearly 300 species of birds and one of the most important stopover points for migratory waterfowl and waders. Most of the participants in the movement, to be sure, probably had not ever visited the area. Just knowing its ecological value, however, served as incentive enough to be involved.

Such enthusiasm, it should be noted, at times clouded the good judgment of the conservationists. ASCONA president Oscar Hutt's public accusation that Carazo was trying to ruin the entire park system, for example, did not really help his cause. And Alexander Bonilla tended to exaggerate when he wrote that Carazo was working for the "elimination" of Palo Verde. Bonilla went on to quote Carazo's words of praise for conservation that he had written in the prologue of Mario Boza and Rolando Mendoza's *The National Parks of Costa Rica* and then added, "Oh what irony! Judge for yourselves, Costa Ricans. Yes, our environmental history is full of ironies."[81]

7 *Crisis Continued*

THE MONGE ADMINISTRATION

Let's consolidate the system of national parks . . . [to] achieve concrete actions in the field of rational use of natural resources and conservation of our biological diversity.

Luis Alberto Monge, 16 October 1982

The debt crisis in Costa Rica hardly evaporated with the election of a new president, Luis Alberto Monge, in the fall of 1981. Monge, of José Figueres' National Liberation Party, had promised to work on improving the economy by increasing agricultural production and putting "unused land" to work—a concept that understandably worried conservationists. So because the SPN wanted no more incidents like Palo Verde, the times now called less for adding new parks to the system and more for improved protection of existing ones. Mario Boza claimed that the service was "moving out of the decade of declaration and into a period of consolidation and refined management of the parks."[1]

Continuing in the tradition of the Oduber and Carazo presidencies, Luis Alberto Monge made thoughtful appointments to governmental agencies responsible for conservation. He named Francisco Morales as head of the Ministry of Agriculture (MAG), who retained José María Rodríguez as chief of the SPN. Rodríguez had been serving as "acting" SPN director during Alvaro Ugalde's graduate school leave, keeping in close touch with him during the absence, but now assumed full directorship duties. Morales had other plans for Ugalde (who had missed the Palo Verde ordeal by being in the United States) upon completion of his studies in Michigan: full-time fundraiser for the parks program with an office in Washington, D.C. Actually, the idea for the job had come from Geoffrey Barnard of the Nature Conservancy, who maintained that Costa Rica's conservation program was developed enough by this time to warrant such a position. The Conservancy worked very closely with Ugalde, the SPN, and the Fundación de Parques Nacionales (FPN) in those days and supplied office space for Ugalde at its Washington headquarters. Glad to have a new administration, Ugalde sent president Monge and his wife Doris their own separate copies of the book *The National Parks of Costa Rica* "as a small showing of our welcome."[2] Meanwhile, Mario Boza continued his work at the National University and became an ever more active president of the FPN. Ugalde in his fundraising position was the FNP's executive director.

Fundraising by the FPN was at the center of national parks activity during the Monge administration (1982–1986). "The economic crisis itself was a new lesson," Ugalde later recalled. "Neither could we trust the national economy or the financial system that we had." Thus, while Costa Rica's economy reached rock bottom in 1982–1983, the FPN launched a five-year $5.5 million fundraising campaign—a drive that made similar efforts during the Carazo years pale in comparison. The goal was to reach $3 million during President Monge's term alone. In a letter to the vice minister of the presidency, Ugalde alerted the administration to the goal and encouragingly noted, "We think this is doable, we are very optimistic." "However," Ugalde continued, "we will depend on the strong moral support of the President of the Republic and of the government in general." A few months later, Ugalde wrote directly to the president suggesting how "indispensable" it was for him "to show that he and his administration were endorsing our efforts." He also asked him to lend his name to the campaign committee as an honorary chairman.[3] Monge agreed to the request.

In February 1982, the FPN issued a "priorities plan" to outline the goals of the fundraising campaign. At the top of the list was what was to become the FNP's principal focus in the early eighties: acquisition of private in-holdings within park boundaries. It was the in-holdings that were needed to consolidate the management of the parks and to better protect their ecological characteristics. Private in-holders, especially in Cahuita, Braulio Carrillo, Poás Volcano, and Santa Rosa national parks, were starting to cut trees on their lands or to develop them in other ways.[4]

The brunt of this legal problem, as in the case of Palo Verde, fell on the shoulders of SPN attorney Ana María Tato. Described by David Rains Wallace as someone with "an almost religious faith in the Park Service's mission," Tato literally worked nights to keep the landowners' demands out of court. She was a "very energetic woman," José María Rodríguez remembered, "although they [the landowners] made her life miserable." He went on to explain how the landowners would call her at home and threaten her because they had not yet been paid for expropriated properties. Compounding the problem was that ASCONA had filed suit against the government (specifically against MAG) for allowing private concessions within national parks. The environmental group pressed all the way to the Supreme Court to force expropriations.[5]

The problem was simply financial. Thus Ugalde's work was laid plainly out for him in his Washington office in 1982. By May of that year, he had met with a variety of international conservation organizations in Washington and New York and reported successful meetings with them. The Nature Conservancy had accepted a proposal to contribute $320,000; the World Wildlife Fund (WWF) had accepted one for $25,000; and the Rare Animal Relief Effort (RARE) and the CCC were considering similar proposals at the time of a report he made to the FNP's executive board. Gerald Leiberman of RARE, Ugalde noted, had also agreed to help him get an article published in *Audubon* magazine to further publicize the need for funds. Later that year, the OTS came up with $50,000 to help with the *zona protectora* land acquisition in Braulio Carrillo National Park. And in 1984, the WWF, the Norway Chapter of the WWF, and the New York Zoological Society contributed a total of $84,000 for help with land purchases at Tortuguero, to list but a few of the donors. "It was breaking new ground," as Ugalde described his campaign effort. "It was not a fad to donate money for conservation in those weird third world countries with unrest and corruption and whatever."[6]

To educate donors, the fundraising campaign became more sophisticated than it had been in the past. The plan now was to bring potential contributors to Costa Rica and show them firsthand what the projects were all about. Such was the approach that Mario Boza took when he directed a grant proposal for the Tinker Foundation in mid-1983. The foundation's president, Renate Rennie, visited the country that summer and, in a memo to SPN and FPN staff, Boza listed specific assignments for each person (who was to pick Rennie up at the airport, etc.), issued a complete schedule of activities for her stay, and directed them "to attend to her well." The grant proposal itself was for $149,050 as "seed money" for the first three years of a national environmental education program (as per one of the FPN's priorities), which would become a permanent, self-supporting fund.[7]

Not all fundraising appeals were as successful. In 1983, for example, the OTS turned the FPN down for a similar request to continue helping with Braulio Carrillo land acquisition. OTS board member Thomas Yuill wrote Ugalde saying that the current situation at Braulio Carrillo was just too "discouraging." He explained that there was too much private land within the *zona protectora* and that the FPN was being "overly optimistic" with its land-swaps plan.[8]

But another benefit to the program came when Mario Boza and Alvaro Ugalde were awarded the Getty Prize (for conservation) in 1983. They accepted the award in Washington at a Rose Garden ceremony presided over by President Ronald Reagan. "Creating a park on paper is easy," Boza stated in his acceptance speech, "preserving it is another story." Ugalde later lamented that there was a lack of press coverage of the event and that Secretary of Interior James Watt was not in attendance because of the troubles he was facing in his last few days in office. Other coverage of the FPN's campaign, and especially of the Costa Rican national parks themselves, did come in the form of articles in U.S. and British conservation journals, which helped to raise awareness of the cause. But to make a long fundraising story short, the FPN's $5.5 million drive succeeded by 1986—in less than the hoped for five-year period.[9]

There is a human side to Costa Rica's quest to consolidate its park holdings. Land was often confiscated for park creation purposes. A representative case in point made it to the office of the presidency in the spring of 1982. Nelly Boza Guadamuz wrote directly to the president begging him to prevent the government from taking over her land in Alajuela province. Writing as a *"campesina,* worker of the land, mother of several children, and becoming elderly in age," the woman cited how she had heard that her "parcel of land" could "be taken away to make into a park, projected to be [named] Garobito" (after a legendary regional indigenous leader). Closing, she wrote emotionally, "I beg you to tell them not to take away what has cost me so much pain and tears." The letter was forwarded to the desk of José María Rodríguez at SPN, who later informed the president's office and Nelly Boza Guadamuz that the area had since been withdrawn from park feasibility study "for its lack of appropriate national park characteristics."[10]

Others who were forced to move for the improved conservation of the country were usually paid for their land (when money was available) and were assisted in the move to another location. The issue became more complicated in the mid-1980s, however, when a gold boom hit the Osa Peninsula in southwestern Costa Rica and prospect miners (*oreros*) flooded into Corcovado National Park. Mining operations in the park environs had been suspended when President Oduber decreed the park's creation. But with the Costa Rican economy in shambles and high unemployment (reaching 79,000 in March of 1982—a 44 percent increase from the previous year), many individuals sought work and wealth mining for gold. A study in 1985, however, estimated that 90 percent of the miners in Corcovado had other sources of employment and that 30–50 percent owned farmland in the region. Permits to reroute the Rincón River for placer mining were denied by the Ministry of Natural Resources (MIRENEM), but that hardly slowed the influx of *oreros,* who set up their own individual mining operations in and around the park. Another study showed that there were 1,500 illegal *oreros* in Corcovado and 3,500 "legal" mining concessions in areas surrounding it.[11]

The problem for the Park Service was that MIRENEM issued a report outlining how public lands could be used for mining. It also encouraged miners to continue their pursuits as long as they had a mining permit and followed certain norms. The report further indicated that the Central Bank in San José would continue to buy gold at international market prices ("representing its importance to the Costa Rican economy"). In October of 1982, Costa Rica had exported 568 kilos of refined gold at a value of $3,558,080. And in 1983 a legislative committee met with members of industry and of the conservation community to discuss what sort of mining could be allowed. It was generally agreed that placer gold mining for small-scale artisanry would be allowed and that water pumps and dynamite would be restricted to certain areas.[12] But when *oreros* continued to stream into the area, the few guards posted at Corcovado could not come close to monitoring permits or seeing whether mining code "norms" or regulations were being followed.

By 1985 Alvaro Ugalde had left Washington, D.C., to resume his duties as director of SPN. He sensed very keenly the growing crisis in Corcovado and wanted to do what he could to protect the park. He commissioned Dan Janzen, an OTS board member and University of Pennsylvania biologist famed for his expertise on the tropical dry forest ecology of Guanacaste, to conduct an on-site study of the *orero* impact on Corcovado. Janzen's research team found significant damage to the park ecosystem: mammal species were nearly eliminated, streams were sterile and muddy from sediment runoff (Janzen learned that a common local saying was "If the river isn't muddy, you're not working hard enough"), organic life in rivers and streams was almost completely absent, and plant communities had been severely altered. The report concluded that "several centuries will pass" before pre-mining ecological conditions could be restored.[13]

Not surprisingly, then, Janzen's study called for the complete removal of *oreros* without compensation. It cited a series of laws that had been violated by having miners in the park and recommended that SPN utilize the Rural Guard to assist in removal. On March 2, 1986, the Rural Guard drove out the *oreros,* destroyed their makeshift shelters, and seized their mining equipment. Later, in 1987, many of the evicted miners camped out for several weeks in San José's central park demanding compensation for the Rural Guard's destruction. The government ended up paying $3,800 to each of the displaced miners. Illegal mining activity resumed in Corcovado and its surroundings in the late 1980s and early 1990s.[14]

One conservation lesson learned from the Corcovado *orero* experience was that the buffer zones surrounding national parks and reserves are as important to the ecological health of the environment to be protected as the park itself. With that in mind, Ugalde and Rodrigo Gámez, a plant virologist active in conservation issues, decided to form an organization dedicated to the protection of ecological buffer zones in 1986. Called Fundación Neotrópica, the foundation began similarly to Fundación de Parques Nacionales (they even shared the same office space for several years), but it had a different focus for raising and channeling funds without government ties. It is a private foundation that works to acquire land for conservation and to promote programs in environmental education. It has also served as a "bank" for debt-swaps and other fundraising activities.

There were also some successes on the legislative front. In the fall of 1982 the Legislative Assembly passed the National Ratification Law (no. 6794) that ASCONA had lobbied for during the Palo Verde situation. President Monge inked it into law at a ceremony on October 16. The speech he gave at that event, however, had been written almost entirely by Alvaro Ugalde upon the request of a Monge aide who had written him asking for ideas. The president, or Ugalde, outlined in the speech a plethora of advantages accrued from conservation practices and ended by saying, "Perhaps I will be the last President of Costa Rica who will be able to create new . . . national parks, biological reserves, and national forests. My successors will only be able to improve them or allow for their destruction." [15]

Other goals were achieved during the Monge administration. In the fall of 1982 the government inaugurated the "Volvamos a la Tierra" (Back to the Land) program to encourage "balance between man's actions and the ecological possibilities and limitations in which they develop" (see Figure 10). It was a program "with profound conservationist ingredients" designed to show how the basic necessities from the land (food, fibers, medicines) could be used "without reducing the natural environment on which we depend." [16]

At the same time, OFIPLAN approved funding a program to research the needs of the country's forestry education. Its goal was to discern "what directions should be taken in forestry research" and to discuss the idea of creating one consolidated university-level forestry program. And in October of 1983 José María Rodríguez noted in an SPN report that significant advances had been made in his department's environmental education program. Some of the achievements included nationwide radio spots, school presentations, university conferences, short television announcements, pamphlets produced for each park, outdoor exhibits and booths at the parks, and a two-week workshop on environmental education held at Poás Volcano. "The results have been satisfactory," wrote Rodríguez, "despite the limitations of budget resources and personnel that we have had." [17]

The nation's financial limitations gave birth to a variety of plans that supposedly would boost the economy. Like gold mining in Corcovado, another controversial environmental dilemma that the Monge administration had to confront was a proposed trans-isthmian oil pipeline (*oleoducto*) that would connect the Caribbean coast with the Pacific. Different plans for such a project had been in the works since the late 1970s. Nei-

Figure 10.   President Monge's "Back to the Land" Campaign (adapted from Manuel Rojas, *Los años ochenta y el futuro incierto* [San José: UNED, 1991])

ther plans for a pipeline near Golfo Dulce (scuttled by President Oduber) nor for one across northern Costa Rica (supported by President Carazo) had ever materialized, thus opening the possibility for a new proposal in 1982–1983. Proponents, including the government, supported the plan as a boon to the economy. Environmentalists opposed it based on potential ecological impacts that could result from the pipeline's construction and possible rupture and spills.

The environmental group ASCONA presented especially strong opposition to the proposal. The group worked to publicize the environmental and economic effects of oil spills in Alaska and Panama. It cited how possible spills in Costa Rica would negatively affect the coastal fishing and budding tourism industries. It showed how the pipeline's construction, and parallel maintenance roads, would augment deforestation, contaminate rivers, and forever damage wildlife habitat. Alexander Bonilla, who dedicated himself in those years to the fight against the pipeline, wrote that "this position is not romantic, unpatriotic, or much less of the extreme left that some sectors of the government have been suggesting it is." [18]

Although no trans-isthmian oil pipeline was ever built, the *oleoducto* controversy caused ASCONA's eventual demise. Bonilla has asserted that "pro-government persons infiltrated" the organization at the height of the campaign and "tried to get ASCONA to adopt an official position in favor of the project," despite its own statutes and history of vigorously opposing such measures in the past. Those people did not succeed in altering ASCONA's position, Bonilla claimed, but through the infighting they generated and negative publicity they caused, ended up breaking the organization. And while the group still exists "on paper" today, Bonilla (who has since left ASCONA) explained, "It does not have any power; the *oleoducto* ruined it." [19]

It was during this same time that Bonilla was active on another environmental cause: the creation of the Costa Rican Ecology Party, or PEC. After years of studies and committees, the political party was formed in 1984 by a group of ambitious environmentalists and university scientists. Calling it a "new hope" for Costa Rica, Bonilla, who served as the party's first president, wrote that the PEC was born "as a new alternative among the traditional political parties whose environmental misinformation, ignorance of the ecological interrelationships of a society, and adherence to an ancestral economic hegemony have been transformed into the depredatory economic principles of the economic, social and political structure of Costa Rica." [20]

The PEC, which was modeled loosely on the concepts of the European "Greens," focuses on national environmental concerns, agrarian reform, and the principles of nonviolence. It urges rigid adherence to Costa Rica's tradition of permanent unarmed neutrality. Bonilla has stated that the PEC goes beyond environmental activism, explaining that "the problem with many ecology groups in Central America is that they fail to address the political and economic problems as part of the environmental problems." But while the PEC has suffered from financial problems and, as another study put it, "not brought with it the fortification of the ecological movement" in Costa Rica, it has made a presence in many local and national elections. It is one of the few "green parties" in Central America.[21]

President Monge did not play a big role in the *orero* situation or the *oleoducto* debate, but he was personally involved in another environmental controversy: the sixth scandal at Santa Rosa National Park. The El Murciélago unit joining the park continued to be used for a military training grounds by the Civil Guard during the Monge administration. By 1983 it had become a staging base for the Nicaraguan *contra* faction of Edén Pastora. Financed by the U.S. Central Intelligence Agency during the Reagan administration, Pastora's forces attacked Sandinista soldiers at the border post of Peñas Blancas just north of Santa Rosa and returned to El Murciélago. That and other border skirmishes caused damage and property loss on Costa Rican soil, which prompted Monge's minister of public security, Angel Edmundo Solano, to crack down on *contra* activity in Costa Rica and Monge to issue a Proclamation of Neutrality on November 17.

Solano, who had gone public with his views that the CIA wanted to militarize Costa Rica's Civil Guard to join President Reagan's efforts against the Sandinistas, worked to enforce Monge's neutrality stance and met with Nicaraguan officials about reducing the border skirmishes. But right-wing groups in Costa Rica (i.e., the Chambers of Commerce and Industry, *La Nación,* and officials in the Ministry of the Interior), as well as U.S. ambassador Curtin Winsor Jr., opposed Solano's interference with the CIA plans and pressed to have him removed. Winsor later admitted under oath that working to have Solano fired was part of his role in the Reagan administration's illegal Iran-*contra* operation and suggested that silencing Solano would help stymie the investigation of Lieutenant Colonel Oliver North's secret activities with the *contras.* Winsor was eventually relieved of his duties "apparently for insufficient subtlety," as Bill Weinberg put it, when he mentioned in a speech that Nicaragua was "an infested piece of meat that attracts insects from all over." Nevertheless, Monge relented (in fact, he shook up his whole cabinet) and named archconservative Benjamin Piza to Solano's position.[22]

Piza was a founder of the Free Costa Rica Movement (MCRL), a John Birch–type paramilitary organization affiliated with the World Anti-Communist League. Immediately into his tenure, he accelerated the anti-Sandinista operations at El Murciélago. When Monge was away on an official trip to Europe, Piza ignored the neutrality stance (and long-range SPN plans to conserve the area for annexation to Santa Rosa, for that matter) and worked with the CIA and the Pentagon to arrange for the arrival of a U.S. Army Special Forces division (Green Berets). Along with West German and Israeli military advisors, the Green Berets conducted ten two-week sessions training 1,000 Civil Guards in jungle survival, counterinsurgency warfare, riot control, and border patrol operations in the fragile environment of the tropical dry forest of Santa Elena Peninsula. The Guard units became known as Batallones Relámpagos (Lightning Battalions) and supposedly were geared for anti-Sandinista warfare and for training other troops. Their staging ground in the forest was off-limits to civilian Costa Ricans, and when the unit was discovered, former president Rodrigo Carazo advised that "these Lightning Battalions should be dissolved . . . because a spirit of militarism is like a contagious disease." [23]

President Monge was reportedly furious upon his return from Europe to learn that Benjamin Piza had converted El Murciélago into a Green Beret training field. But, as was discovered when the story started to unravel after his term had expired, that was not all the Santa Elena Peninsula was being used for. Monge had approved the construction of a secret *contra* resupply airstrip to be built on land that had been earmarked for national park expansion (Santa Rosa scandal number seven). The 6,500-foot airstrip, part of the whole Oliver North "Contragate" drugs-for-arms disgrace, was built in an ecologically sensitive part of Guanacaste where wildlife seasonally migrate between the Pacific dry forest and the cooler highlands of the volcanic slopes. The peninsula is home to rare species of vegetation that have evolved over time due to the fact that the ground there has been above the ocean longer than elsewhere in Central America. [24]

President Monge claimed he had sanctioned construction of the airstrip because officials from Washington had warned him of an imminent Sandinista invasion of Costa Rica. The landing field, he believed, would be used to airlift border defense supplies into Costa Rica. Lewis Tambs, who had replaced Curtin Winsor as U.S. ambassador to Costa Rica, pressured Monge to approve the plan by threatening to cut off U.S. aid— an unattractive scenario during the economic crisis. [25] In hearings of the Tower Commission, which the U.S. Senate used to investigate the "Contragate" scandal, Tambs admitted that he and Oliver North had also threatened Monge's successor, Oscar Arias, with a cutoff of U.S. aid if he

Figure 11.   Political Cartoon, Santa Rosa Secret Airstrip (reproduced by permission of *Tico Times*)

went public with the airstrip's discovery. Arias refused to be intimidated and held a press conference to announce not only the strip's existence but also its closure. U.S. aid, however, did decline; it dropped from $180 million in 1986 when Arias came into office to $85 million by 1987.

Then representatives from a Panama-based "dummy corporation" called Udall Research (engineered by Richard Secord and Albert Hakim of "Project Democracy") arrived in the town of Liberia, Guanacaste, to solicit cooperation from the local Civil Guard commander. They informed him that they were preparing to build a tourist project on the Santa Elena Peninsula and needed his support to transport workers, construction materials, and heavy equipment through Santa Rosa National Park. Advised by Public Security Minister Benjamin Piza to cooperate, the commander then pressured park officials for compliance and lent Guardsmen to assist with the airstrip's construction. The U.S. construction crew and Costa Rican Guardsmen, however, hardly respected the environment. They set forest fires in the area, hunted deer without permission, dined on rare Kemp's Ridley sea turtle eggs, and, at least on one occasion, shot a tapir for sport.[26]

The affair finally came to light when local residents became suspicious in the fall of 1986. After repeatedly seeing large military transport aircraft flying low and landing (especially at odd hours) and military trucks moving fuel drums and other equipment in and out of the area, they alerted officials who discovered the secret strip. Via the Tower Commission hearings and an investigative committee of Costa Rica's Legislative Assembly, facts surfaced regarding how the strip was used not only as a base from which to fly U.S. arms for the *contras* into Nicaragua, but also allegedly to fund Manuel Noriega's drug-smuggling operation with funds from an arms sale to Iran. The Legislative Assembly barred Oliver North, John Poindexter, Richard Secord, Lewis Tambs, and CIA Costa Rica station chief Joe Fernández from ever returning to Costa Rica. It also indicted Benjamin Piza and the Liberia commander who were a part of the team.

By early 1987, the new president—Oscar Arias—had declared his intent to work with the SPN to develop the region into Guanacaste National Park. Such a plan was to be the start of a whole new administrative restructuring program that would characterize the future of Costa Rica's conservation agenda. For their part, the individuals who had been so instrumental with conservation programs during the last two administrations would continue to be involved, if not in the same capacity, inside or out of the government. Alvaro Ugalde, for example, who in 1985 had returned to his position as SPN director to work on the Corcovado crisis, left again in 1986 at the end of Monge's term, "burnt out" from the work and emotional toil involved with the *orero* evictions. For the next four years he worked in a variety of nongovernmental conservation positions, including ones at the Conservation Foundation and the Nature Conservancy, as an advisor to conservation programs in Paraguay and Guatemala and even as a national parks guide for a major ecotourism firm in Costa Rica. Vera Varel succeeded Ugalde as executive director of Fundación de Parques Nacionales. She later served in the same capacity at Fundación Neotrópica. José María Rodríguez decided to take a leave of absence for his own training and professional development in 1984. Following in Ugalde's footsteps, he left the SPN for graduate work at the University of Michigan. Luis Méndez, a biologist who had been serving as SPN assistant director since the late 1970s, assumed acting directorship duties for 1984, moved over when Ugalde came back in 1985, but then was named SPN director by the new Arias administration in 1986. Mario Boza remained active with the environmental studies program at the National Open University and as president of the FPN.[27]

The people and organizations like the ones mentioned in these last two chapters played an indispensable role in seeing Costa Rica meet the challenging goals of conservation through crisis. The experience gained from the 1978–1986 fundraising efforts was not shelved in the coming years. New opportunities and ideas for the 1990s and beyond would mean drawing on past lessons and successes to continue and expand on the way the country's environment could be protected.

8 *Restructuring and Decentralizing Conservation*

In just a few short years we have been able to consolidate a system of protected areas. . . . But we should recognize that until now the concept of sustainable development has not formed part . . . of the ways implemented for socioeconomic development.

Oscar Arias Sánchez, "Palabras del Presidente de Costa Rica"

When Oscar Arias was elected president of Costa Rica in 1986, the national parks program of his country was in the beginning stages of undergoing a philosophical change in strategy. What conservationists and politicians now saw as the coming role of national parks and preserves was their ability to be incorporated into the nation's larger socioeconomic context. Daniel Janzen perhaps best explained the new phenomenon when he wrote, "The traditions of tropical conservation in general, and certainly in Costa Rica specifically, have to evolve with urgent haste to a mode where the integration of the park into the social consciousness is dominant and central to the entire [management] plan."[1] The ideas of Arias and Janzen here reflect the growing attention to "sustainable development" that started to flourish in international conservationist thought by the mid-1980s and would set the tone for environmental policy making in the next three administrations: Oscar Arias Sánchez (1986–1990), Rafael Angel Calderón Fournier (1990–1994), and José María Figueres Olsen (1994–1998).

One of the first testing grounds where the principles of sustainable development would be incorporated into the management plan of a protected area was with the creation of Guanacaste National Park. When President Arias was handed the Green Beret and "Contragate" airstrip scandals at Santa Rosa from outgoing president Luis Alberto Monge, he was confronted with decisions that had to be made for the long-range use of the Santa Elena Peninsula and surrounding areas of tropical dry forest. To the east of Santa Rosa (and east of the Pan American Highway), plans had been in the offing since 1985 to develop a vast area of dry forest and sloping volcanoes into a large conservation area based on "tropical restoration."

The plan was the brainchild of entomologist and tropical ecologist Daniel Janzen, who had been working, researching, and living in Guanacaste for over twenty years. He usually spent half the year in Costa Rica and other half back at his post in the biology department at the University of Pennsylvania. His research focus had centered on the life history of saturniid moths and on coevolution (plant-animal-insect adaptations and interdependencies). But after an invitation by the government of Australia to study that country's dry forests (which were rapidly becoming extinct) and after his research in Corcovado that Alvaro Ugalde had requested he do for the National Park Service in 1985 (which alerted him to how endangered an ecosystem can become), Janzen became converted to the gospel of conservation. Before, "I never gave a second thought to conservation," he mentioned to one reporter. To another he admitted that he "used to chainsaw big trees just to count rings for my research with no more thought than you'd flick an insect off your sleeve." It was then that he witnessed with greater concern how the Pacific dry forest that once had spanned much of the west coast of Mexico and Central America was at the brink of ecosystem extinction.[2] Wasting no time, Janzen authored a study in 1986 entitled *Guanacaste National Park: Tropical, Ecological, and Cultural Restoration* as a format to present to the Costa Rican government in hopes the area would be considered for conservation status. Janzen noted in the work that only 2 percent (or 6,600 square miles) of the original 330,000 square miles of Mesoamerican Pacific dry forest yet remained relatively undisturbed and that only .08 percent (or 264 square miles) existed in legally protected areas—in Santa Rosa National Park and several small reserves in Costa Rica and other countries.[3]

The ecosystem disappearance, of course, was due to intensive burning and agricultural development. Since the days of the Spanish encounter, the tropical dry forest of Costa Rica had been used more than the country's rainforests for farming due to its vast savanna clearings and long dry season. It is a windy, leafless, and brown environment from November to April and lush green and wet from May to October. The area has been cleared with annual fires for four hundred years, which kept saplings down and moved the grasslands farther into the forest margins. Answering his own hypothetical question concerning what would happen if the Guanacaste National Park Project (GNPP) area were not preserved, Janzen wrote: "We retreat to Santa Rosa (the Murciélago area will be roasted off the map by the wildfires) and carry out all of the goals for Guanacaste National Park on an inferior scale and in a gradually decomposing habitat. All of the inventory and other biological studies for Guanacaste will be priceless as salvage biology, and at least tell future generations what they lost." [4]

Thus, his goal was to "put biology back into [the local people's] cultural repertoire—back on the same status with music, art and religion" as opposed to their current preoccupation with rice, cotton, sorghum, and cattle. And looking at the larger picture of Guanacaste's importance for Costa Rica and for the study of ecology in general, Janzen asserted that "to lose the abundance of tropical dry forest to the demands of agriculture is comparable to processing the books in the Library of Congress to relieve a temporary paper shortage." [5]

What made the park specifically different from others was that its management plan retained some local economic uses. Cattle grazing, for instance, was allowed (although managed to prevent pasture depletion). Janzen saw it as beneficial for seed dispersal, grass control, and generating local support. Burning and hunting, however, were banned and reforestation projects launched as preliminary methods to restore the ecosystem. The plan was to plant just a few trees in the pastures that once had been forests and to let nature take care of the rest. Janzen's research found that the wind and the manuring effect of seed-dispersing animals (deer, monkeys, peccaries, agoutis, cotton rats, bats, and magpie jays, which eat fruits and nuts and then defecate seeds elsewhere) could work to start the restoration process in roughly ten years. Restoring the entire area with "all the plants and animals that were here when the Spaniards arrived," however, would take hundreds of years. [6]

This kind of a management scheme breaks from the past experience of Costa Rican national parks, which were modeled after their counterparts in the United States and thus espoused a "caretaker" philosophy.

The "parks basically have been taken care of by a police force," Janzen argued in 1988. "They have not been managed with regard to their bio-logical needs." Such thinking has not always endeared him to SPN em-ployees, and the government requested that he leave Costa Rica for a while. But at Guanacaste National Park, Janzen set up programs for local schoolchildren such as field trips to the beaches for biology lessons. Some of the children even helped pick seeds out of horse dung to be planted later where needed. He also employed area workers to help collect and catalogue specimens from the park's plant and animal life and to be on fire control teams ("broom squads") during the dry season. "The fire crew is deadly," he told a reporter in 1989. "Only six percent of the GNPP burned this year, as compared with the traditional thirty percent barbe-cue." Some local farm families elected to stay on their farms but work for the park—adding to the complete "self-supporting . . . biocultural resto-ration" of the environment. "We have to integrate the park into the minds and pocketbooks of the community," he added.[7]

The pocketbook of the government at the time Oscar Arias took office, however, could not sustain purchasing the amount of land called for in Janzen's proposal. Janzen had approached Arias about the park idea and received his blessing for it, but was informed that the government could not support it financially at that particular time. Undaunted and satisfied to have Arias' support, Janzen launched his own fundraising blitz. Mario Boza at Fundación de Parques Nacionales (FNP) gladly endorsed the idea and enlisted the support of his organization. Alvaro Ugalde (soon be-fore his departure from the National Park Service) was less enthusias-tic at first—based on the number of other pressing needs at SPN—but warmed to the idea later after an on-site hike with Janzen. Fundación Neotrópica, the organization that Ugalde helped found, also joined the effort. With his "engaging personality and eccentricities," as one reporter described him (he was known to wear a snake bag with specimens on his head, share his specimen-cluttered home/laboratory in Guanacaste with skunks, and utilize a rich and colorful vocabulary), Janzen became the darling of international conservation organizations. He was the subject of a BBC television documentary and many newspaper and magazine ar-ticles. Thomas Lewis, who interviewed him in 1989, wondered "whether a man who spent much of his life probing the secrets of animal excre-ment, for clues to the distribution of seeds, was prepared for truly dis-tasteful tasks such as asking for money and dealing with journalists." Janzen explained to Lewis that "you see something that needs doing, and you do it." Thus, as Lewis put it, "Janzen undertook a metamorphosis worthy of one of his beloved moths: from reclusive biologist to garrulous after-dinner speaker."[8]

Janzen's efforts resulted in major contributions from the Nature Conservancy, the World Wildlife Fund (WWF), and other groups amounting to $3 million by 1987 (one-fourth of his goal) one year into his fundraising drive. In that time he had convinced many farmers and landholders in the area to sell their land to the government for the park. By the end of the decade the park was complete.[9]

One of the biggest financial boosts came with the innovative introduction of "debt-for-nature" swaps in the late 1980s. An idea conceived by WWF's Thomas Lovejoy in 1984, debt swaps were intended to help developing countries reduce their foreign debt while at the same time increase their budgets for conservation. Under the plan, foreign banks sold off loans they had made to deeply indebted nations to international conservation organizations. For Costa Rica, the loan notes went for seventeen cents on the dollar, which were then donated to Fundación Neotrópica. The government's Central Bank then issued bonds to Neotrópica for seventy-five cents on the dollar (using *colones*), which multiplied the value of the discounted loans and allowed Neotrópica to use them as collateral that drew 25 percent interest. Meanwhile, the U.S. Internal Revenue Service sweetened the incentives for banks by ruling that they could write off the swaps as partial charity contributions. The Fleet Bank of Rhode Island, for example, retired a portion of Costa Rica's debt to the bank by donating $250,000 for land acquisition and park management.[10]

With this kind of program in gear, the Arias administration formed the Costa Rica Debt Conservation Plan in 1987. By 1991 over $40 million of external debt had been erased by purchases from international organizations. Costa Rica was the third country in the world to participate in the swap program and the first to receive European support when the Netherlands and Sweden forgave their government loans. Sweden's contribution was specifically earmarked for restoration of the Pacific dry forest in Guanacaste. The Nature Conservancy worked as an intermediary with Sweden and the United States on these swaps and parlayed $5.6 million of Costa Rican debt into a $784,000 sale. Geoffrey Barnard, the Conservancy's director for Latin America (and the group's former Costa Rica field representative), stated at the time that Costa Rica was chosen over Panama and Nicaragua—countries with equal if not greater conservation needs—because of the security of the investment with Costa Rica's stable government. Environmental activist Alexander Bonilla supported such swaps, saying that the approach allowed the "wealthy nations of the North to take their share of the responsibility for tropical forest restoration" and was a way "to avoid both the twin global disasters of economic collapse brought about by massive debt default and ecological collapse brought about by rampant deforestation."[11]

Fundación Neotrópica's end of the business was handled by Mario Boza, who had become its director during the Arias administration. "Debt swapping is the most important tool to achieve conservation," he stated in 1988. "You multiply money by five. It's a lot of money that's free. We can use it to buy land, pay personnel, and do everything. It's an incredible scheme."[12]

He went on to relate how the funds were to be used not only at Guanacaste National Park but at other areas as well. They were needed to improve the parks to attract more tourists and scientific research projects. FNP's primary goals were to enlarge existing parks and to protect the parks' buffer zones.

Buffer zone integration into the park system was a relatively new conservation ideal. At the same time efforts were mounting in the United States to protect areas around national parks (like the Greater Yellowstone Ecosystem movement in the early 1980s), similar attempts were under way in Costa Rica. UCR biologist Sergio Salas had argued for "park ecosystem" protection in 1981 at the First Symposium on National Parks. Daniel Janzen, another outspoken proponent for what he referred to as "edge biology," advised that protecting up to approximately three miles depth surrounding parks was essential to the natural integrity of the parks themselves. Without managing the buffer zone of Santa Rosa effectively, for example, Janzen warned that a scheduled oak reforestation plan there would have "as much chance to influence the overall climate of the park [to improve environmental conditions] as [would] an ice cube."[13]

Thus, the overall plan for Guanacaste National Park was for it to combine with Santa Rosa to form an ecosystem "mega-park" of tropical dry forest. This was the beginning of SPN's new focus on restructuring conservation to fit biological realities. To achieve this goal in Guanacaste meant acquiring lands to the west of the Pan American Highway also—the land on the Santa Elena Peninsula that had been used for military training during the Monge administration. In 1987 President Arias announced that the "Udall Research" land where the clandestine airstrip had been constructed would be annexed to adjacent Santa Rosa National Park. It required financial negotiations—what Janzen termed "bureaucratic chug-along"—with the North American investors from whom "Udall" (i.e., the CIA) rented the land. The deal was completed one year after the scandal was uncovered. On the other hand, Arias decided against incorporating the El Murciélago hacienda into the park. It remained a Civil Guard training facility, although minus the Green Berets.[14]

But the Relámpago Battalion controversy near Santa Rosa was not the end to the U.S. Army Special Forces' experience in Costa Rican national parks. In the summer of 1989 the Green Berets were in a remote part of Braulio Carrillo National Park at the request of President Arias' minister of public security to train Civil Guards in anti-narcotrafficking tactics. The park had recently been consolidated when former president Monge, as one of his last acts in office, approved the annexation of the *zona protectora* that Rodrigo Carazo had decreed years earlier. Likewise, in February of 1988, UNESCO had declared a central portion of the park as a World Biosphere Reserve. Thus, when news of the Berets' presence there reached the press, conservationists were stunned.

The surreptitious military training was discovered in August 1989 when a Costa Rican naturalist with two American ecotourists stumbled onto the training session while hiking in the cloud forest. After the soldiers escorted the trio from the area, one of the members of the party told a reporter for *Mesoamérica* that "We didn't understand why Americans in camouflage uniforms were throwing us out of a national park in Costa Rica. We thought it was outrageous." The park director at Braulio Carrillo was equally appalled and told reporters that the Green Berets and the Civil Guards had no permission to enter the park as per Forestry Law clauses that prohibit military maneuvers in protected areas.[15]

But while the Green Berets went home and an embarrassed Arias administration dealt with damage repair (it was only two years earlier that Oscar Arias had received the Nobel Peace Prize for his efforts to halt the wars in Central America), the U.S. Army was also conducting activity with environmentally dangerous implications in southern Costa Rica. In 1989 the Army Corps of Engineers began building and improving roads on the Osa Peninsula as part of its "Roads for Peace" mission. The plan was actually part of the Reagan administration's paranoia about communist infiltration in Central America—believing improved roads in the region could assist U.S. military efforts in the event its presence was needed to counter some aggressive force. In addition to the unrealistic philosophy behind these scenarios, the project alarmed Costa Rican environmentalists because the roads that the Corps was constructing led directly into Corcovado National Park. With the gold mining situation still not firmly resolved, the concern was that the road would be a conduit for *oreros* to bring further ecological destruction to the park.

The conservationists had reason to worry. Despite the efforts of the SPN to rid Corcovado of mining activity during the Oduber and Monge administrations, in 1987 the government hosted the International Gold Conference in San José as a means to lure investment to the Osa Peninsula. A recent joint UCR/U.S. Geological Survey study had confirmed the presence of large deposits of gold on the peninsula, a fact that was highlighted at the conference. The *Tico Times* reported that Arias' minister of natural resources, Alvaro Umaña, told the conferees, "If we're going to develop the industry, we must also protect the environment. However, the majority of the area is certainly open to exploitation." [16]

The problem was that if the area was open to mining, it was easy for an *orero* to cross over into Corcovado. In 1988 eighty some miners were arrested in the national park. Fifty more were caught inside park limits in September 1989, including two who had held park guards hostage overnight. Actually the problems illustrated very clearly the need for what Daniel Janzen and others were calling for: park management guidelines that included socioeconomic criteria. The problem was bigger than *campesinos* wanting to strike it rich; it reflected an absence of agrarian reform. Alexander Bonilla explained that "a clear vision" of sustainable development was needed—one that recognized that "humans are animals first; that they are a part of nature" and therefore should hardly be excluded from park use plans. "We need to find the point of equilibrium," he advised. "Without it there will always be socio-economic problems. . . . Conservation with hunger is impossible." [17]

Although Corcovado's management plan did not include small-scale gold panning (even Janzen had recommended *total* removal of miners), the National Park Service did start to consider locally based economic park uses during the Arias administration. One of the new tactics that the SPN worked on was a "mixed management" program to integrate people who lived within or near the borders of protected areas into the park planning itself. For some residents it meant being trained as tourist guides or to help with agroforestry projects. Eric Ulloa, assistant to the minister of natural resources in the Calderón administration, stated that this plan was part of the "new criteria . . . to create protected areas where the people living there will not be expelled." The idea was to help them to develop an economic base using the local natural resources.[18]

The ministry where Ulloa served, Ministry of Natural Resources, Energy, and Mines (MIRENEM), was a new branch of the government conceived during the Arias administration. The president created and the Legislative Assembly approved the agency to restructure and unify the management of Costa Rica's public lands and to deal with other conservation issues outside of agriculture. The plan moved the Park Service and the Forestry Directorate (DGF) out of the Ministry of Agriculture and Livestock (MAG)—a move roundly applauded by conservationists and something that Mario Boza had been urging for years. Also falling under MIRENEM's umbrella were the Department of Wildlife, the Department of Geology and Mines, and the National Zoo. During the Calderón administration MIRENEM relocated to the vacant ten-story Hotel Talamanca near downtown San José and SPN moved its offices into an adjoining house—moves that saved millions of dollars and conserved natural resources that would otherwise have been used for the building of a new facility. MIRENEM's name was changed to the Ministry of the Environment and Energy (MINAE) as part of the government's ongoing restructuring process when José María Figueres was elected in 1994. Its offices have remained at the MIRENEM building.

Arias appointed Alvaro Umaña to head the newly created ministry. A Stanford-educated economist and environmental engineer, Umaña took a very hands-on administrative role with the departments in his agency. He kept Luis Méndez as SPN director for the first few years of the term but replaced him in 1989 with Alfonso Matamoros, a DGF official, when the Park Service was starting to slide. Alvaro Ugalde, who came back to SPN in the Calderón administration, explained that in the Arias years "the power rested in the minister (Umaña) and his advisors. . . . Policy was made without consulting the Park Service." Budgets continued to be too small for needed services, the SPN could not afford to hire additional park guards, and employee dissatisfaction was on the rise. Park Service personnel went on strike in April 1990, shutting down the offices and the parks for a few days in the process.[19]

Administrative constraints aside, Umaña carried the ball for the process of restructuring the administration of protected areas, especially given the new emphasis placed on "mega-park" connectedness. Working with other MIRENEM officials, he developed a system of regional conservation units (Unidades Regionales de Conservación, or URCs) to incorporate the parks and reserves within a geographic area into a new administrative district. The URCs included all of the parks, biological reserves, forest reserves, wildlife refuges and indigenous reserves within that district. The plan called for a management strategy for each URC that included community input from people who lived in or around the protected areas and from park personnel there, as opposed to management decisions coming only from San José. It was the birth of decentralized park administration.

Umaña was also a foot soldier for incorporating the theory of sustainable development into the policy-making duties of his agency. More than just a verbal proponent of the ideal, Umaña was active in promoting what he called an "aggressive" and "ambitious" reforestation program in parts of the denuded countryside as a way to prevent erosion, restore farmland, and protect hydrologic resources. In a press release in the fall of 1987 he made known that in the administration's first year alone (1986), almost 15,000 acres had been reforested—double the acreage of 1985 and more than in all the years since 1969. He also oversaw a MIRENEM study that created and implemented the National Conservation Strategy for Sustainable Development. The strategy was the offshoot of Costa Rica's participation in the 1980 World Strategy for Conservation, jointly sponsored by the U.N. Programme for the Environment, the IUCN, and WWF (see Appendix 5). Its objective was to "change the thrust of development toward a more sustainable form" and promoted an evolving effort to keep up with advances in technology and discoveries.[20] Implementation and enforcement of its recommendations are under way, but time and ecological restoration will be the litmus test of its success.

The strategy's emphasis on balanced agricultural production is evidence that the government's attention to conservation during the past three administrations has not been limited to parks and reserves. Studies and practices of sustainable farming are an equally important contribution to Costa Rica's conservation history, especially given the largesse of the agricultural scene. Agriculture remains the country's top industry, accounting for over half the country's land use and two-thirds of its national economy. Thus research, training, and development of sustainable practices have become important factors for farmers and policy makers.

A study that originated during the Arias administration came to have special significance on this subject. Entitled "Natural Resource Management in Costa Rica," the study came up with a system of geographical land use capabilities (LUCs). It identified five land types "where the most intensive use that a piece of land is able to sustain on a continuous basis without suffering from degradation" was possible. The categories included land for clean-tilled crops, pastureland, permanent crop cover areas, forest, and protected reserves. Using soil studies, drainage data, topography reports, and climate information, the study was able to discern the size of each land use category and to define their locations across the country. This type of data had useful implications for policy making. For example, the study showed that 4,656 square kilometers were viable for pasture but that 19,000 square kilometers—almost one-third of the country—were presently being used in that capacity. It showed very graphically the degree of deforestation caused by the expansion of the livestock industry. But that the study identified the importance of agricultural land (three of the five LUCs) shows that conservationists were interested in more than just fencing off areas and taking land out of production. The goal was to show how production could be sustainable and less harmful to the environment.[21]

Sustainable development was also the theme of the Seventeenth General Assembly of the International Union for the Conservation of Nature (IUCN, presently called the World Conservation Union), which took place in San José in 1988. Members of the Costa Rican conservationist community were proud to host this event and showcase their accomplishments. They actively participated in different conferences and panels presented at the gathering of conservationists who attended from all over the world. Alvaro Umaña, for example, spoke on how "the concept of sustainable development" was an important "new style" of meeting the challenges of agriculture in the tropics. "It used to be that conservation meant preservation without [the presence] of man, that land should be kept in a bubble," Umaña stated, "but in Central America, that's not possible." [22] It was at this conference that Costa Rica's first debt swap plan was announced.

The campaign for sustainable development was the result of a satellite photography study that showed how acute the problem of deforestation was becoming. Instead of the 8 to 9 percent of forested land that aerial photos showed to exist outside of parks and reserves (bad enough as that was), the satellite images showed that only 5 percent remained. The cause for such destruction was pasture expansion and logging. Alvaro Umaña explained to reporters that much of the logging was illegal and that he had ordered the Rural Guard to be put on duty to conduct surprise searches. Their work resulted in the discovery of illegal cuts in and around national parks, trucks hauling logs out of restricted areas by night, the practice of hiding logs under agricultural produce on truck beds, and the common use of forged logging permits. The problem grew so out of hand that in 1988 officials from the Forestry Directorate petitioned President Arias to declare a national state of emergency. Agreeing to do so the following year, the proclamation empowered the DGF to suspend all permits to fell trees outside of private plantations and to prohibit the export of unfinished wood products. The declaration also freed government funds to beef up the enforcement of these policies, again making use of the Rural Guard. As expected, the timber companies reacted negatively and conservationists very positively to the measures. [23]

At the root of the problem was an obsolescent forestry code. In 1983, during the Monge administration, the Legislative Commission on Agricultural and Natural Resources Affairs convened to consider a "total reform" of the 1969 Forestry Law. That law established national parks, forest reserves, and other land use limitations, but did not do much to control the logging or livestock industries, especially on private forested land. Diputado Carazo Paredes recognized the urgency of legislative reform and told fellow commission members that after seeing "more and more logging trucks" in the country, he was "worried that total deforestation" would soon follow "if we don't put a stop to it now." "If the forest disappears," he reminded the committee, "so will everything else." [24]

There were others who supported reforming the Ley Forestal. Alexander Bonilla of ASCONA lobbied for reform, emphasizing the problems of unregulated burns. The DGF supported it because it would grant that agency more power to intervene against timber exploitation. Nonetheless, most debate on the bill centered around the question of regulating private property. Three years later, after considerable discussion and amendments on these points, the commission sent the bill to the Assembly. It was approved there and signed into law in 1986.

It hardly went over well in certain sectors of the public. The logging industry and various landowners complained that it violated the Constitution of the Republic by infringing on their rights as private property holders. Roxana Salazar, one of Costa Rica's leading environmental attorneys, explained that at issue was the right of the government to impose "limitation on private property." Those opposed to the measure presented several cases to lower courts, but because the matter was of a constitutional nature, it ended up being resolved by a Constitutional Tribunal (Sala Constitucional) made up of Supreme Court judges. In 1990 the tribunal ruled that the new Forestry Law did, in fact, violate the Constitution by imposing the restrictions on private land. The Legislative Assembly had the power to make such a law, but it required a two-thirds vote on the third debate of the motion. The Assembly had approved the bill by a majority of thirty-seven votes in 1986—one vote short of the required two-thirds needed. Thus, the tribunal annulled the reformed Forestry Law and reincarnated its 1969 predecessor.[25]

According to Salazar, the environmentalist community in Costa Rica did not react very strongly to the tribunal's decision. "It was more of a blow to the government," she explained, in that legislative committees had to go back to the drawing board, a bill would have to trudge anew through the legislative process, and agencies like the DGF were denied the meaty authority needed to slow deforestation. Luis Fournier, on the other hand, was annoyed. Fournier, a member of the original committee that hammered out the Ley Forestal bill in the late 1960s, mentioned that the ruling was based "more on the letter of the law than on the spirit in which it was made." But, as he added, "you have to work with [the court's] decisions."[26]

The work fell on the Legislative Assembly, which raced to put a "Band-Aid" provisional law together until a new, authoritative forestry law could be enacted. A team of *diputados* prepared a study outlining the good and bad points of the 1986 law and what needed to be changed. The *diputados* concluded that consolidating state forestry policy, more strongly regulating the logging industry, and filling in the gaps of the 1969 law were advantages of the recently annulled law that needed to be continued but that its constitutional faults outweighed any benefits accrued. Thus, as "a very urgent" measure, they proposed an alternative forestry policy that arrived at a plenary session of the Legislative Assembly on June 5, 1990—an apropos date since it was the International Day of the Environment, a point aptly exploited by more than one speaker during that session.[27]

The proposed law's principal objective was "to guard for the protection, conservation, exploitation, industrialization, administration, and development of the country's forest resources in accord with the principles of rational use of renewable natural resources." The bill gave the DGF authority over those broad responsibilities and established an interdisciplinary Forestry Council (in some ways similar to the one José Figueres had created in 1949) to serve as an advisory committee for policy implementation. The council was to be made up of various forestry industry associations, representatives of forestry cooperatives, university scientists, and government agency officials and was to be headed by the minister (or vice minister) of MIRENEM. And finally, among other duties, the law clarified state and private forestry categories and how regulations would apply to each. The tone of the section on private property was one of encouraged cooperation. It urged industry representatives to maintain relations with government agencies and to participate in research and policy forums.

As in 1969, speakers supporting the proposed law on the floor of the Assembly exploited references to "future generations" and "for the future of all Costa Ricans" as reasons why they were in favor of its passage. Other Assembly members, however, were quick to point out that the proposed law did not seem too different from the 1986 version, which was deemed unconstitutional. But like the other forestry bills preceding it, Law 7174 received wide support from municipal leaders and conservationists around the country and was approved by the Legislative Assembly after a third reading on June 28, 1990.[28]

It was approved with provisions. The most important one for this study was Provision VI, which, because the law was temporary in nature, required that a report be made by a special commission to study and propose reforms. The commission got right on the job, but in the meantime there had been a change of government with the election of Rafael Calderón as president. Oscar Arias left office after having revamped the government's public lands management and environmental agencies

Figure 12.   Arenal Volcano at Arenal National Park

(MIRENEM, URCs), after having supported the protection of tropical dry forest ecosystems with the Santa Rosa expansions and the creation of Guanacaste National Park, and after having overseen the integration of sustainable development policies. Before his term expired he also decreed the creation of the National Biodiversity Institute (INBio) to inventory the nation's biological wealth (see Chapter 12) and Arenal National Park.

Arenal, the country's most consistently active volcano, is located in the Tilarán Mountains not far from the Monteverde Cloud Forest Reserve. It took several years to complete the land expropriations needed for Arenal's designation (not all landowners in the area had consented to sell), and the courts nullified Arias' original proclamation. Today it is a restricted-access national park because of the danger its eruptions present. It is also part of a corridor protection plan for endangered cloud forests, as it is linked with the Children's Rainforest project and the Monteverde Preserve.

The new president, Rafael Calderón Fournier of the conservative

United Social Christian Party (PUSC), was the son of former president Rafael Calderón Guardia (arch rival of "Don Pepe" Figueres in the 1940s) and the godson of ousted Nicaraguan dictator Anastasio Somoza. He was elected president in 1990 after two unsuccessful tries in the previous elections against PLN winners Luis Monge and Oscar Arias. He won this time in a very close and bitter race with the help of campaign manager Roger Ailes (the mastermind behind George Bush's negative campaign for president against Michael Dukakis), who worked to link the PLN with complicity in narcotrafficking and had Calderón appeal to the populist sentiments of *campesino* voters.

Calderón's conservative résumé and positions logically worried Costa Rican conservationists. They were further alarmed when the environmental group ASCONA came out with reports that Calderón's PUSC supporters in the Osa Peninsula had promised area *oreros* access to Corcovado National Park. Calderón denied the charges, but the director of the park told reporters for the *Tico Times,* "We've identified these people as Calderón people, and they were telling the goldminers that Corcovado National Park would be given to them."[29]

Calderón did not mention Corcovado gold panners in his inaugural speech, but he did talk about preserving Costa Rica's "untold ecological riches" and his interest in creating a "new ecological order of international cooperation." These words surprised conservationists since in none of his three campaigns for president had he ever given much attention to environmental concerns. But he made some appointments that seemed to please the conservationist community. While he named outsider Hernán Bravo (a beverage company executive from Cartago) as the new MIRENEM minister, he appointed Mario Boza as MIRENEM subdirector, retained Alfonso Matamoros as head of SPN, and named Alvaro Ugalde as head of the Wildlands and Wildlife Department, a newly created office that was part of the administration's reorganization scheme. Ugalde was transferred back to the directorship of SPN in the spring of 1991—less than a year into Calderón's term—to utilize his expertise in the day-to-day management of the park system.

Back in the government saddle again, Boza and Ugalde wasted no time in working to influence conservation policy. The most important policy under consideration at the time was the reworking of the emergency Forestry Law that the Legislative Assembly's Special Commission was engaged in during that summer of 1990. When Boza was called on to testify before the commission on July 28, he brought his slide projector with him. In it were pictures rendered from the Land-Sat images that had been taken from over five hundred miles above the earth and that showed the extent of Costa Rican deforestation. Edward Cyrus, chief of MIRENEM's Technical Services Department, also came to the meeting to interpret some of the satellite images. He talked about the waste involved in deforestation and explained that while 63 percent of the timber cuts were destined for industrial purposes, in reality only 34 percent of the wood made it to the various industries and, of that, only 17 percent was converted into "products that reach the consumers."[30]

The commission members were receptive to the data presented to them. They had recently learned that there were only 617,500 acres of forest remaining in Costa Rica outside of protected areas—far less than had been estimated earlier. They knew, then, that Boza was not exaggerating when he told them that his office received "letters daily from all over Costa Rica from groups and citizens who were worried and upset about deforestation in their area." He continued, "The people say 'come, see this, do an investigation, stop the culprits, buy out the land, position some guards,' which is almost impossible for us to do . . . we just don't have the economic means . . . to acquire more land, which is the only effective protection in this country." Therefore, he urged the commission to pass a tough forestry bill on to the Assembly—"an effective instrument to manage what natural forest we have left."[31]

It was at this particular hearing that Boza introduced a compelling new argument: changes in land use were the most destructive for the environment. He showed that farming, ranching, and logging could occur in certain areas without ecological damage because the land was being properly managed for those uses. It was when a radical change took place (i.e., clearcutting) that the long-term damage started to mount which eventually not only affected the forest but also caused erosion, flooding, and loss of hydrologic resources.

The greatest problem, according to Boza, was still with agricultural colonization and specifically with the IDA (Agrarian Development Institute, formerly ITCO), which continued to help peasant families move onto public lands without suitable guidelines on sustainable farming and forestry. Other forestry officials present at the hearing testified that DGF was pushing hard for reforestation of native tree species—as opposed to teakwood or other tree farms. Boza closed the presentation by reiterating the importance of including "no change of land use" language in the new forestry law. "Without it," he advised, "we have nothing legal to enforce the law."[32]

The Special Commission continued to meet into the fall of 1990 and on into 1991. Evidently the two-month deadline had been extended since deliberations continued for the next few years. Boza addressed the committee members again in September 1990 with a renewed concern about Corcovado National Park. Mincing no words, he said, "Either we do something very soon, . . . or within four to five years [the park] will be an island surrounded by pastures." This type of testimony reflected the evolution of conservation thought in the early 1990s. The concern for the area surrounding Corcovado National Park was more than just arguments for buffer zone protection; it was a concern for optimal park size. Conservationists like Boza and Ugalde were now questioning the ideal park size for protecting an entire ecosystem. New MIRENEM minister Hernán Bravo addressed this concern in a letter to Special Commission chairman William Cordero in which he told of how his agency was working to create "conservation areas" (an expanded version of the URCs from the Arias administration).[33]

Along those lines, then, Boza prepared the Renewable Resources Action Plan for the Calderón administration. In it he wrote that the "ultimate goal" was to maintain 25 percent of Costa Rica's forests outside of protected areas. It advocated integrating national wildlife refuges into a park system that would link biological reserves, national parks, and forest reserves into these large conservation areas. Its long-range goal was to form a corridor of forested areas in Costa Rica that would connect with protected areas in Panama to the south and with Nicaragua to the north, eventually to form "a biological migration corridor throughout Mesoamerica." The plan also included sections on ecotourism and environmental education and proposed that ICT be actively involved with planning and promoting the protection of natural areas.[34]

Meanwhile, President Calderón was working to advance another item on his administration's conservation agenda: promoting Costa Rica as the headquarters of a proposed Earth Council—part of the "New Ecological Order of International Cooperation" that he had alluded to in his inaugural address. The plan was to present such a proposal in the form of a resolution to the U.N. Conference on the Environment and Development (the "Earth Summit") that was held in Rio de Janeiro in June of

1992. The plan also had the support of the delegates from other Central American nations who cosponsored the resolution. MIRENEM minister Hernán Bravo introduced the resolution, which outlined how Costa Rica could be the administrative seat of the Earth Summit to follow up on agreements reached in Rio de Janeiro. And in a speech to the assembled delegates, President Calderón boldly invited the rest of the world "to emulate Costa Rica . . . [where] ecology enjoys a long tradition and solid prestige." The international delegates, made up of over 100 heads of state and over 9,000 representatives of nongovernmental organizations, approved the resolution.[35]

In addition to the honor of hosting the Earth Council in recognition of Costa Rica's active commitment to environmental conservation, many Ticos believed that the Earth Council would generate important economic and educational resources for the benefit of the country. Full-page ads in Costa Rica newspapers congratulated President Calderón and Minister Bravo for their efforts and success in Rio. An editorial in *La Nación* soon after the U.N. conference proclaimed that "Calderón has obtained his greatest foreign policy victory with the Rio Summit's designation of Costa Rica as the permanent seat of the Earth Council. We are converting ourselves as a nation into one of the principal centers of world ecology."[36]

Not everyone agreed with this assessment. Leaders of Costa Rican environmental groups were quick to point to contradictions in policy. For example, the Calderón administration had done little to discourage another U.S. Army Corps of Engineers road project—this time in the Sarapiquí area—just three months earlier. The *Tico Times* reported that this "Bridges for Peace" project was actually aiding the multinational banana companies by constructing roads and bridges in previously inaccessible lowland forests so the growers could expand banana plantations. Thus ASCONA's César Castro maintained that "the government is scrambling for eleventh-hour strategies." The director of the Costa Rican Ecological Association (AECO), Orlando Avila, called the Earth Summit idea "demagogic and opportunistic" and was more succinct in his specific criticism: "While the government is promoting Costa Rica abroad as a model of environmentalism, the rape of natural resources continues at home without the political will to stop it." And Guillermo Barquero of the National Organization for Wildlife and Conservation, who had earlier called Calderón's Earth Council idea "a rhetorical plan," now stated that

"Costa Rica is creating a myth, without meaning or content in practice, in legislative and environmental policy." Likewise the conservationists complained that the environmental groups had not been consulted in the planning process of Calderón's proposal.[37]

There is a side note to the story that produced bold headlines in Costa Rican newspapers at the time. The government discovered before the start of the Rio Conference that a resort project under construction on Costa Rica's far southeastern Caribbean coast had improperly crossed (or had ignored) the legal boundaries of the Kekóldi Indigenous Reserve and of the Gandoca-Manzanillo National Wildlife Refuge. The resort, to be called "Ecodesarrollo" (Ecodevelopment), however, was the project of Maurice Strong—the Canadian businessman and self-proclaimed environmentalist who had brainstormed and organized much of the Earth Summit in Rio. Pictures of the bulldozed area crossing the property lines of the protected areas were emblazoned across front pages and added to the irony of the timing. Strong later claimed that the whole affair had been blown out of proportion in that the bulldozer had inadvertently crossed into a protected area and caused little ecological damage.[38]

Strong's alleged transgressions notwithstanding, the Earth Council did headquarter in Costa Rica following the Rio Conference. Original plans called for the seat to be located at the University for Peace near Ciudad Colón but instead the Consejo de la Tierra was set up in a vast office space on the eleventh floor of a government building in San José. The arrangement was temporary. Plans as of 1996 were for the construction of a new headquarters building to be completed by the turn of the century that would be designed to use solar energy and other environmentally friendly construction concepts. Local materials and local construction firms will be used. According to one official there, the organization will continue to benefit the host country as was originally hoped by its proponents in the Calderón administration. Fifty percent of the employees who work there are Costa Rican (and, as the official assured, they are not solely in secretarial and janitorial positions—they include department chiefs, administrators, assistants, etc.). Gerardo Budowski and Alvaro Umaña serve as Costa Rican representatives to the Earth Council Institute. The Earth Council's mission is "to operationalize the Earth Summit agreements and sustainable development through the empowerment of civil society." Its charter calls for "a world-wide participatory process . . . that will guide people and nations . . . [and] will be the

Sustainable Development equivalent to the Universal Declaration of Human Rights."[39]

President Calderón's success at landing the Earth Council in Costa Rica was not matched by the passage of a new forestry law during his term. That legislation would have to wait for the administration of José María Figueres, who became president in 1994. With the new administration came new appointments to conservation positions and a continued restructuring of environmental agencies. Mario Boza left MIRENEM to head the Mesoamerican Biological Corridor Foundation in its San Pedro office. Alvaro Ugalde left the National Parks Service to work for the U.N. Environmental Programme (UNEP), whose Central America office is located in Pavas, a San José suburb. Hernán Bravo left MIRENEM to serve in the Legislative Assembly after winning a seat from his home district in Cartago.

President Figueres replaced Bravo with René Castro, who oversaw his ministry's change of nomenclature and direction. When MIRENEM became MINAE (Ministry of Environment and Energy) in 1996, the agency combined the SPN, DGF, and Wildlife and Wildlands office into one subagency called Sistema Nacional de Areas de Conservación (National System of Conservation Areas, or SINAC). The government leased a large 1950s-style mansion two blocks from the MINAE tower to house SINAC's offices, which were formerly scattered at DGF and SPN facilities elsewhere.

Part of the reason for the reorganization project was due to the multiplicity of bureaucratic agencies. Between the office of the president, the Legislative Assembly, and the "megastructure" of environmental agencies involved, there was, according to UCR biologist Sergio Salas, who often worked with government agencies, "too much diffusion of responsibility." By the early 1990s there were twenty-seven different divisions, councils, offices, institutes, and *juntas* that rarely acted in cooperation with each other. The different offices often had conflicting or overlapping results. Further, many ministries developed their own environmental sections in response to their required duties.[40]

The creation of MIRENEM as an umbrella organization did not seem to correct the problem. Even the assistant to President Calderón's minister of MIRENEM, Eric Ulloa, pointed out that there was "too much duplication of efforts, especially between MIRENEM and MAG. Likewise, we have a commission on Women in the Environment and recently the of-

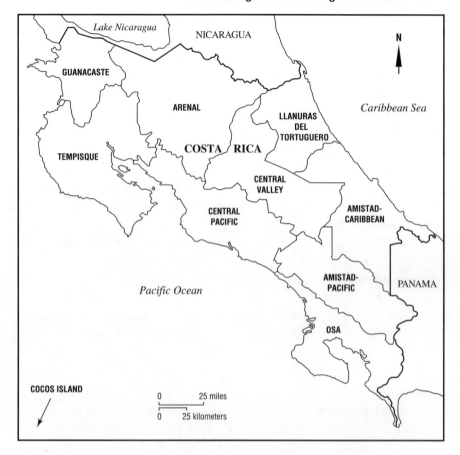

Figure 13. Costa Rican System of Conservation Areas (*source:* SINAC)

fice of the First Lady [Señora de Calderón] has created a similar council."[41] There was also duplication of efforts within certain departments
via planning commissions, councils, and committees with overlapping
responsibilities.

Thus SINAC was the result of the government's drive to restructure
and decentralize conservation policy in Costa Rica. It was a direct descen-
dant of the URC (regional conservation units) concept started at the tail
end of President Arias' term. Like the URCs, the new system divided the
country into ten Conservation Areas (ACs) based on geographical characteristics (see Figure 13). Each AC was assigned its own director to be
over several subdirectors charged with promoting conservation policy
for different parts of the area.

The mission was "to consolidate a National System of Conservation Areas, integrated and planned with other MINAE agencies where authority and duties will be delegated to the regions to give wider participation to the local society." Or, as SINAC literature proclaims, its goal is to follow "the three D's"—"deconcentration, decentralization, and democratization" of the nation's conservation policies.[42]

At stake in the new system's goals was whether a policy that advanced economic development via sustainable use of natural resources could mesh with the ideals of conserving biodiversity. The apparent contradiction was not lost among some conservationists. The environmental group AECO, for example, has been an outspoken critic of the reorganization scheme and has criticized the duality of SINAC's mission. Current AECO director Alvaro León explained that one of his group's concerns was that the Directorate of Geology and Mines was *not* incorporated into SINAC—"excluding that agency from the decision-making process because of the boom in gold." Thus, with decentralized authority and increased local input, León contended, mining interests in the Osa Peninsula were able to exert more influence in the management scheme of that AC at the expense of the buffer zone protection goals and biodiversity preservation talk of SINAC officials. He also claimed that the plan would result in increased exploitation of resources, especially by the U.S. and Japanese paper industries, and increased construction of resort hotels in pristine areas—events that many local residents would actually oppose. So instead of increased local decisions, there would be increased external influence for economic development projects being exerted on regional AC personnel who could make their own decisions without regard for stricter national environmental standards, León said.[43]

Anselmo Flores Reyes, a native leader from the Térraba Indigenous Reserve on the west slope of the Talamancas in southern Costa Rica, corroborated León's point. He mentioned that commercial deforestation continued to be a problem in and around the reserve: "There's a great deal of logging, watersheds are endangered, there are laws but they're not enforced, the wood-cutting regulations are not put into effect, the police do not help." He said he did not know much about the new reorganization system but mentioned that the forestry officials from the regional AC office "do not visit very often; they go when they want and then don't do very much." In the past, however, he claimed that preconsolidation DGF personnel regularly visited the area to inspect and control the woodcutters. He also mentioned that he knew of no indigenous people on any of the SINAC study commissions—the government solicited little input from the Talamancan Térrabas.[44]

AECO's Alvaro León voiced another concern his group had about the agency restructuring process: it had no legal foundation. He remarked that the Legislative Assembly had never passed any law allowing MIRENEM (or MINAE) officials to consolidate and regionalize the government's conservation arms. This point was also made by former MIRENEM official Eric Ulloa, who during the Figueres administration was serving as a legislative assistant to Hernán Bravo, his former MIRENEM boss and now a *diputado* in the Assembly. "It's a fatal disaster!" Ulloa said of the whole SINAC organization. "It's never been approved by the legislature, it's part of the new president's goals [and] very typical of how this administration ignores laws." He went on to lambaste how MINAE had gone from one extreme of central coordination to the far other extreme of "way too much regionalism." And he related how a decentralized SINAC was decreasing Costa Rica's prestige abroad among international lending organizations. The government of Canada, for example, "was so bothered" by the potentially environmentally harmful policy changes that it diverted a financial aid package from Costa Rica to Nicaragua; the government of the Netherlands was considering a similar move. These decisions were made despite MINAE Minister René Castro's written explanation to the commission studying the changes that a benefit of the restructuring process would be "to guarantee international credibility to donors." Before the Rio Conference, "it was only Costa Rica," Ulloa remembered, "but now there's a lot of competition" for international funds.[45]

Environmental attorney Roxana Salazar disagreed with León's and Ulloa's contention that SINAC was an extralegal entity. "No, there's no problem with legislative law," she rejoined, "MINAE can [legally] make changes" in the administration of the agencies under its domain. In fact, Salazar praised the direction SINAC was taking: "It's good; it's a different vision, more independent . . . that will allow greater local participation." Luis Fournier agreed. He admitted that there will be "problems at first," but went on to suggest that "local people know much more [than San José environmentalists]." In the long run, then, the decentralized policies "are going to be a benefit in the future," he added.[46]

Most conservationists concurred with Fournier. Fellow UCR biologist

Jorge Cortés said that SINAC was "good" for bringing about more local input and keeping resources in the area instead of "disappearing" at the central office. He also applauded the agency's plans to hire area residents and to have conservation personnel living and working closer to the protected areas. Overall, Cortés thought SINAC would be a "benefit for national parks" but agreed that "corruption like [gold] miners" would continue to be a "difficult" problem to deal with. Gerardo Budowski said he liked "the idea of joining together" the different government agencies and "decentralizing the regions into one administrative organ." But, agreeing with Ulloa here, he warned that the changes could be "a pendulum [going] from one extreme to the other—there's the danger of losing central authority for policy control . . . and the tendency to think on a short-term basis." Alexander Bonilla said he too believed in "the importance of decentralizing—it will help, it's positive to have more spaces in which to promote conservation." But "it's going to take more than laws," he continued. "SINAC is good only if put into practice." Stressing that sustainable development could be explained by understanding "society, economics, and ecology" as the three points of a triangle, Bonilla said that many groups look only at one point; he criticized environmental groups for often seeing only the ecology point: "Environmentalists are not the owners of truth." Thus, SINAC was on the right track "to have connections with the private sector." But he also suggested that "globalization" was "important to consider" for protecting the environment in places like Costa Rica. "We have the right to develop," he concluded. "Northerners do not have the right to complain."[47]

Another SINAC proponent, but one who came to support it a bit more slowly than others, was Mario Boza. While he may have been philosophically opposed to the URCs when they were first implemented, Boza said that he was "in agreement" with SINAC—that it was "an old idea going back many years." He cited how he had been a member of the committee that originally had worked to bring it into existence. "It's under way," he stated, and "it's a better system with the regional input." He explained that he agreed with SINAC's work to dispel the "compartmentalization" theory of managing protected areas "like islands." Representatives of the conservation foundations where Boza had been so instrumental in the 1970s and 1980s more or less agreed with this assessment. When asked about her organization's reaction to the SINAC changes, an official at Fundación de Parques Nacionales said that the system had "advantages and disadvantages" but that, overall, FNP approved of it and supported it. An official at Fundación Neotrópica said "we're waiting to see." He stated that his organization was "more nongovernmental" and that it would work with whatever changes the government came up with. "What's important," he said, "was to continue to apply for and receive grant money" to support Costa Rican conservation efforts.[48]

About at the same time that MINAE and SINAC started functioning as new agencies (1996), the Legislative Assembly finally passed a new and revised Forestry Law. The same Special Commission (albeit with different members across the years) had continued to meet to discuss the proposal and had convened over eighty hearings. Important points of the law included outlining the duties of a new Forestry Administration (within SINAC)—conserving forest resources, approving management plans, establishing guidelines for the prohibited use of endangered tree species, and a variety of other administrative functions. The law created a National Forestry Office and replaced the National Forestry Council with Regional Environmental Councils in the spirit of the government's decentralization emphasis. The councils would authorize wood-cutting permits. Very important, different articles of the law dealt with conservation and reforestation incentives and various tax and penalty restrictions.

Perhaps one of the most important new tenets of the law was its language concerning forests on private land. Because it was the big stumbling block of the 1986 version, the issue had to be handled carefully but firmly. Title III of the law specifically dealt with this point and spelled out that "on lands covered with forests, a change in the soil use of the area will not be permitted, nor will forestry plantations be established." The wording was intended to impede the process of deforestation for agricultural purposes and made two options available to owners of the 494,000 acres of private forested land left in the country: the owners could leave their forests untouched and receive a [government] incentive "so that the land will stay for eternity as forest"; or the landowners could "manage their forests—prohibiting the change of soil use" and every few years undergo an intense management review process.[49]

There was actually very little debate in the plenary sessions of the Legislative Assembly. One of the new Forestry Law's greatest proponents was Diputado Hernán Bravo, who, as minister of MIRENEM under President Calderón, had worked unsuccessfully to see it pass years earlier. He explained in one debate that the law would not prohibit logging, but would make "us look for how to protect the forest, not just the trees." It passed on 5 February 1996 by a vote of forty-four to one.[50] Eight days later, President Figueres, like his father before him in 1969, signed the forestry bill into law.

By the end of the decade, however, Costa Rican environmentalists were attributing new problems to the 1996 law. "The old law allowed us to fight more effectively for conservation," argued Carlos Calvo, manager of Protected Wildlife Areas in the Tortuguero AC, but "with the new legislation, loggers are now awaiting to pounce like bees around the honey pot." He claimed that the previous legislation allowed only landholders with legal property titles to apply for timber-cutting permits. But the new law requires only that one have sworn testimony from witnesses to prove possession, which has increased logging in areas like Tortuguero, where the cut logs are then floated down the waterways of the national park. Seeing this kind of logging operation worried former park ranger Herman Hay, who now works as an ecotourist guide. "Two weeks ago [February 1998], a shipment came through dragging about eighty logs. As guides, we are constantly singing the praises of Costa Rica's conservation policies, so it's embarrassing when something like this happens. The tourists I was with took pictures and asked questions, but what could I say?"[51]

A similar pattern has developed on the Osa Peninsula, where logging continues to threaten Corcovado National Park. The timber permits there (both legal and illegal) have created a checkerboard of clearcuts around the peninsula that have caused the rivers to turn brown with uncontrolled runoff and destroyed important fisheries and wildlife habitat. The silt eventually makes its way to the sea where sedimentation is beginning to choke out the coral reef in the Golfo Dulce. Cecilia Solano, of the Association for the Defense of Natural Resources of the Osa, summed up the situation: "Unfortunately, we have a new forestry law that does not benefit us. On the contrary, it has made the problem worse. The new law has been a disgrace for this country, for the forests, and for those of us responsible for conserving the next generation." And reporter John Burnett has written that the problem is not only grounded in the new law, but is part of the wide ramifications of the government's decentralization program. "Under the old law, landowners had to request cutting permits from federal forestry engineers in San José. But the procedure was slow and riddled with corruption. To decentralize the permit process, lawmakers took away the federal authority, and split it between the municipalities and private forestry engineers." And, he continued, "the result has been chaos: the municipalities are handing out permits, though they have no experience in forest management, and the private foresters . . . are just as corrupt as the federal foresters were." By August of 1997 the situation had grown so bad that MINAE director René Castro imposed a temporary cutting ban on the Osa and created a commission to investigate illegal logging. Environmentalists, Burnett reported, "cautiously praised" the moratorium, but "are worried what will happen when it expires."[52]

The passage of the new Forestry Law and the implementation of the administrative restructuring process bring to a close another chapter in Costa Rica's conservation history. The changes will have to be evaluated in the future to see if they brought with them the hopes dreamed of by their advocates or the disadvantages predicted by their opponents. Moreover, the election of the new, conservative (PUSC) President Miguel Angel Rodríguez in February 1998 may have implications that affect these policies. Environmental issues did not play a large role in his campaign. Thus, the verdict is still out on the application of sustainable development and its implications for Costa Rican conservation. These ideals and experiments await future debate and will be the center of studies for years to come.

Meanwhile, it seems appropriate here to evaluate other aspects of Costa Rica's conservation history that are not related to policy. If we consider that conservation policies and institutions are the foundation of a green republic, then these other points (environmental education, nongovernmental organizations, ecotourism, and biodiversity inventorying) are its building blocks. They are the subject of the chapters in Part II.

PART

2

Building a Green Republic

9 Environmental Education

FRAMEWORK FOR THE FUTURE

Environmental education has surfaced as an indispensable instrument to create conscience and to internalize our conduct, attitudes, and capacity to make decisions for the rational and creative management of nature's resources.

Estrella Guier, "La conservación como elemento educacional para el desarrollo"

"Environmentalizing" the Public

History and its lessons are dynamic. To learn from past experiences and to plan for the changing needs of the environment, Costa Rica has implemented a strong educational program. Environmental education, according to Estrella Guier, who is a professor in the Environmental Education program at the National Open University, seeks to understand "the balance between the natural environment and that which was created by man." In Costa Rica this has become an "innovative" process serving as a "link between social and natural sciences, which traditionally have been taught in a totally isolated form." Put another way, environmental activist-attorney Roxana Salazar writes that environmental education "is an essential element in all forms related to the environment and natural resources." Its overarching goal, she states, is "to forge a . . . consciousness necessary for a true protection of the environment."[1]

While the independent, and often erudite, study and instruction of Costa Rican natural history and biosystematics can be traced to the middle of the nineteenth century, environmental education is a relatively recent addition to the curricula of public schools and universities. Its legal foundation, however, goes back to the 1950s and 1960s. The 1957 Fundamental Education Law (Law 2160) stated that the Ministry of Education had the obligation to ensure the instruction of methods to protect places of scenic beauty and to conserve and develop the historic and artistic patrimony of the nation.[2] But the rather nebulous wording of the clause provided no specific examples of what was to be protected or how instruction could be integrated into the classroom.

The 1969 Forestry Law also mandated that the government be involved in the instruction of natural resource use and protection. It required the Ministry of Agriculture to establish continuing education programs on the importance of forest resources but again spelled out no specific guidelines. Schools and universities have had to develop their own curricula for the instruction of the broader and more interrelated concepts of environmental education. Professor Guier referred to this as an "integrated approach" for the "environmentalization of the curriculum." She added that the idea was to conceptualize "environmental education as the integrating axis of other disciplines. . . . In other words, the environment should be considered with a holistic perspective where each variable should be considered within a total context, and forming a scheme of interactions. The fundamental characteristics of each environmental situation can be defined as multi-, inter-, and transdisciplinary."[3]

A variety of programs has emerged in Costa Rica to address the need for an integrated approach to environmental education. The University of Costa Rica's School of Biology emphasizes applied ecology and instructs within many different biological disciplines. It maintains a tropical forest field station to allow students to gain hands-on experience with research projects. Its School of Agronomy deals with environmental issues in agriculture and sustainable development. Many of UCR's projects are in part funded by the National Council for Scientific and Technological Research (CONICIT). The Legislative Assembly created CONICIT in 1972 as the grant-supporting arm of the government. One of its important components is its Natural Resources Commission, which has actively funded research on a variety of environmental and conservation projects.

The National University (UNA), located in Heredia, offers a more specifically integrated program through its much-respected School of Environmental Sciences. According to one professor there, the school was established in response "to the urgency of educating the public which forced conservationists to discuss environmental themes and to give [them] dimensions of totality." With grant assistance from CONICIT, the school has been especially involved in researching forest and marine science issues. UNA has tried to fill a historic void in Costa Rican research on marine biology and maintains research stations in coastal areas. The School of Environmental Sciences also offers degrees in wildlife management and is a leading institution for the identification, study, and protection of endangered species.[4]

In the mid-1980s UNA established a specific commission—the Commission on Natural Resources and the Environment (CORENAMA)—for studying and promoting environmental conservation. The "general objectives" for CORENAMA included "contributing in any positive way to pro-environment campaigns and conservationist programs, contributing to research on national ecological issues, developing plans to increase environmental education nationally, and lending support to government conservation agencies." Alvaro Ugalde, as head of the SPN, took the UNA students and staff up on their offer and requested their service as members of a "planning team" for Chirripó and La Amistad national parks.[5] UNA's School of Environmental Sciences also publishes a monthly environmental update called *Ambien-Tico* and maintains a large video library with over 150 films on environmental topics. The *videoteca* is open to the public.

The National Open University (UNED), in collaboration with the conservation group ASCONA, founded the Program for Environmental Education in 1977. Mario Boza was its first director. This program grew out of the "emerging necessity for younger generations to study the relationships of their surroundings, [and] to create an awareness and an ability to confront the problems that they generate." The program was started to develop curricula, literature, and audiovisual aids that could be transferred to classroom settings for a wide range of age groups. It has enjoyed popular support and high enrollment among Costa Rican students. Like their counterparts at UNA, UNED students and faculty are often called upon to assist in government conservation programs. In 1984, for example, a UNED team completed research on a fire management plan for SPN. Another UNED entity is CIDA, the Center for Environmental Information and Documentation. As mentioned earlier, CIDA was created by the Carazo administration as a joint function of UNED and the National

Park Service (today SINAC) as a data-collecting and -storing service for information on natural resources.[6]

There are other schools of higher education and programs that offer environmental education. Costa Rica's Institute of Technology, primarily an engineering school, deals with industrial planning and environmental pollution and it also has a Forestry Engineering Department that teaches students about environmental silviculture. The University for Peace has an integrated conflict resolution/natural resource management program, and students there can study for a master's degree in peace and ecology. Most of Costa Rica's other colleges and universities offer some coursework in environmental sciences. Having research organizations headquartered in the country has been another useful source of disseminating environmental education. The Organization of Tropical Studies (OTS), Tropical Science Center (TSC), Agricultural School for the Humid Tropics (EARTH), Center for Environmental Study (CEA), and especially the Tropical Agronomical Research and Education Center (CATIE) have had ongoing training programs via conferences and in-field studies to advance new ideas in conservation and sustainable agriculture.

Environmental education in Costa Rica is not limited to the college level. The Ministry of Public Instruction is involved with disseminating environmental curricula to elementary and secondary schools. Based on his work entitled "Preliminary Considerations for the Elaboration of a National Environmental Education Plan," Orlando Hall developed the Center for the Improvement and Teaching of Sciences (CEMEC) within the ministry, funded in part by CONICIT. CEMEC not only promotes the instruction of sciences but also helps public schools educate people about the care of their tropical environment. Another training program is the Latin American Center for Environmental Education (CLEA), which was founded in Costa Rica in 1982. Using Latin American and North American guest instructors, CLEA focuses on offering teacher in-service training on environmental issues. It prepares course materials, environmental books and guides, and field trips for teachers to acquaint them with how to teach environmental topics.[7] Evidence of student involvement on ecological topics is seen throughout the country. Students' artwork often graces city walls and sides of buildings and is exhibited at the national zoo.

Other youth programs in environmental education exist. One of the more noteworthy ones is the National Youth Movement's involvement with national parks in ecological projects, education, and maintenance of park services and forests. Instruction on and field visits to the national parks are part of the official programs of Costa Rican elementary and secondary schools. The *Tico Times* reported that one high school in Costa Rica, Liceo de Alajuita, formed an Ecology Club in 1992, which was the first of its kind in the nation. Its members are involved with informational programs and environmental service projects.[8]

Other Costa Rican media are utilized for the environmental education of the country. Environmental literature, including a host of journals and magazines, has flourished in Costa Rica. The principal ones are *Biocenosis* (a publication of UNED's Program for Environmental Education), *Brenesia* (a publication of the National Museum), *Zurqui* (a periodic environmental supplement to the daily newspaper *La Nación*), *Agronomía Costarricense, Revista de Biología Tropical, Tecnología en Marcha, Turrialba* (a CATIE publication), and *Neotrópica* (of the Fundación Neotrópica). Numerous nature guides, national park books, wildlife literature, and posters of endangered species abound in book stores and tourism shops. Posters of the Costa Rican life zones (created and distributed by Fundación Neotrópica) or of pristine beaches and volcanoes (produced by Costa Rica's tourism institute, ICT) grace hotels, travel agencies, book stores, department stores, schools, offices, and restaurants, continually reminding citizens of their country's natural areas.

In the 1980s and 1990s the print and electronic media kept active guard in keeping abreast of environmental issues and informing the public. Newspapers like *La Nación,* the *Tico Times,* and others maintained regular environmental features and columns. Costa Rican television aired many programs dealing with wildlife and nature. One station, Channel Six, proclaimed itself the "canal ecológico" (the ecology channel) and almost exclusively featured environmental programming. MIRENEM even used to maintain a national telephone hotline, called "teléfono ecológico," which citizens could call twenty-four hours a day to be updated on various environmental issues and to report abuses they observed. A commonly seen environmental slogan on billboards, buses, and bumper stickers was "Naturaleza, Belleza, y Paz: Todo en Uno— Costa Rica" (Nature, Beauty, and Peace: All in One—Costa Rica). There were other public and private campaigns to encourage recycling ("¿yo reciclo, y usted?"/I recycle, do you?) and to control pollution and litter ("no a la contaminación"/stop pollution).

Government proclamations of special days and weeks likewise have been a means to educate, inform, and alert the public. Arbor Day has been used for decades to encourage reforestation. As early as 1950, the government declared a National Week for the Conservation of Natural Resources. The fifth of June (World Environment Day) was especially commemorated in 1992 to correspond with the Earth Summit taking place at the same time in Rio de Janeiro. Many Costa Rican scout groups marked the day by planting trees in deforested areas. And the fourth Monday in July has been proclaimed National Wildlife Day with similar attention given to it by the media and environmental groups.

Environmental groups themselves have been another key source of environmental education in Costa Rica. A directory of nongovernmental organizations lists some fifty different groups across Costa Rica that engage in promoting environmental education programs. The groups offer workshops and courses to their members, to schoolchildren, and to the general public. Many organizations have been involved with the variety of national and regional conferences on conservation topics that Costa Rica has hosted in the last twenty-five years. Journalist Shirley Christian pointed out that "here in Costa Rica, some kind of conference on the environment takes place almost every week."[9]

Critics, however, have complained about the inherent bureaucratic inability to translate ideas and decisions from conferences into workable, enforceable strategies for environmental protection. Inadequate funding for agencies to implement the suggested proposals has also impeded their complete success. But the alternative seems worse. The absence of continuing dialogue could potentially stifle creative thought and could lead to even greater governmental inaction. It could also decrease the opportunity for professional, interdisciplinary participation in the decision-making arena. And the conferences have at least displayed an awareness of, and a willingness to deal with, the vast dilemma of development versus protection.

From National Parks to a National Environmental Ethic

Which came first? Did a national environmental ethic lead to the development of national parks, or were national parks a catalyst for the development of an environmental ethic? This "chicken or egg" question can be analyzed only in light of Costa Rica's evolutionary conservation history: the ethic evolved over time from a simpler form with periodic mutations along the way.

That Costa Rica's geographic and historic uniqueness shaped the unfolding pattern of conservationist thought in the beginning does not account for the surge in environmental awareness experienced in the last twenty years. It explains its background and indeed was a germ in its formation, but another element was surely at work to nurture its rapid growth. Luis Gómez and Jay Savage believe that a greater environmental awareness occurred through "the changes in Costa Rican national attitudes in the past two decades, the dedicated young biological scientists and conservationists who have helped in developing the nation's environmental consciousness, and the emerging national concern for basic knowledge of the environment and its biota."[10]

But the reason "the past two decades" is so frequently cited is because of that threshold legislation from 1969—the Ley Forestal, which established the basis to create national parks. It was destined to be a cyclical phenomenon. Once parks were created, they became, as Gerardo Budowski has described them, "a source of pride for the majority of Costa Ricans"—whether they necessarily visited them or not—which in turn inspired them to demand more protected areas and other environmental policies.[11]

One of the most important ways in which the national parks actively led to an increased environmental ethic among Costa Ricans was via their educational capacity. Mario Boza, speaking at the 1972 IUCN national parks conference, said that publicity via the national media and park visitor centers soon after the designation of the first two national parks (Poás Volcano and Santa Rosa) was "a tremendous success in our country." Ten years later Douglas Cuillard (a U.S. National Park Service liaison to SPN) told the delegates at the First Symposium on National Parks and Biological Reserves that creating awareness was the most important mission of Costa Rica's national parks. He emphasized that interpretive facilities ("visitor centers, exhibits, hiking trails, guided nature walks or . . . virtually any planned activity intended to transmit the citizen's relationship to the parks"), television and radio programs, traveling exhibits, movies, and newspaper articles were "all understood by the public and [were] the best investment SPN [made] to create a conservationist conscience." [12] Tactfully placed signs in national parks remind visitors of their environmental stewardship. Examples include:

> Costa Rica es nuestra casa, ¡no la ensuciemos!
> (Costa Rica is our home, let's not pollute it!)

> ¿Refleja su comportamiento diario esta responsabilidad?
> (Does your daily behavior reflect your responsibility?)

> Produzcamos oxígeno, plantemos árboles.
> (Let's produce oxygen, plant trees.)

Concerning endangered species:

> Pero ¿por cuánto tiempo más?
> (But for how much longer?)

> Quedamos pocos, muy pocos . . . ¡protegemos!
> (We are left with few, very few . . . let's protect them.)

To continue the push, the National Park Service inaugurated an environmental education department in the late 1970s. An important study in 1979 resulted in a report on the directions SPN would take to use national parks as tools of environmental education. One of its general objectives was "to develop an environmental ethic." The report concluded that it was "necessary to divulge knowledge of the environment among the greatest number of people possible due to the fact that our communities—the whole world, in fact—are being confronted with a serious threat: the degradation of the environment." It was hoped that such an ethic would enable citizens to understand their "relationship with the natural world" and would lead to a better understanding of how to take care of it. National parks would help "to immerse the people in nature" and SPN would work with the Ministry of Public Instruction to use a variety of media to introduce Costa Ricans to issues concerning the destruction of the environment—deforestation, pollution, etc.—to help them understand how and why to protect it. The report ended by saying that the national parks and other protected areas would "play a determining role" to fulfill the goal by being a part of the educational system via curricula in both primary and secondary schools.[13]

In 1981 the role of national parks in disseminating education was the topic of a regional multiweek conference. SPN hosted the Regional Mesoamerican Workshop on Interpretation and Environmental Education at Manuel Antonio National Park. It was designed specifically for teaching representatives from other countries which interpretive services worked well at Costa Rican national parks and how those could be developed elsewhere. Again, emphasis was placed on how to familiarize the public with nature and to help people understand environmental stewardship.[14]

Likewise, SPN joined hands with the National University's School of Environmental Sciences to develop a special course, "Interpretation of Natural History." The course was designed to help students learn how to create exhibits, how ("and how not") to prepare and give slide presentations, and how to arrange field trips to national parks and museums. It also provided tours of radio and television studios to acquaint students with how to utilize the media for making spot announcements, special programs, and interviews.[15]

These and other programs were continued through the 1980s and into the 1990s. In his annual report of 1983, SPN director José María Rodríguez wrote of how his Environmental Education Department had expanded the work of interpretation centers at national parks for "the consciencization [sic] of the public in terms of the rational use of valuable resources and of the natural and cultural heritage of the country." He listed a variety of conferences, workshops, television and radio programs, publications, and outdoor exhibits and booths that the department had been active in during the year. Topics of the publications and programs ranged from threatened and endangered wildlife species to the role of national parks in protecting the environment.[16]

By the late 1980s, when SPN's direction shifted to "socioeconomic park uses" and "sustainable development," special emphasis was placed on acquainting the people who lived near the parks with the parks' resources. U.S. Peace Corps volunteers became instrumental in this regard. They organized trips into the parks for local residents to develop support and to encourage the parks' recreational activities like hiking and sightseeing. One Peace Corps volunteer, Cyndi Hypki, prepared a training booklet entitled "Manual for Interpretation and Environmental Education" that the SPN used for many years. Estrella Guier stated that these plans were a way "to fortify" the national parks and a way "to project themselves into the nearby communities." Agreeing with that judgment, Susan Place, a geographer who has studied the impact of parks on the lives of Costa Ricans, affirmed that "local participation from the beginning of conservation projects was critical to their success."[17]

Familiarizing local residents with the benefits of conservation areas and integrating them into national park design were never easy tasks. Former President Carazo explained that because Costa Rica was agriculturally steeped for centuries in a "European mentality for deforestation," there was a great deal of "legislative and community opposition" that slowed acceptance of park ideals by many citizens. Mario Boza claimed that the program developed "despite a persistent shortage of funds and of qualified personnel, and in the face of the belief, which most of the country originally shared, that nature conservation is a superfluous activity." He later described this condition as "widespread apathy, particularly among decision makers." And, as Gerardo Budowski observed, many of the parks and protected areas that were established "went relatively unnoticed and even caused resentment in certain private and public sectors."[18]

However, little by little (and due to successful environmental education programs and the work of environmental groups), much of Costa Rican society came to accept and support conservation. By the mid-1980s many Costa Ricans had become what one Peace Corps volunteer called "patriotically proud" of how their nation was becoming a world leader in tropical conservation, even though many were not really "familiar with the parks themselves." According to Karen Olsen de Figueres, this kind of "soft support" resulted from a growing environmental ethic even if it did not always lead to nationwide bandwagon activism for policy reform.[19]

There have been many instances, however, of public activism that did help to shape policy. Certainly government leaders were well aware of the public's opinion on the Palo Verde National Park and *oleoducto* controversies. There was a great deal of public response to various versions of the Forestry Law. And university students by the late 1970s and 1980s realized that they too could be a force for environmental reform. Not only did students petition the government against the Palo Verde separation and for passage of the Forestry Law and other policies, but they also became involved with protesting pesticide abuse that was leading to nonpoint pollution. In 1984, for example, the University of Costa Rica's Association of Biology Students complained to SPN officials that fumigations on cotton plantations in Guanacaste were adversely affecting Santa Rosa National Park. The students' findings showed that toxic pesticides had caused the death of fauna—facts that they hastened to bring to the attention of the Legislative Assembly, the Ministry of Justice, the UCR School of Chemistry, the Colegio de Biólogos, and to radio and television stations. Over seventy students signed letters of petition to SPN chief Alvaro Ugalde demanding "an investigation and quick action" on the problem.[20]

In other cases, students have volunteered to be of assistance to the park service. The Mountain Climbing Club of the National University worked with the Fundación de Parques Nacionales on certain projects and assisted SPN. The government has also taken advantage of a program designed to use schoolchildren in protected areas. Daniel Janzen pioneered the program in Guanacaste National Park, and the idea has caught on elsewhere. One study reports that the program "enlists student volunteers in the protection and maintenance of national parks [and] as a result, the young people frequently become advocates of tropical forest conservation."[21]

The SPN (now SINAC) has been an untiring leader in the efforts to use conservation programs to educate the public about environmental issues. Its successes with park development, management, and education were discussed in Bali, Indonesia, at the 1982 Third World Congress on National Parks (an overt play on words indicating that it was the third in a series of ten-year conferences and that its theme was for encouraging park development in the Third World). Many changes had taken place in the ten years since Mario Boza had spoken of his country's new parks program at the IUCN-sponsored Second World Congress. In Bali, one Costa Rican panel presented a report on strategies to establish a national wildlands system, and another presented a "do's and don'ts" strategy plan for conserving areas in the "Neo-Tropical Realm." Once again, Costa Rican conservationists had volunteered to share the strengths of their programs with other developing nations.[22]

Lest the ideals immortalized in these actions and words become stale,

Daniel Janzen proffered the following advice for reminding a nation of its environmental stewardship:

> It is traditional . . . to identify biologically important habitats, obtain title, fence and patrol them and view the task as largely complete. Such an act is functional if society at large is pre-programmed to recognize the jewel thus bestowed upon it. . . . If not, and this is the general case in tropical conservation, the story is only halfway through the first chapter of a long book. Those areas we view today as endangered are probably already extinct, and those we view as securely preserved are at best on the endangered list. They will remain there until they are viewed in the same breath as churches, libraries, and democratic government.[23]

The question remains, then, are Costa Ricans such a "pre-programmed" people? There are no consistent answers. Luis Fournier posits that thirty years ago there were few who stood with him on environmental issues, but that now "in all parts of the country" there is a "very strong environmental awareness" despite how some individuals and groups are "more enthusiastic than knowledgeable." He is encouraged by the growing environmental law community and movements that advocate sustained uses of resources.

Gerardo Budowski agrees but is more guarded. He sees an environmental ethic as a "nebulous and arbitrary" entity that is more characteristic of Costa Ricans with higher education—although he is quick to admit that Costa Rica has a very high percentage of high school and college graduates. "There's less in the rural areas," he stated in a recent interview, "especially with older people there who are used to other uses of the environment, who have believed that 'industry is always good.'"[24]

Alexander Bonilla recently stated that "yes, there's an environmental ethic, but it's poorly understood in certain conditions." His main point is that now people's awareness for the environment "needs to be oriented"—to be directed toward understanding how people fit into the larger picture of being a part of nature. "We need to involve everyone more so they can understand world environmental problems to survive on this planet," he added. And others, like historian and environmentalist Orlando Castillo, are not as sure that a true environmental ethic exists. Castillo told this author that the ethic is more of a "cassette in the mind, in the imagination—a cassette made in the United States." Clarifying, he said that many Costa Ricans "admire natural beauty from a distance, say from the mall in San Pedro. . . . Only a few truly understand the natural harmony of the cosmos, of all natural landforms." [25]

This diversity in thinking on conservation of the environment is manifested very clearly in the makeup of Costa Rican nongovernmental organizations. It is to the history and development of these groups that attention should be given next.

10 The Nongovernmental Approach

The expansion of the Costa Rican environmental movement and conservation organizations is a natural growth. [Like] a tree given roots,
sunshine, fertilizer, water, and allowed to grow, the movement has
become what it is today.
                    Karen Olsen Beck de Figueres, personal interview, 29 June 1992

The Active Role of NGOs

Nongovernmental organizations (NGOs) abound in Costa Rica. Local
groups, national associations, and international environmental organizations play a vital role in monitoring the government and working to
lobby for (and to fund) conservation efforts in Costa Rica. There has
been a very dramatic proliferation of NGOs in the last fifteen years.
The 1994 *Directorio de organizaciones, instituciones y consultores en el sector
de recursos naturales en Costa Rica* lists eighty-eight nongovernmental,
nonuniversity-sponsored environmental groups that are active throughout the country. Historically, these organizations have stemmed directly
from people's perception that the government has been unable to address adequately the country's deteriorating environmental conditions.
They also have served to gauge public opinion, endorse or reject governmental policies, and encourage the public to become involved.[1]

The Association of Biologists (Colegio de Biólogos), founded in 1968,
is considered to be Costa Rica's oldest "environmental organization," although it was not originally created as such. It was organized by Univer-

sity of Costa Rica biologist José Alberto Sáenz as a professional association of biological scientists, but it soon became involved in lending technical advice, scientific expertise, and professional assistance to conservation causes. It became an especially important entity in the 1970s and 1980s for championing the defense of the Costa Rican environment. Members of the association lobbied the Legislative Assembly for environmental policies and national park designations and conducted and publicized research on a wide range of conservation topics.

ASCONA (the Costa Rican Association for the Conservation of Nature) was the country's first "grassroots" environmental organization—that is, the first citizens' action group. It was established in response to the 1972 U.N. Stockholm Conference on the Human Environment by what Alexander Bonilla, one of its founders, called a "group of university youth whose goal was to foment a new attitude about man's relation with nature." Since its inception in 1972, it has been a volunteer organization made up of "all levels of the population." Its central focus has been to serve as a watchdog for environmental policy and to offer assistance to both public and private sectors in the conservation of natural resources. The group's five principal goals have been to promote the rational use of natural resources—insisting on "development without destruction" (the group's motto); to help educate Costa Ricans about the importance of conserving the environment and its unique biodiversity; to promote the creation and enforcement of environmental protection laws; to collaborate with state and private institutions for the conservation of nature; and to monitor the restoration and protection of the "physical, biotic, and cultural environment for the benefit of present and future generations."[2]

In addition to being one of ASCONA's founders, Alexander Bonilla served as its first president throughout the 1970s and its conservation director in the 1980s. During these years, the group was involved in a broad range of issues, which included the creation and protection of national parks, urban planning, reforestation, soil conservation, and watershed protection. ASCONA members lobbied the Legislative Assembly for such environmental policies as pesticide abuse laws, industrial pollution regulations, mining policies, and public health standards. They were also involved in performing environmental impact assessments and in providing sustainable forest management education to local *campesinos*. The group enjoyed a good working relationship with ICE (the electricity institute) on watershed and reforestation projects. Former National Park Service director Alvaro Ugalde suggested that the group offered "a more critical" approach toward government programs and conservation efforts and that it was a "help to the cause in a different way." An outside study found that ASCONA "grew to be one of the most respected and powerful environmental groups in Latin America."[3]

Certain preserved areas are directly attributable to ASCONA efforts. The Puriscal, Quepos, and San Carlos reforestation projects were major ASCONA successes in the late 1970s and early 1980s. The group also worked diligently to protect Costa Rica's ecologically vulnerable coastal mangrove swamps by working to pass a bill in the Legislative Assembly that created the Zona Marítima-Terrestre, which also provided for oil-spill prevention and cleanup measures and coastal pollution controls. In fact, ASCONA is best known for its 1983 campaign against the trans-isthmian *oleoducto* proposal (see Chapter 7).

The group was instrumental in helping form the National Committee Against the Pipeline and mounted a nationwide publicity campaign to educate Costa Ricans about its possible environmental consequences. The Committee Against the Pipeline succeeded in preventing construction of the *oleoducto,* but ASCONA's involvement in the campaign caused its eventual demise. The group had been the recipient of financial support from the U.S. Agency for International Development (AID), which required that salaried staff be a precondition of aid. While this proved successful for some of its projects, it also led to the decline of its volunteer-based organization and a big membership loss. AID funds to ASCONA were cut off during the *oleoducto* controversy because the U.S. government supported the pipeline's construction. This caused a split within ASCONA ranks as some members sided in support of the project. A Peace Corps volunteer working with ASCONA at the time recalled that "the pipeline got it [ASCONA] in trouble, from which it never completely recovered."[4]

ASCONA is still listed in the *Directorio* of active conservation groups and it maintains a small office in Tibás (a San José suburb), but the scale of its activities is much reduced from its heyday of the 1970s and 1980s. Research and legal action are still two of its primary foci, however. Projects in the early 1990s included conducting environmental assessments on coal mining in the Talamanca Mountains and on a road construction project in La Amistad National Park. It has also worked to investigate sources of pollution in the Tarcoles and other rivers. Recent priorities include monitoring the banana industry, researching ecotourism, and providing environmental education programs.

Other environmental groups were important assets on Costa Rica's conservation front in the late 1970s and 1980s. Although the important roles played by Fundación de Parques Nacionales (founded in 1979 by Mario Boza) and Fundación Neotrópica (founded in 1985 by Alvaro Ugalde and Rodrigo Gámez) have been discussed in some detail in previous chapters, it would be remiss to omit mention of them here. Both organizations were formed specifically to support the development of national parks but have branched out to other conservation concerns in the past decade. FPN's mission has been to seek and distribute national and international funds (grants and donations) for national park projects. Much of the fundraising has been for purchasing private in-holdings within national parks to ensure the ecological integrity of the area itself.

More recently it has funded sustainable development projects and environmental education programs. Fundación Neotrópica has promoted activities that are directly related to the conservation of Costa Rica's natural heritage. Its goals have included acquiring private lands for nature reserves, protecting endangered species of flora and fauna, promoting ecological education through its publications branch—Heliconia Press (which publishes many of the guides to Costa Rica's national parks), and promoting resources for scientific tourism. It has become known for its promotion of sustainable development in communities near the national parks by providing a market ("Nature Stores") for local artisanry and products made from forest resources.

In terms of grassroots activist organizations, the void created with ASCONA's decline has been filled in many ways for the past ten years by the Costa Rican Ecology Association (AECO). According to the group's literature, AECO was formed in 1988 "to promote the development of an ecological conscience in Costa Rican society [by] facilitating knowledge and analysis to clarify the causes and effects of the environmental crisis." Its two central objectives have been "to generate initiatives" and to stimulate "ecological practices that will renew man's traditional relationship with the environment, which in turn will allow a true and democratic participation of the people in the country's process of development."

Using a "multidisciplinary and multisectorial vision," AECO has set out to accomplish these goals by attempting to be a very inclusive organization. Membership is open to "all people in agreement with [the group's] principles and objectives," and solutions are sought via open discussions with scientists and lay people, on both national and local levels, and taking into consideration the diversity of opinions on how development should proceed. The objective is to integrate not only "social, technological . . . and economic factors," but also to include ones that are uniquely "Tico" into a formula for change. The underlying principle here is the belief that "environmental problems have their origins in the mistaken models of development [that were] imposed on [Costa Rican] society" and that thus require "a social transformation that changes the model [and] proposes alternative experiences." To that end, the group has written an "Institutional Development Project" that traces the historic and "socio-environmental" nature of Costa Rica's past agricultural and economic history. It evaluates the history and ecological consequences of Europeanized agricultural development and calls for a return to native, traditional crops and practices for the long-range sustainability of the country's economy.[5]

AECO has engaged this philosophy by promoting a variety of so-called "activities in the defense of the environment." These have included environmental education programs, research and training workshops, lobbying campaigns, sustainable development incentives, youth programs, and citizen involvement promotions. Specifically, AECO assisted the community of Tibás to fight for halting the pollution caused by a metal manufacturing firm. It has been involved in the continuing fight against the illegal importation of certain pesticides. It has fought against the "uncontrolled expansion" of the banana industry, campaigned for modifications of the tuna fishing industry, assisted the effort in northern Costa Rica to halt Tico Fruit's dumping of pollutants in the Aguas Zarcas River, and was successful in blocking Stone Container's plans to build a giant port facility in the Golfo Dulce. Likewise, it has published several books on environmental subjects, including a poetry anthology called *Dejen al sol brillar* (Let the Sun Shine) and a book on the views of Latin American youth concerning the environment and development. It publishes a magazine called *El Ecologista*. According to AECO director Alvaro León, the organization's current priorities are to work for improved forestry management plans and to work with local communities on fitting environmental policies into their local needs. The group is also monitoring very closely the government's recent restructured and decentralized national parks and conservation areas management plans (SINAC) and has been critical of granting regional administrators too much authority on environmental decisions.[6]

There are too many Costa Rican NGOs to go into similar detail about here. Many of the groups are area-specific in nature or are concerned with the conservation of a particular species or place. There are NGOs that concentrate specifically on alternative and organic agriculture, forestry issues, rural and urban social problems, national parks and other protected areas, sustainable development, pollution control, energy issues, environmental education, coastal resources, mining, indigenous issues, environmental legislation, ecotourism, and wildlife protection. Most seem to be identified with a requisite acronym. Some of the more prominent, national groups include the following:

Asociación Protectora de Arboles (ARBOFILIA)
Asociación Costarricense para la Protección de los Riós (PRO RIOS)
Asociación Naturista de Costa Rica (ASNAT)
Asociación para la Conservación de los Recursos Naturales de
    Costa Rica (ACORENA)
Asociación Preservacionista de Flora y Fauna Silvestre
    (APREFLOFAS)
Asociación Pro Conservación Acuática de Costa Rica (APROCA)
Asociación Pro Desarrollo y Ecología (APDE)
Asociación de Voluntarios en Investigación y Desarrollo Ambien-
    talista (VIDA)
Asociación de Voluntarios para el Servicio de las Areas Protegidas
    (ASVO)
Fundación Costarricense para la Conservación de la Naturaleza
    (AMORA)
Fundación Forestal Costarricense

A development on the NGO scene in the late 1980s and 1990s was the increase of attention given to environmental law. Fundación Ambio and the Center for Environmental and Natural Resource Law (CEDARENA) were both formed in 1989 to concentrate on legal aspects of environmental problems. Fundación Ambio has organized training courses on assessing environmental impact and has been especially attentive to cases of pesticide abuse in the banana industry. Its director, Roxana Salazar Cambronero, is one of Costa Rica's leading environmental attorneys and has authored or coauthored a variety of books and reports on the legal aspects of pesticide abuse, public health, hazardous waste disposal, biodiversity, sustainable development, and environmental human rights. CEDARENA focuses on some of these same issues and is involved more with natural resource legal issues.

Another species of NGO that has gained popularity in the 1980s and 1990s is the volunteer organization. Both ASVO and VIDA organize groups of volunteers to do conservation projects in national parks and biological reserves. ARBOFILIA volunteers work with local residents in various parts of the country to help teach alternatives to clearing forest. One newspaper article reported that ARBOFILIA members working on a project near Carara Biological Reserve in 1992 "share[d] talent, time, and knowledge of agronomy and ecological biology . . . in exchange for the people's promise not to cut down the trees or burn the land."[7] Other groups like Amigos de Lomas Barbudal (Friends of Barbudal Hills) and Asociación para la Conservación de los Cerros de Escazú (Escazú Hills Conservation Association) are responsible for managing conservation areas. And finally there is a growing number of youth organizations that organize conservation projects for children and teens. Among those are the Alianza de Niños para la Protección del Ambiente (Children's Alliance for the Protection of the Environment), Asociación Cristiana de Jóvenes (Christian Youth Association), Ecojoven (Ecoyouth), and the Boy Scouts and Girl Scouts of Costa Rica.

In 1989 representatives from various NGOs met to consider forming an umbrella organization that would unite the environmental movement and promote increased cooperation and communication among the myriad groups. The result was the formation of the Costa Rican Federation for the Conservation of the Environment (FECON). FECON publishes the annual directory of environmental groups and works to coordinate interorganizational activities. It also sponsors workshops and conferences on a variety of environmental topics and has given technical and financial assistance on a number of conservation initiatives. There are nineteen member organizations.

International NGOs have also had a historic and ongoing role in Costa Rican conservation. Since its charter membership in the International Union for the Conservation of Nature (IUCN) in 1948, Costa Rica has welcomed advice, finances, and attention from the international environmental community. As described earlier, international NGOs were of tremendous assistance to Costa Rica in the early years of national park development and during the years of economic crisis. This trend has continued into the 1990s as many international NGOs have tropical conservation priorities and often have research programs in Costa Rica. Some of these include the Nature Conservancy, Conservation International, IUCN, Audubon Society, Rainforest Alliance, Rainforest Action Network, Sierra Club, and the World Wildlife Fund (WWF), which maintains an office in San José.

Some international NGOs have Costa Rican chapters. Friends of the Earth (Asociación Amigos de la Tierra de Costa Rica) and the Audubon Society are active in the country. A more common trend is the affiliation of international NGOs with national and local groups. AECO, for example, has a close relationship with Friends of the Earth. Fundación Ambio is affiliated with the Canadian Association of Environmental Attorneys. And many different groups list WWF and IUCN as affiliate organizations from which they receive technical advice and financial support.

But while financial contributions from international NGOs, U.N. programs, and government lending agencies have been indispensable to Costa Rican conservation efforts, pitfalls have emerged in their type and scope. Mario Boza has written that the donations often have "serious drawbacks" when the NGOs and agencies "decide how they will be used." He notes that Costa Rica's greatest financial need is for acquiring more land—purchasing park in-holdings, expropriating buffer zones, and creating biological corridors. Yet the global environmental community, he explains, often avoids donating funds for land purchases. Instead they give money for research. He has calculated that "for the cost of technical advisory services by a United Nations expert for one month . . . we could purchase twenty hectares [fifty acres] of tropical forest to be added to a national park." He concludes, "We simply do not need to be told over and over again what we must do; instead, all the organizations interested in the environment should start looking for funds to make environmental conservation a reality."[8]

Regional NGOs are a more recent addition to the Costa Rican conservation scene. In 1978 the Mesoamerican Federation of Conservationist Associations was formed at a regional gathering of environmentalists in

Guatemala City. In 1987 the Regional Network of Non-Governmental Conservationist Organizations was created at the First Central American Conference for Environmental Action in Managua, Nicaragua. Costa Rica participated in both and also is home to the offices of the Plan de Acción Forestal para Centro América (PAFT-CA). Outside of Central America there are two other NGOs that specifically address environmental issues of the region. The San Francisco–based Environmental Project on Central America (EPOCA) investigates a wide range of conservation issues, including ones pertinent to tropical conservation in Costa Rica. The other is Policy Alternatives for Central America (PACCA), which is based in Washington, D.C., and deals with many political, social, and environmental issues. Likewise, there are Central American offices of UNEP and the IUCN in Costa Rica, and the Mesoamerican Biological Corridor Foundation is working with the Caribbean Conservation Corporation (CCC) on the pan-regional Paseo Pantera project out of its San Pedro, Costa Rica, office.

Opinions vary on the twenty-year history of NGO involvement in Costa Rica. "Twenty years ago there were no NGOs here," Alvaro Ugalde remembered, "and now there are heaps." Eighty-odd organizations, their conservation accomplishments, and their ability to stimulate grassroots public involvement cannot be ignored; yet the redundancy of their efforts is obvious. The unified and integrated efforts of FECON may continue to yield successful results on the conservation front and may generally benefit Costa Rica's conservationist community in the long run. A criticism is that most NGO members are highly intellectual and perhaps do not represent a broad cross-section of Costa Rican society. Luko Quirós, a professor of environmental sciences at the National University, suggested in 1989 that this cultural gap could be bridged by giving more attention to local groups and projects instead of concentrating on large-scale national agendas—a goal that has been in large part realized with the proliferation of such groups in the last decade. In a different study, Bill Weinberg faulted Costa Rican NGOs for their overattention to publicity-generating rainforest issues and insufficient attention to the "ecocide" occurring on the country's agricultural landscape. His study showed that in the mid- to late 1980s, the NGOs tended to be selective in their causes, especially with the *orero* controversy, when an estimated 1,500 gold panners (with 3,500 legal mining permits) invaded areas in and around Corcovado National Park. "The environmental movement supported their ouster," Weinberg wrote, "but did nothing about the large mining companies nearby."[9]

Finally, Alexander Bonilla, now a private consultant, offers a particularly poignant analysis of the present state of NGOs. He divides the organizations and their members into four categories. First, there are those who "truly believe in conservation" and work with an "environmental spirit." These are the "merchants of conservation—the environment is their business." Second, there are the "Post-communist" conservationists who with "failed ideologies" are working to "re-enact their own agendas." These are the people who "use ecology to seize international [financial] resources [and] to defend indigenous groups," but whose lifestyles have not changed—"they still want to drive a Mercedes Benz" and have the benefits of a capitalist world system. A third category consists of those who want to "maintain the status quo." They support the government and are successful in soliciting funds for conservation projects, but they are not critical; they are not activists—"they do the easy part, the nice part." And fourth is the research branch of the conservation movement. People or groups who fall into this category are consultants, biologists, advisors, and other "environmental experts" whose research is used as proof for the need for policy changes, but who are not always the activists lobbying for them. This is a growing group in Costa Rica.[10] The FECON *Directorio* lists twenty-eight pages of private conservation consultants.

Obviously not all NGOs and their members fit neatly into the Bonilla categories, but in general it is a realistic scheme for outlining the basic structure of the environmental movement. Likewise, there is duplication of efforts and overlapping of goals among the groups, but repetition can also represent the breadth of national support for particular causes. Either way, the number and scope of the NGOs reflect the "greening" of the republic, even if the hue is not always consistently even.

Campesino and Indigenous Movements

In addition to the traditional environmental NGOs, Costa Rica has witnessed the growth of *campesino* and indigenous movements that focus on conservation in a different, but equally important, way. These groups have advocated a return to traditional agriculture in some rural regions of the country and have tended to support sustainable development of native crops to reach that goal. They are also active in promoting organic farming and other "agro-ecological" practices. Some of the principal groups involved are the following:

Asociación de Pequeños Agricultores de Talamanca (APPTA)
Asociación Nacional de Agricultores Orgánicos (ANAPAO)
Centro Nacional de Acción Pastoral (CENAP)
Consultoria de Investigación y Capacitación para el Desarrollo
  Agrario Alternativo
Coordinadora de Organismos no Gubernamentales con Proyectos
  Alternativos de Desarrollo (COPROALDE)
El Productor R.L.
Fundación Guilombe
Taller Experimental en Producción y Comercialización Agrícola
  Alternativa (TEPROCA)

In the late 1980s, however, there were barriers that prevented full-scale implementation of sustainable agriculture. Carlos Brenes Castillo, a sociologist at the Technological Institute of Costa Rica, suggested four areas that stood in the way: an absence of capital that prevented initial investment; problems in dispersing available technology; "lucrocentric" legislation that favored big corporations and monocultural production; and the problem of dealing with some Costa Rican cultures that were based on subsistence farming and seemed unwilling to diversify.[11]

The good news was that different sectors of Costa Rican society started to grapple with these barriers. First, to deal with the issue of capital investment, the government provided tax incentives, and banks made loan credits more easily available to farmers practicing soil conservation and other sustainable methods. Likewise, the government urged forest industries to diversify their capital investments to include locally produced smaller wood products.[12] Different methods were also introduced to make new advances in technology more available. NGOs like ARBOFILIA used trained volunteers to help teach area farmers about sustainable practices. The Programa de Diversificación near Turrialba similarly showed farmers how to raise sustainable crops for export. Spices, nuts, medicinal plants, cacao, and natural coloring plants are examples of such crops that have enjoyed increased international demand. And Costa Rica's universities continued to play a leading role in researching, publicizing, and offering training in pesticide-free farming and integrated pest management (IPM). Recently, the University of Costa Rica has been actively exploring organic farming options through its experimental program TEPROCA. In this program, IPM experiments with frogs proved successful to control insects, and the program touted chicken manure as an effective alternative to chemical fertilizers.[13]

To counter the influence of the large companies and to join together in a united front, many small-scale farmers formed agricultural unions and cooperatives. These unions strongly promoted natural fertilizers, sustainable crops, and the elimination of agrochemical dependency. They also pressed the government for tax incentives, professional training, and market expansion of local crops. One of the larger organizations, UNSA (the National Agricultural Union), became vocal in its efforts to get national attention and government support. UPAGRA (the Atlantic Coast Agricultural Cooperative), a small-scale farmers' union, also led protests to seek support for sustainable development and against chemically dependent big agriculture. Likewise, among other groups, APROADAP was established as a *campesino* cooperative comprised of "agroforesters for agricultural diversification."[14]

The *campesino* movements likewise have addressed the fourth barrier, cultural opposition based on subsistence agriculture. Indigenous tribes historically have been rooted in traditional agricultural practices based on a subsistence model. Actually, instead of a barrier, Indian methods were an earlier contribution to sustainable agriculture. William Soto believes that the current agricultural dilemma "demands that we look not with nostalgia, but with respect and a clear sense for the future at how Costa Rican indigenous cultures solved the problems of survival." The problem was that native tribes had been forced to acculturate into an Iberianized Costa Rica. Left without many of their traditional lands and natural resources, some tribes clung to subsistence methods that have not proven sufficient for life in contemporary Costa Rica. UCR anthropologist María Bozzoli de Wille laments that "the Indian can no longer make use of his environment in the way passed down from his ancestors; his lands are completely dominated by systems which treat the environment differently than the traditional indigenous ways." Thus, some native groups have sought help from the *campesino* unions and have experimented with agricultural changes. The Costa Rican government, via its National Commission on Indigenous Affairs (CONAI), has not been consistent in its help to these native peoples. In an interview,

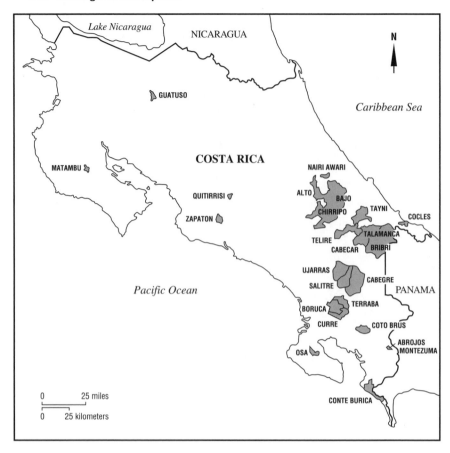

Figure 14. Costa Rican Indigenous Reserves (*source:* CONAI)

Dr. Bozzoli called the government's policies toward Indians "ambiguous—sometimes helping the Indians and sometimes not." [15]

The government formed CONAI in 1973. It is an autonomous agency (not under any ministry) created to be the government's link to Costa Rican indigenous people—by CONAI sources, 36,350 people—and to oversee the administration of the nation's twenty-two indigenous reserves (see Figure 14 and Appendix 6). An additional law, the Ley Indígena of 1977, established important legal parameters for the reserves. It stipulated that no non-Indians could own land on the reserves, but it did not appropriate the funds to buy in-holdings owned by other people. "Buying the land is very difficult," CONAI official Mario Alvarado Sánchez admitted, "but we must do it to refortify the indigenous presence—to give them more land for their own survival." He went on to explain that the government has the right to expropriate lands to be added to the reserves at market prices, but that "it just does not allocate the money to do it."[16]

Land, agriculture, and survival are three of the big reasons that indigenous people have formed cooperatives and associations aimed at, as one organization of Cabécar Indians put it, "conservation of culture and of the environment." That group, KABEKWA, also provides legal assistance and education programs to support local, smaller indigenous groups in "strengthening communal and organizational" skills. Another group, Asociación Cultural Sejetko de Costa Rica, works "to strengthen Costa Rican indigenous culture, to orient education for the protection of the environment, to defend indigenous land, [and] to promote and develop the indigenous cosmovision." It hosts training seminars and workshops in native languages on environmental education and conservation topics. The World Council of Indigenous Peoples works on similar projects in Costa Rica and maintains an office in San José. Its focus is on indigenous rights and on the international program of PIMA, or Pueblos Indígenas y Medio Ambiente (Indigenous People and the Environment). Most Indian groups are affiliated with the Costa Rican Association of Indigenous Peoples. CONAI's Mario Alvarado estimated that there are nearly fifty local, national, and international indigenous groups active in the country.[17]

The problem with the well-intentioned international groups, however, is that their financial support often does not reach the indigenous people. Térraba Indian leader Anselmo Flores mentioned that "CONAI really helps us a lot, . . . but the money from the government or the international NGOs does not go to the Indians." He cited cases of contributions that ended up being spent on new office equipment for agency use in San José while Indians were struggling to come up with the resources to buy such needed supplies as seeds. Some of the nation's mainline environmental NGOs also claim to prioritize indigenous conservation issues. But as Flores mentioned, "The environmental groups really don't help." His concern was that the NGOs have no power to control the growing amount of logging that occurs near the Térraba Reserve in southern Costa Rica—the greatest threat to his people's goals of long-term sustainability. "We believe in sustainable agriculture," said Flores, who is the president of the Association of Integrated Indigenous Development of the Térraba Reserve, "but we do not have all the necessary resources in each Indian community. . . . It's absolutely impossible to have complete agricultural subsistence."[18]

In a different region of the Talamancas, however, a *campesino* organization and an environmental group are working with Bribri Indians to overcome "language barriers, trade bureaucracies, and a lack of working capital" in their struggle to remain physically and culturally alive. The Talamanca Small Producers Association (APPTA) and the ANAI Association (a local conservation organization affiliated with the Nature Conservancy) have assisted the Bribri in developing organic cacao and other Talamancan produce for export to the United States. APPTA has helped construct a community-based cacao processing plant and storage facility near the Bribri Reserve and has helped them enter into trade relations with North American chocolate companies that buy organically produced cacao. According to one report, the region has become the largest supplier of organic cacao to the United States. APPTA has also worked with local people in the area to diversify their crops to include organic bananas, ginger, nutmeg, and cinnamon and has helped link these crops with markets in Europe. "And that's just a step," stated APPTA's Walter Rodríguez. "Tomorrow's product is healthy communities."[19]

Meanwhile, ANAI and the Nature Conservancy have included the Talamanca region in their Parks in Peril project, which seeks to connect La Amistad International Park and its surroundings into a biological corridor stretching to the Caribbean. ANAI's Bob Mack claims that the corridor project will protect not only the region's complex biodiversity but also the region's Indian communities, which comprise 65 percent of Costa Rica's indigenous population. And Walter Rodríguez added that personal and environmental health are at the heart of the organic agriculture and biological corridor project: "People concerned about their own health are buying our organic produce, yet they're showing concern for the health of the Talamancans and *their* environment." CONAI's Mario Alvarado observed that "many of the national parks were created near indigenous communities in the South because of their [the Indians'] good maintenance of the environment." "What does this tell us?" he asked hypothetically. "That there is a narrow relationship—the Indians kept the land well."[20]

Friction between Indians and government conservationists (and NGOs) sometimes occurs, however, on the issue of indigenous hunting rights. Many conservationists have a difficult time appreciating such Indian practices as hunting tapirs, gathering turtle eggs, and eating "quetzal soup," but as Juan Carlos Crespo, former president of Fundación Neotrópica, pointed out, "Their hunting is subsistence, not commercial or sport. . . . It is part of their cultural roots." The real problem with hunting, he continued, is in areas outside of reserves where non-Indians hunt with specialized hunting dogs. Mario Alvarado agreed and suggested that while some Costa Ricans have accused native people of "overhunting and overfishing, the truth is that they have maintained an equilibrium like they have done for centuries; they really know the biodiversity." Put another way, as Bribri activist Doris Ortiz mentioned, "for us, development isn't roads and bridges, it's being able to hunt a guan for dinner."[21]

Alvarado also stated that despite the Indians' "tranquil nature," they are very "concerned about logging and mining in and around their reserves." In June of 1992, for instance, a delegation of native people from the group La Voz del Indio (Voice of the Indian), one of the largest indigenous organizations in the country, traveled to Rio de Janeiro for the Earth Summit to make known their concerns and demands. The Indians called for more "tribal" autonomy, for more control over the natural resources in their domain, and for support in the production of more traditional, sustainable crops. One month later, there was an Indian protest march in San José. Cherokee Indians from the United States and different native peoples from Mexico and Guatemala joined with Costa Rican Indians to protest logging on Indian reserves and to demand changes in government policy toward native people.[22]

The Indians marching in the 1992 protest called for the abolition of CONAI. Other Indians would rather reform the agency and grant more authority to individual "tribal" governments. Such was the message of one of the largest Indian protests in recent Costa Rican history, which was staged on 3 July 1996 in front of the Casa Presidencial in the San José suburb of Zapote. Called the "National Indigenous March," hundreds of Indians converged on the San José area from many parts of the country. Alvarado mentioned that, for many, it was the first time they had been to a city and that "they were amazed at the tall buildings and other aspects of city life." They marched to lobby the executive branch to strengthen CONAI by purchasing more land for Indian reserves and to give increased attention to education and health, and to lobby the

Legislative Assembly to respect indigenous rights. The major complaints of the protesters centered around insufficient indigenous input into CONAI's administration and the need for more land. In response, Guido Rojas, chairman of CONAI's governing board of directors, mentioned that the government recently had purchased 300,000 hectares (741,000 acres) to be added to the reserve system. "We can't fix what has dragged out for five hundred years," Rojas admitted, "but we have fought to buy more land for the Indians and to promote the development of their communities."[23]

Nonetheless, one of the organizers of the protest, Alejandro Swaby of the Asociación de Talamanca, complained that CONAI was "a poor administrator" since it had "done very little for the indigenous people" and that the newly acquired reserve lands were "of poor quality." Other complaints were voiced concerning title and in-holding problems of some of the new parcels added to the reserve system. The protesters denounced how in "the majority of indigenous territory, more than 80 percent of the land was in the hands of whites" and that extraction of natural resources was continuing on Indian lands.[24]

And thus the native struggle continues in Costa Rica. It is symbolic that only one Spanish-language newspaper, *Al Día* (not one of San José's larger papers), reported the national protest. This was frustrating to CONAI officials who had worked with the Indians in organizing the event. "The press gave us very little attention," Alvarado lamented, "because they usually go for things that sell more papers." Gerardo Budowski stated that the Indians had legitimate complaints and that the government only pays lip service to Indian laws—"they really mean nothing." Most important, however, is that CONAI is working toward what Alvarado called "a double sharing" between the Indians and the agency officials; they are actively working to include a greater indigenous presence in the commission's administration. "We have to respect the indigenous mentality," he advised.[25]

CHAPTER 11

¡Oro Verde!
Ecotourism for
Economic Growth

"Yo visito y apoyo los parques nacionales, ¿y usted?"
Bumper sticker on car in San José

(I visit and support the national parks, do you?)

Tourism is one of the multiple use concepts under which Costa Rican national parks and protected areas are managed. While restricted access is still a fundamental tenet of the management plans, the parks and reserves are open to the public—a phenomenon that has sparked an exponential growth of Costa Rica's tourism industry since the mid-1970s. Mario Boza remarked that the role played by national parks and biological reserves in this economic development was that of being "the base of ecological tourism and of scientific research." Various terms have been used over the years to describe such activity. The "biotourism," "scientific tourism," and "academic tourism" of the early years of park development and tropical research projects have been replaced in the last two decades with "nature tourism," "adventure tourism," "selective tourism," "alternative tourism," and, most important, "ecotourism."[1] Hector Ceballos-Lascurain of the World Conservation Union (formerly the IUCN) has described ecological tourism, or "ecotourism," as implying

a relocation to zones that are relatively little altered and contaminated, with the specific purpose of studying, admiring, and enjoying the scenic beauty, the flora and fauna, and existing cultural aspects (past and present) found in the areas. [It] implies a scientific, aesthetic, or philosophical appreciation without the ecological tourist necessarily being a scientist, artist, or professional philosopher. A principal point is that the person who practices ecotourism has the opportunity to enter into contact with nature, in a very different form than they experience in their urban or routine lives.[2]

Early into his conservationist career, Mario Boza started to understand how concepts such as Ceballos-Lascurain's could have a positive impact on Costa Rica's economy. When the Forestry Law that allowed for national parks to be created was up for debate in the Legislative Assembly in the spring of 1969, Boza, new at his desk at the Ministry of Agriculture, wrote a guest editorial in the San José daily *La República* in support of the proposed law. As if forecasting the future, Boza noted, "Although from a commercial viewpoint parks might seem an unnecessary investment, they could become one of the major sources of revenue for the nation. East Africa, by having more vision than us in this field, increased its annual income from tourism by fifteen percent. What couldn't our country do, being closer to the main sources of tourists in the world?"[3]

What could Costa Rica do? Create national parks, capitalize on pristine beaches, advertise viewable wildlife, promote a tropical experience, "and they [tourists from all over the world] will come" and spend millions of foreign dollars. Indeed national parks and the tourism they generate did become one of Costa Rica's major sources of revenue. By 1988 tourism generated $164.7 million in foreign currency for Costa Rica, making it the third largest industry in the country—often referred to as "the industry without chimneys"—after coffee ($316.2 million) and bananas ($248.7 million). By 1997, however, statistics showed that tourism was the largest industry (worth $700 million).[4] This kind of capital influx into Costa Rica, called *oro verde* (green gold), was the hope of people like Luis Fournier, Mario Boza, presidents Daniel Oduber and Rodrigo Carazo, and others in the conservationist community, who saw the potential to make the parks and preserves become self-supporting and assets to the general economy and, therefore, more widely accepted among the public.

An important question to be asked here is whether all tourism in Costa Rica is ecotourism. Carole Hill, in a study she conducted on the topic, cites a growing faction of "cocoon tourists"—those who prefer "to be sheltered from the native physical and social environments" and who would rather stay in large resorts.[5] The problem is in semantics and statistics. Many resort tourists choose to visit Costa Rica to experience the rainforests, watch birds, and go on day hikes, but they like to stay in comfortable accommodations. They are ecotourists made in a different mold than the backpackers and beach campers.

Tamara Budowski, the cofounder of Horizontes Nature Tours in Costa Rica and an industry spokesperson, has created a visitor taxonomy to classify ecotourists that is useful here to clarify this issue. She finds that there are two "relatively distinct" groups. Scientific tourists are "scientists and students who travel for education or research reasons and who, therefore, generally remain [in Costa Rica] for longer periods of time, make use of regular services (family restaurants and public transportation), and stay in moderately priced hotels." Nature tourists are "people whose passion for nature is personal rather than professional." A subgroup of nature tourists that Budowski calls "soft nature" tourists is the fastest-growing sector of ecotourists. They travel "more for 'fashion' than from a genuine interest in nature" and have less knowledge and preparation for the sites and parks they visit. The "adventure tourist" subgroup also represents a robust sector of the market, although she argues that it is "debatable" whether these visitors "can rightly be considered ecotourists" given that sports like fishing "consume" part of a natural resource and other activities may "detract somewhat from the philosophy of 'observation without destruction.'" On the other hand, catch-and-release fishing is becoming more popular and, as she notes, "more adventure tourists are becoming interested in learning about the natural history and environmental problems of areas visited." All in all, nature tourism generates the most visits to Costa Rican national parks and other protected areas, and among U.S. tourists who travel abroad, it is the fastest-growing type of tourism.[6]

It can be concluded here, then, that tourists who come to Costa Rica to spend part of their time in the natural, tropical surroundings that they do not have at home are different from the crowd who tours, say, London, Paris, and Rome to visit museums, cathedrals, and open-air cafés. In fact, visitor surveys and data from ICT (the official Costa Rican tourism bureau) support these points. One ICT survey conducted in 1985 showed that 75 percent of the foreign visitor respondents claimed they visited Costa Rica for the natural beauty, 66 percent for the culture and political environment, and 36 percent for its flora and fauna. The first and third categories easily fit "ecotourism" definitions. In 1987 a different study showed that visitations to the principal national parks had increased by 50 percent in two years.[7] Clearly, it is no coincidence that tourism in general in Costa Rica has increased so dramatically since the development of national parks.

The business and investment community in Costa Rica did not fail to notice this market niche. Ecotourism agencies, resorts, and lodges abound throughout the nation. As Yanina Rovinski (from the World Conservation Union's Central America Office) noted, "When Costa Ricans want to sell something, they paint it green," and "the prefix 'eco' is featured in almost any ad dealing with tourism these days." A sampling of these include Ecoadventure Lodge, Ecotourism Costa Rica, Ecodesarrollo (Ecodevelopment), and Eco-Lodge, S.A. Prospective tourists are lured to various agencies and resorts with such slogans as one lodge's "visions of man successfully joined with nature," or an expensive hotel and country club's "excellent service in unison with exuberant natural beauty." Or "for those who love the sea, the sun, and *untouched* nature," one can stay at the Punta Cocles Caribbean "Jungle" and Beach Hotel (which also offers "research and education in tropical biology") or get the "complete rainforest package" at the Casa Rio Blanco. The Selva Verde Lodge offers "a naturalist's paradise . . . to enjoy the wonder of the forest." One can stay at the Punta Leona Hotel and Club "where the *virgin* forest meets the sea." And, perhaps most unique, the Hotel Chalet Tirol comes "with the only private rain forest *and* a superb French gourmet restaurant" (emphasis added).[8]

A more recent innovation is the development of "eco-lodges" in Costa Rica. According to Fundación Neotrópica's Katiana Murillo, an "eco-lodge" (or *ecoalojamiento*) does not necessarily cater to ecotourism and is not a commercial term. It is a term used to describe "a hospitality establishment, such as a hotel or lodge, for tourists concerned about environmental protection and interested in getting to know and interact with local culture." They are built with "appropriate technologies . . . recycled materials, and products native to the region, [and are] constructed in harmony with the landscape." Costa Rica hosted the Second International Forum and Seminar-Workshop on Ecolodging in 1995, which drew specialists in architecture, design, and planning from many parts of the world. The event was sponsored by the World Ecotourism Society, whose president is Gerardo Budowski of Costa Rica. One of the important conclusions of the conference was that "tourism should not be viewed as an isolated productive activity [but rather] should complement other nature friendly activities that generate income" and that encourage the participation of local residents in nearby communities.[9]

The history of how ecological tourism developed in Costa Rica is multidimensional with origins in the governmental, scientific, and private sectors. It starts in 1955 with the passage of Law 1917, which established the Instituto Costarricense de Turismo (ICT) under the jurisdiction of the Ministry of Industry and Commerce. The law authorized ICT to promote tourism in general and granted it the power to create national parks, although it never did. Its functions included protecting and promoting historic sites and scenic areas and making foreign tourists feel welcome "in their search for relaxation, fun or entertainment."[10]

Scientists working on research projects through the Organization for Tropical Studies (OTS) may not have started coming to Costa Rica in the early 1960s for fun or entertainment, but their dollars added to the foreign tourist trade and helped to launch a thriving academic tourism business. With the establishment of its La Selva, Palo Verde, and Las Cruces biological stations and the Robert and Catherine Wilson Botanical Garden, OTS created a permanent base that came to host over 2,500 foreign biologists and studies by the late 1980s. La Selva can accommodate seventy-five people at a time and has recorded an average of thirty-six persons per day studying and staying there. In 1989 alone, La Selva counted 20,000 person-days (a formula of number of visitors and time spent at the place). These figures translated into between $2.9 million and $10.2 million of annual transactions in Costa Rica, with $3.4 million being directly injected into the national economy and the remainder spread out as secondary spending through an economic multiplier. In 1990 that meant that OTS accounted for 2 to 3 percent of all tourism receipts and just under .03 percent of the nation's GNP.[11] Another study showed that 60 percent of OTS visitors have returned to Costa Rica and that 69 percent have persuaded others to visit also. Return travel alone until 1987 accounted for $7.51 million worth of revenue.[12]

Straight west of La Selva in northwestern Costa Rica's Tilarán Mountains is the country's top ecotourist destination: the Monteverde Cloud Forest Preserve. This 5,000-acre private reserve was established in 1972 by the Tropical Science Centre (TSC). It has been expanded several times since, growing to five times its original size, approximately 25,000 acres, by 1990. In its first few years, only scientists and university students (primarily from the United States) visited the area to conduct research on tropical subjects and to study rare plant and animal species. The biologists' publications on the tropical wonders of the area soon started to attract the more casual nature tourists, and from then on tourism has boomed in the region. Monteverde's dramatic rise in popularity is clear from its visitation figures:

1973	300 visitors
1978	1,616 visitors
1980	2,700 visitors
1989	17,574 visitors
1991	40,000 visitors
1995	50,000 visitors [13]

While financial benefit figures like those for OTS were unavailable for Monteverde, the "off the graph" visitation numbers speak for themselves in terms of the economic impact on local communities near the preserve and for Costa Rica in general.

Meanwhile, the government enacted other laws and policies that led to an increase in the country's ecotourism. The 1969 Forestry Law was the vehicle that prompted national park designations and the preservation of scenic and historic places as well as wildlife habitat. When national parks started to be developed in the early 1970s, tourists interested in nature started coming to see them, although the parks are in many ways different from their counterparts in North America, Europe, or Africa. They are not used as vacation spots in the same way they are in the United States, have far less human intervention, and support much more scientific research. Many of the parks and preserves (like Corcovado, Cabo Blanco, La Amistad, and Guanacaste) are difficult to reach; visits entail hiking for miles on unpaved roads, which are often pure mud during much of the year. And most of the wildlife preserved in the parks is nocturnal and never seen by visitors—unlike the so-called charismatic megaspecies easily viewed in places like Yellowstone, the Canadian Rockies, or East Africa.

The National Parks Act of 1977 (which created the National Park Service, SPN) was also a boon to tourism as it allowed more focus to be

placed on the creation and management of parks and on visitor interpretive facilities. The government's shift to sustainable development
and socioeconomic park uses in the late 1980s also meant that protected
areas could "pay their way" by boosting tourism and by creating new
markets for local products and services. In 1997 the national parks paid
their way by earning $4 million in entrance and research fees. Environ-
mental education initiatives also clearly have led to an increase in nature
tourism as young people and adults have learned more about their natural heritage, national parks, and tropical conservation and have visited
the parks as a result. And to assist the government in general, and the ICT
specifically, in 1987 the Arias administration created the National Tourism Advisory Commission to advise policy makers and to coordinate activities between the government and private institutions (resorts, tour
agencies, lodges, etc.) on the protection of natural resources.[14]

The history of these private ecotourist operations corresponds to government initiatives. Two of the "pioneers" in the field were Jack and
Diane Ewing, who created the Hacienda Baru near Dominical in southern Costa Rica "to give visitors nature." The Ewings had left the United
States in the early 1970s to settle in this remote, tropical setting and
opened up their "hacienda" to visitors for rainforest hiking, bird watching, and helping hired biologists conduct wildlife studies. A 1993 newspaper article referred to the Ewings' operation as an example of "sustainable tourism."[15]

Larger ecotourism outfits started opening in Costa Rica in the late
1970s. Michael Kaye was one of the first entrepreneurs to market Costa
Rican nature tours abroad and was instrumental in opening up the whole
ecotourism industry in Costa Rica. He founded Costa Rica Expeditions in
1978 to offer whitewater rafting adventures on the Pacuare and Reven-
tazón rivers. But the more Kaye's clients from North America and Europe
enjoyed his river-rafting excursions, the more he learned that they were
looking for other nature tourism opportunities in rainforests and at tropical beaches, volcanoes, and other "off-the-beaten-track" natural areas.
By 1990 Kaye's firm was the largest ecotourism agency in Costa Rica.
Seventy-five percent of his clients, representing some 20,000 visitors a
year, came exclusively for tropical experiences and tours. One study reported that each client spent an average of $148 a day while in Costa
Rica—illustrating once again the impact of ecotourism's *oro verde* on the
nation's economy.[16]

Other outfitters soon followed in Kaye's footsteps. Tikal Tour Operators, one of Costa Rica's larger tourist agencies, moved from general tourism to ecotourism in the early 1980s and marketed tropical experiences to foreigners with bright, colorful brochures and advertisements. Tikal's "ecoadventures" included birdwatching, natural history, rafting, biking, national parks, fishing, diving, and "trekking." Like Tikal, Central American Tours (CAT, with a jaguar as its logo) moved into ecotourism at about the same time. CAT promised "the most exciting tours to experience in Costa Rica," ranging from "jungle adventures" to tours of oxcart factories. By the mid-1980s there were over a dozen agencies in the ecotourism market.[17]

Two individuals who started their own ecotourist facilities were Sergio Miranda, near Corcovado National Park, and Amos Bien, near Braulio Carrillo National Park. Miranda's Marenco private "biological reserve" and lodge was established to host visitors traveling to Corcovado who wanted simple cabinlike accommodations. At first Miranda thought he would market his place to scientists wanting to conduct research on the Osa Peninsula, but he soon discovered that U.S. travel agents were interested in marketing Marenco as a destination for nature tourists. Today Miranda offers "guided rainforest hikes," horseback riding, and bird watching on his 1,500 "private acres of virgin forest."[18]

Amos Bien, a tropical biologist who came to know the Braulio Carrillo area from the time he spent doing research at OTS's La Selva, purchased land near the park and established a private reserve he named Rara Avis as an experiment in "rain forest conservation for profit." Guests at Rara Avis spend time in Bien's alternative forest crops (ornamental plants) and observe what he calls sustainable forestry practices. He estimates that Rara Avis generates approximately $80,000 a year in revenues to the area and to the nearby community of Horquetas, making it one of the community's largest sources of income.[19]

Another agency, started by Ticos and dealing exclusively with ecotourism packages, is Horizontes Nature Tours. Tamara Budowski and Margarita Forero opened Horizontes "to serve the purpose of leading naturalists to the country's most attractive wildernesses." Their company, whose motto is "for natural encounters with tropical wonders," was established specifically to cater to scientists, students, and nature lovers and has become one of the major nature tour companies in the country. Budowski spent much of her childhood growing up in Switzerland, where her father, Gerardo Budowski, was director of the IUCN. The younger Budowski enjoyed the beauty of the Swiss Alps and countryside but was "astonished" by its lack of wildlife. Returning to her native Costa Rica, she witnessed the combination of wildlife and beautiful scenery and decided to enter the ecotourism business.[20]

Tamara Budowski points out that ICT and the national airline LACSA became two of the country's biggest ecotourism promoters in the 1980s and 1990s. ICT launched a major promotional campaign with the slogan "Costa Rica [with the national orchid draped between the two words] is . . . natural." It printed thousands of large posters picturing some of the country's major national parks and scenic wonders and sent tens of thousands of brochures to travel agencies and tour companies throughout the world. ICT's aggressive "Escape to Paradise" advertising campaign in the 1980s brought thousands of foreign tourists, as Tom Barry has written, "seeking a peaceful tropical nirvana." And in the early 1990s ICT began a campaign aimed at bringing in more tourists during the off-season (May to November), which is Central America's winter and is usually quite rainy. Avoiding the rain image, ICT concentrated on that time period being the "green season" and printed literature welcoming tourists to "go for adventure in the Kingdom of Green—it's even more exciting in the green season." LACSA, likewise, published brochures and booklets extolling Costa Rica as a haven for nature lovers and dedicated ample space in its in-flight magazine, *LACSA's World,* to articles and advertisements on ecotourist establishments.[21] The map in Figure 15 locates the principal ecotourism destinations in Costa Rica.

ICT and the National Park Service have always had a rather tenuous relationship. Over the years ICT certainly has promoted the national parks, but it has not been involved in lobbying for park expansion, buffer zone protection, or any of the other ecological mainstays of the parks' designations. Likewise, conflicts have occasionally arisen between the two agencies regarding tourist zones (hotels and resorts) in and around natural areas and the whole question of defining ecologically friendly tourism.

There has also been disagreement among park service personnel as to the role tourism should play in national parks. Mario Boza has generally supported it. As early as 1972 he requested information from Gerardo Budowski at the IUCN on how "scientific tourism operated in Africa" and how it could be applied to Costa Rica. There are few records, however, to

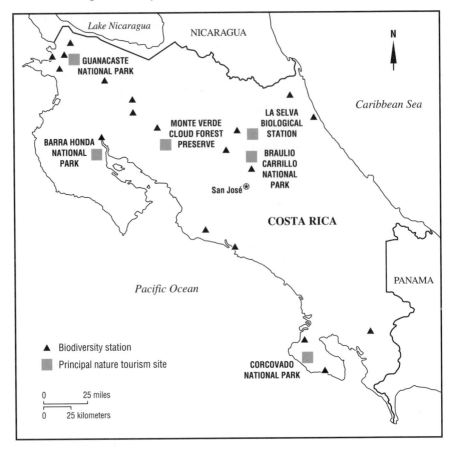

Figure 15. Principal Ecotourism Destinations and INBio Biodiversity Stations (adapted from maps in Tensie Whelan, ed., *Nature Tourism* [Washington, D.C.: Island Press, 1991], and from INBio Office, Santo Domingo, C.R.)

show that his office ever had much interaction with ICT. Alvaro Ugalde generally opposed park-based tourism when he was SPN director. In 1982 he told a reporter for the *Tico Times,* "I will not resort to tourism as a way to maintain parks. Management of the ecosystem in parks in perpetuity is the Park Service's main goal." Ugalde later mellowed somewhat on this attitude. When he was between government positions in the late 1980s, for example, he served as a national parks guide for a San José–based ecotourist operator. And back at the helm as SPN director in 1992, he told this author that one of his most important roles was "to convince the legislature that national parks were a great help to the economy."[22]

Whatever ICT's involvement, ecotourism has continued to grow in a variety of market sectors. In her essay on the subject, Tamara Budowski disentangles some of the demographics of the industry. She argues that most ecotourists in Costa Rica are foreign "baby boomers," "yuppies," and "DINKS" (couples between their twenties and forties with double income, no kids) and that the market is rapidly expanding for retired adults. Likewise, national park use is becoming more popular with Costa Ricans, although Budowski admits that the visitors come from a well-educated, middle- or upper-class segment of society.[23]

An earlier study conducted by geographer Susan Place showed that "the majority of visitors to most Costa Rican national parks [were], in fact, Costa Ricans," which reflected their "increasing domestic interest in environmental issues and conservation of the country's unique biological endowments." During the early years of park development, this was especially true since foreign tourism had not yet begun to expand into the Costa Rican market. At Poás Volcano, the country's first national park, over 82 percent of the visitors between 1974 and 1978 were from Costa Rica. But while Poás is rather close to the major population centers of the Central Valley, records at parks at considerable distance from San José and without easy, drivable access also showed a Costa Rican visitor predominance. Place found that the records at Tortuguero National Park revealed that from 1980 to 1985 2,850 Costa Ricans visited the park compared with 2,600 foreigners. And records at the Los Patos entrance on the far northwestern side of Corcovado National Park (accessible only by foot three hours up the Rincón River or by path through the heart of the park) showed that of the 1,750 visitors registered there, 72 percent, or 1,260, were Costa Ricans.[24]

But as the data in Table 2 show, park visitations by Costa Ricans have hovered around half of the total in the past five years. Moreover, there has been some disparity between the parks Costa Ricans have selected to visit and those selected by foreigners. As Table 3 indicates, Costa Rican visitations range from as low as 3.6 percent of the total at Tortuguero National Park to as high as 83.8 percent at Guayabo National Monument (based on Place's study of the mid-1980s when Ticos surpassed their foreign counterparts at that particular park). And despite visitations to the Los Patos station of Corcovado National Park, overall Costa Rican visitations to that park as a whole represented only 17.7 percent of the total. This seems to have been the case at other more "remote"

Table 2. Comparison of Costa Rican and Foreign Visitors to National Parks

	Total Visitors	Foreign Visitors	Costa Rican Visitors	Costa Rican Visitors (%)
1992	639,753	338,109	301,644	47
1993	772,025	404,342	367,683	47
1994	700,434	378,286	322,148	54
1995	614,081	251,740	362,341	59
1996*	342,711	147,589	195,122	57

*First six months only.
Source: Compiled from annual records, SINAC, Departamento de Mercadeo, July 1996.

Table 3. Comparison of Costa Rican and Foreign Visitors to Selected National Parks and Equivalent Reserves, 1992 to Mid-1996

	Total Visitors	Foreign Visitors	Costa Rican Visitors	Costa Rican Visitors (%)
Tortuguero National Park	81,750	78,572	2,998	3.6
Carara Biological Reserve	159,167	132,694	26,473	16.6*
Corcovado National Park	57,602	47,394	10,208	17.7
Cabo Blanco National Park	38,412	30,040	8,372	21.8
Manuel Antonio National Park	655,907	412,928	242,979	37.0
Isla del Coco National Park	7,949	4,161	3,788	47.6
Volcán Poás National Park	811,712	372,301	439,411	54.1
Irazú National Park	538,320	207,670	330,650	61.4
Santa Rosa National Park	185,729	63,309	122,420	65.9
Tapanti National Wildlife Refuge	99,931	22,640	77,291	77.3
Guayabo National Monument	96,644	15,287	79,357	83.8

*Large cruise ships often dock at Puntarenas and allow their North American and European passengers to be bused to the park to view scarlet macaws and experience a tropical rainforest.
Source: Compiled from annual records, SINAC, Departamento de Mercadeo, July 1996.

parks also—for example, at Cabo Blanco National Park, where Ticos represented only 21.8 percent of its total visitors, but not at the most remote park (and most expensive to get to), Isla del Coco, where national visitation was nearly half the total. At the top three most visited national parks, Poás Volcano, Manuel Antonio, and Irazú, Costa Ricans accounted for nearly half of the visitations. The same is true for national visits to the private reserve of Monteverde. In 1978, for example, 49.5 percent of the tourists there were Costa Rican.

International tourism rapidly expanded in Costa Rica in the late 1980s. Industry officials suggest that the boom started in 1987 when President Oscar Arias was awarded the Nobel Peace Prize. The award drew a great deal of international media attention to Costa Rica as a stable democracy in a beautiful tropical setting in the midst of a war-torn region. The image was further enhanced the next year when Costa Rica hosted the Twelfth General Assembly of the IUCN, which drew delegates and press coverage from all over the world.[25] ICT records based on tourist arrivals at San José's Juan Santamaría International Airport show that the number of foreign tourists in Costa Rica more than tripled in the decade between 1986 and 1995—from 260,080 to 784,610 arrivals. Table 4 reveals that the greatest number of these foreign travelers hailed from the United States, followed by Central America, Europe (dominated by tourists from Germany, Spain, and Italy), and Canada.

The large influx of foreign travelers has resulted in the economic boon dreamed of by the tourism promoters. The goal, according to Rodrigo Gámez, former environmental advisor to President Arias, was "to make the conservation idea attractive to those Costa Ricans who fear[ed] that conservation would inhibit their economic prospects." In her study on the impact of national park development in Costa Rica, Susan Place warned that tourism had "to be organized in such a way that a large number of local people [would] benefit from the influx of tourists rather than merely bear the burden of its costs." Some residents living near Tortuguero National Park, for example, at first experienced a general decline in their standard of living when the park was created due to less available farmland, firewood, and game meat, Place reported. Over the years, however, the economy of the area as a whole increased through "tourist trickle-down" businesses. "As a result," Place concluded, "both the people and the environment may face a more secure future." Former Ministry of Natural Resources official Eric Ulloa referred to this as "arriving at a central line" between the long-range advantages to the environment and the economic benefits to local communities.[26] Moreover, the government raised foreigners' entrance fees to national parks in the summer of 1994. For years international visitors paid the ridicu-

Table 4. Arrival Statistics of International Travelers, Juan Santamaría International Airport, 1986 to 1995

Regions & Countries	1986	1987	1988	1989	1990	1991	1992	1993	1994	1995
Grand total	260,840	277,861	329,386	375,951	435,037	504,649	610,591	684,005	761,448	784,610
North America	93,105	104,841	123,551	153,112	191,284	223,126	274,061	302,741	332,602	349,307
Canada	5,551	7,310	13,037	20,285	30,892	37,187	42,029	44,236	49,091	41,898
United States	81,722	90,581	102,822	124,284	150,224	173,626	217,693	242,546	263,568	287,434
Mexico	5,832	6,950	7,692	8,563	10,168	12,313	14,339	15,959	19,943	19,975
Central America	106,825	108,543	124,728	135,376	139,913	164,809	187,790	193,512	221,384	218,023
Guatemala	9,663	11,095	12,251	14,977	14,695	16,079	19,010	22,664	22,207	24,305
El Salvador	6,408	6,838	7,689	8,359	8,986	11,299	15,668	18,248	21,755	22,340
Honduras	8,687	9,429	10,203	10,066	8,894	10,475	13,238	12,930	14,925	15,876
Nicaragua	26,437	23,537	31,568	38,812	48,395	73,558	78,011	81,875	107,851	102,557
Panama	55,630	57,644	63,017	63,162	57,943	53,398	61,863	57,795	54,846	52,945
Caribbean	3,957	3,438	5,103	4,387	4,192	4,679	5,344	6,442	7,425	7,125
South America	21,272	21,768	26,150	28,644	32,575	32,891	42,657	52,921	54,043	58,600
Europe	29,026	32,354	41,396	45,355	57,177	67,319	88,301	113,943	129,580	132,057
Other areas	6,655	6,917	8,458	9,077	9,896	11,825	12,438	14,448	16,414	19,498

Source: ICT, Departamento de Estadística, July 1996.

lously low fee of $1.50 per person; SPN raised it to a more practical and revenue-producing $6.00 a head, which helped to cover expenses and maintenance.

But the influx of tourists has also created an economic-environmental dilemma. What Carole Hill has called "the tug between preservation and profit" are the dangers of oversell. With the millions of tourist dollars have come problems with sewage disposal, waste management, and inadequately regulated zoning. Because Costa Rica's rich coasts are attracting hundreds of thousands of tourists a year, environmentalists are worried that shorelines will become littered with cheap hotels and beach bars like those of Spain, Portugal, or Mexico. Their fear is grounded in the fact that only 7 percent of Costa Rica's coastlines have any kind of regulatory plans. Roxana Salazar warns of health problems caused by the increase of garbage at beaches and other public places and of the effects on marine ecosystems of increased waste flowing into the seas. Her studies on tourist areas indicate increased levels of noise pollution caused by the rise in airline and vehicular traffic, an increase in crime, drug addiction, and prostitution, and negative impact on the flora and fauna in and around areas of greatest tourist presence. The increase in foreign-owned and -operated resorts, likewise, concerns her as a possible impediment that would preclude some of the promised economic benefits. A *Tico Times* article thus concluded that tourism is becoming "the goose that laid the golden egg."[27]

The dilemma came to a head in 1991 when the French firm Eurocaribeña planned to build a large resort complex on the Caribbean near Gandoca-Manzanillo National Wildlife Refuge in extreme southern Limón province. Gandoca-Manzanillo is home to some of Costa Rica's finest Caribbean beaches and protects Costa Rica's largest and most diverse coral reef system not far off shore. The planned resort, according to University of Costa Rica marine biologist Jorge Cortés, who completed a study of the area, however, would cause severe environmental consequences to the coastal and off-shore ecosystems. Moreover, Eurocaribeña was proceeding with construction of the complex without conducting any planning studies on how it would mitigate the environmental impact—a scenario that Cortés called "pirate development." Cortés' study recommended "absolute protection" for the fragile coral reef system, beaches, and mangrove swamps, which meant eliminating contaminant-heavy runoff from streams and rivers that drained into the Caribbean from that region.[28]

Adding to the problem was Eurocaribeña's plan to pipe waste directly from the resort to the open Caribbean—a fact discovered by novelist and environmental activist Anacristina Rossi, who owned land near the project under construction. "It's not possible that they were permitted to construct a drainage system without any knowledge of the soils, and that [drainage] from the septic tanks would go directly to the sea," she told a reporter for *La Prensa Libre,* which ran a picture of the sewage ditch. Enraged, Rossi filed a complaint with the Forestry Directorate (DGF) and the Special Commission on the Environment and sent a copy to Mario Boza, who, at the time, was assistant director of the Ministry of Natural Resources (MIRENEM). In her letter, Rossi demanded answers to a variety of questions related to Eurocaribeña's designs. She wondered how what was supposed to have been a small development of only "two charming bungalows" ended up as a major resort project. She inquired "what DGF was planning to do with the sewage and soapy waters from a restaurant one hundred meters from the sea." Explaining that other residents of the area were offended by the plans, she said that the local people were of the opinion that "we can't go from being landowners to employees and let them destroy our land, too." She also believed that the Gandoca-Manzanillo situation represented Costa Rica's larger problem of "tourist development without planning."[29]

Rossi went on to write a short novel called *La loca de Gandoca,* which dealt with the issues surrounding the controversy at Gandoca-Manzanillo. Jorge Cortés said in an interview that Rossi's descriptions of the event in her novel were "exactly right," although she changed the names of the people involved. Cortés remained closely involved with the situation and was disgusted at the Calderón administration's response. MIRENEM director Hernán Bravo ended up supporting Eurocaribeña, a move that made Cortés wonder "who got to him." The resort was built, but thanks to people like Rossi and Cortés, with stricter environmental standards.[30]

A similar scenario unfolded a few months later on the opposite side of the country—at Tambor on the Nicoya Peninsula. There, the Barcelona-based investment firm Grupo Barcelo was proceeding with plans to construct a large beachside resort complex on the Pacific Ocean. To do so meant filling in a mangrove swamp, razing part of a tropical forest, and bulldozing the side of a mountain that faced the sea. The fact that ICT supported the project enraged conservationists. Representatives of the environmental group ASCONA sought a probe of the resort project and threatened to file suit to stop it. Speaking on behalf of MIRENEM, Mario Boza even went on Costa Rican television and admitted that there had been "a lack of coordination" between MIRENEM and ICT on the issue.[31] But despite these words and conservationists' angst, Grupo Barcelo was never stopped from building the resort.

The Tambor controversy ended up generating some negative international press for Costa Rica. Two German environmental organizations, Robin Wood and Pro-Reganwald (Pro-Rainforest), awarded their annual Environmental Devil prize in 1993 to ICT director Luis Manual Chacón for his support of such an environmentally unfriendly project. The prize, which included a trophy of a devil emblazoned with the words "for the most hypocritical ecotourism to the government of Costa Rica," was handed to Chacón in person on a visit to Germany he was making, ironically, to promote Costa Rican tourism to Europeans. A shocked Chacón was quoted in *La Nación* as saying that he was "pretty astonished" by the award but that he was trying to "conceal his disapproval." The article quoted an ASCONA spokesperson who said that the prize was "ridiculous and offensive." The *Tico Times* quoted Chacón as having stated that the award "was based on information coming out of Costa Rica, but it's totally erroneous and tries to hide the efforts that we are doing in different fields." He went on to point out that ICT had forced Grupo Barcelo to halt construction on a different project that was "within the inviolable fifty-meter mark of high tide." The Catalonian firm there had been accused of dredging rivers, illegally removing beach sand, and filling in a swamp.[32]

The dilemma is also very visible in places like Manuel Antonio National Park and Carara Biological Reserve, which have suffered because of overcrowded conditions. Table 3 shows how nearly 150,000 people a year visit Manuel Antonio—one of Costa Rica's smallest national parks. Michael Kaye of Costa Rica Expeditions lamented that "people pollution" at Carara had caused an overall degradation of the tropical forest experience there with busloads of tourists clamoring to catch a glimpse of scarlet macaws. Yanina Rovinski reports that these conditions have caused some conservationists in Costa Rica to call for carrying capacity studies to be performed at national parks. "A park is like a movie theatre," she writes, describing this philosophy. "If its capacity is 150, visitor 151 will not fit in and will endanger the security of the others." Managers at the Monteverde Cloud Forest Reserve completed carrying capacity studies when tourism there got out of hand in the late 1980s. In response to their findings, they created different trails to help them manage the flow of hikers and constructed improved visitor facilities.[33]

A newer dilemma that has developed is the recent surge in privately (often foreign) owned nature reserves, forest preserves, and "rent-a-parks." Some areas charge visitors up to seventy-five dollars a day, which excludes most Costa Ricans. Fencing in these private reserves worries conservationists, but the government to date has not regulated the industry and supports the influx of capital it brings. AECO director Alvaro León said that the "tendency to privatize" reserves was "very dangerous" since the government lacks the regulations, manpower, and financial resources to monitor them. World Ecotourism Society president Gerardo Budowski claimed that in Costa Rica the private reserves represented less than one percent of all land protected in the country; most are adjacent to lodges and hotels that cater to nature tourism. In some ways they are positive, he argued, because they can provide buffer zones or be part of biological corridors and are better than deforested livestock pastures. The problem, however, according to Budowski, is that some tend to be irresponsibly managed due to the lack of regulations. He cited the "dangerous" practice of "feeding wildlife." And forestry ecologist Luis Fournier mentioned that some private reserves were not managed for ecotourist use, but instead were strictly for ecosystem conservation and were good for helping to expand corridors for wildlife habitat. He lauded the University for Peace's forest reserve as a noteworthy case in point. And if nothing else, he added, the trees in the private reserves or ecotourist complexes were at least adding to the oxygen supply and increasing the hydrologic potential of the region where they are found. Likewise, many of the private-reserve owners and ecotourism lodge operators have "a great love for nature" and know the ecology of their area.[34]

To assist preserve owners, environmental consultant Roberto Wells founded the Conservation and Management of Private Forests Association (COMBOS) in 1992. COMBOS serves as a network of private reserve owners, implements programs on the industry's developments, and promotes ecological forest management. Only recently has MIRENEM (now MINAE) issued some policy guidelines, and those are for private wildlife reserves. The regulations require prospective entrepreneurs to complete formal applications, agree to allow their facility be monitored by government conservation officials for an initial five-year period, and abide by all national wildlife laws.[35]

A related issue is that of private reforestation plantations. Since the 1970s, teakwood plantations have sprouted up all over Costa Rica's lowland humid regions (on the Pacific and Caribbean sides). Typical of the industry is Reforestadora Buen Precio, S.A., in Limón province, which advertises for people to "Invest in green gold, tomorrow's most valuable asset: land/nature." Buen Precio's literature asserts that teakwood is a "promising answer for the XXI Century," especially since Costa Rica is the "ecological capital of the world," replete with all the "geographical, political-cultural, and social-economic conditions that are basic to fully guarantee long-range sustainable development." It states that Buen Precio believes in "integration of industrial reforestation" and that the plantation "has always been closely involved with proper management of woods and lumber," making it "a new model for development and secure investment." Pictures of the plantations show neat, even rows of the uniformly tall, quick-growing teakwood and tropically attired young women warmly embracing the trees. The *Tico Times* ran a series of articles in the summer of 1993 that questioned the economic and environmental benefits of such plantations. Those reports, combined with his own research, prompted University of Wisconsin botanist J. Robert Hunter to conclude that "Despite high-pressure propaganda asserting that these plantings are the best means of reforesting worn-out or cutover land, monocultural stands of untested trees (chiefly exotics) at unproven spacing are no more real forests than plantations of African oil palm or sugar cane."[36]

A final analysis of the long-range effects of ecotourism and private reserves awaits time and future research. Conservationists and ecotourism proponents agree that the Costa Rican government needs a well-regulated set of guidelines to monitor the industry. They conclude that ecotourism cannot go unplanned or unchecked and that regulations for proper waste disposal, zoning, and environmental impact assessments are sorely needed and must be enforced. Yanina Rovinski writes that some ecotourism operators have come up with their own self-imposed regulations: "Nature-oriented tours are to be led by biologists or other natural history experts. Groups are to be kept small and manageable.

Carrying capacity has to be respected for protected areas. Accommodations should be built at a considerable distance from parks and reserves, and money has to be spent as close to the wildlands as possible, in order to engender local support." The problem, she points out, is that the rules are self-monitored with some regulations being respected and others not, while "ecotourism continues to grow without planning or oversight." Likewise, ICT has been incapable of regulating the industry. Rovinski refers to the agency as a "mammoth institution" preoccupied with such issues as transportation, infrastructure, foreign investment, and advertising.[37]

Some individuals and groups have called for improved ecological education for tourists and ecotourism operators. To that end, the Costa Rican Audubon Society hosted a series of "ecotourism seminars" in 1992. The group's director, Richard Holland, stated that the ecotourism "buzzword" was actually "nebulously defined" and "largely uncontrolled," and he called for greater monitoring of the tourism companies. Calling tourists "the natural allies of conservationists," Holland also believed that they should be properly educated for visiting Costa Rica. The Audubon Society thus issued a Code of Environmental Ethics for Nature Travel, which advocated responsible visitation with the overall goal of minimizing human impact. Many travel and tourism agencies in the country have promoted the code and have encouraged their clients to report violations.[38]

A common tourist complaint concerns Costa Rican roads. Indeed the country's "highways" are among the worst in all of Central America in terms of potholes, broken pavement (or no pavement), and general disrepair. It takes hours to go short distances. According to an editorial in *La Nación* in June of 1996, the Pan-American Highway between San José and Puntarenas was so bad that it was starting to have a serious negative economic impact on the Pacific Coast tourism industry. Even President José María Figueres alluded to the bad roads in a televised national address in July of that year. Saying that he was "proud" of the country's 36,000 kilometers (21,600 miles) of roads, he pointed out that "of course now we have to concern ourselves with their maintenance."[39]

The dilemma, however, is that improved roads would bring even greater number of tourists to already overcrowded and overstressed national parks and preserves. The issue was debated by Monteverde officials as tourism agencies and foreigners complained of the long, bumpy, and dusty road from the main highway to the cloud forest preserve. After

Figure 16.   Ecotourist Site, Parismina Lodge, near Tortuguero National Park

considerable consideration of the matter, the Monteverde officials nixed plans to improve the road as they were already dealing with overly high tourist numbers. Roads were also the topic of a 1988 meeting of the Costa Rica–American Chamber of Commerce (AmCham). AmCham officials invited Jeb Bush, son of the former U.S. president, to advise them on how to petition the U.S. Agency for International Development (AID) for more tourism loans. Bush suggested that the Costa Rican government build more roads to beaches to hustle the tourists to the resorts. And, finally, the roads dilemma surfaced during the legislative debates on the 1996 Forestry Law. Diputado Victor Hugo Núñez from Limón province argued strongly for roads to be constructed through Tortuguero National Park to the town of Tortuguero, accessible only by boat or air. "Sure, [the lack of roads] is great for those who have their yachts and planes and other very luxurious transportation equipment," Diputado Núñez complained on the floor of the Legislative Assembly, "but the poor, humble folks there have to travel three hours on their old boats." He told the Assembly that it was his "responsibility" to see that Tortuguero "gets a road like every other Costa Rican city."[40] No roads have as yet been constructed through the swampy plain.

Promoting nature is, as Alexander Bonilla has called it, an "unsubstitutable capital" resource for Costa Rica.[41] But while "conservation for profit" is inadequately regulated now, the visible benefits to education, enjoyment, conservation, the economy, and as a vehicle to instill a sense of an environmental ethic can be the products of ecotourism, which can certainly be considered an important ingredient in the growth of a green republic.

12 *The National Biodiversity Institute*

> We need to change people's attitudes to nature toward a greater level of complexity. To change attitudes, we need to know what we have, because one doesn't value what one doesn't know, and the tragedy of tropical forests has been that they have had no value more than the wood in them and the land they grow on. . . . [L]et's prove that we should conserve the biodiversity of the country because we know it and use it.
>
> Rodrigo Gámez, quoted in David Rains Wallace,
> *The Quetzal and the Macaw*

In analyzing the conservation history of Costa Rica, it is fitting to conclude with a brief discussion of the most recent addition to the environmentalist makeup of the country: the Instituto Nacional de Biodiversidad (National Biodiversity Institute, or INBio). A discussion of this unique institution is included here because it is a direct result of the use of national parks and forests in the development of a national environmental ethic. In this case, the conscious protection of natural resources for the future environmental stability of the country starts with knowing, and understanding as much as possible about, exactly what organic resources exist.

According to an INBio brochure, the institute was planned by an interinstitutional commission that president Oscar Arias named in June of 1988 "to specialize in understanding and helping society use . . . Costa Rica's extraordinary biodiversity. There are at least a half million species of organisms in Costa Rica. . . . [H]owever, we understand only a minute fraction of these species. What they eat, what they do and how they do it, [and] how they can fit into the agroecosystem diversification that Costa Rica must sustain, are unopened books written in strange languages. . . . By understanding biodiversity, we can protect it, manage it, and help society use it."[1]

Prior to INBio's creation, biological and social scientists often had cited the need to inventory biological resources for improved resource management in Costa Rica. That officials in Costa Rica developed a way to do this, the first tropical country in the world to do so, indicates their sincere determination to secure the environmental welfare of the country. Or as internationally acclaimed botanist Peter Raven put it regarding INBio, "Once again Costa Rica has emerged as one of the world's leaders in tropical conservation."[2]

To accomplish this goal, INBio was established as a private organization. The INBio brochure explains that "the current framework of government structures did not seem appropriate for many of the INBio tasks—such as the magnitude and complexity of the inventory, the publicizing of Costa Rican biodiversity, the urgent demand for speed, and the critical need for a flexible organizational structure designed for the task."[3] Hence, in October of 1989 the INBio Association was legally registered with an Assembly of Founders and a Board of Trustees. The board hired former University of Costa Rica (UCR) botany instructor and Fundación Neotrópica president Rodrigo Gámez (who earned a doctorate in plant pathology from the University of Illinois) as INBio director. To house the institute and to secure a place to perform laboratory and data storage operations, the board built a large facility in Santo Domingo, northwest of San José.

Rodrigo Gámez has been an outspoken and well-publicized INBio proponent. His background leading up to his appointment as its director led him to understand the relationship that protected areas should have in the overall social economy of the nation. He had worked closely with the national parks system via his service as an advisor to Fundación Neotrópica. He explained that he got to know Mario Boza, Alvaro Ugalde, "and others of what might be called the 'conservation cartel'" who put him to work on fundraising and guiding visitors to national parks. "I was very impressed with what had been created there," Gámez said in an interview, "but I asked myself, 'Why do we want parks? What do we want to do with them, really?'" He has also written that "preserving areas does not guarantee perpetual conservation" and that the environment will be protected only by a "multiparticipatory effort . . . conducted by the people responsible for and expected to benefit from the conservation of their own biodiversity." To put this belief in motion, he developed a three-point credo for INBio: save biodiversity, know what has been saved, and put it to work for the improvement of society.[4]

Protecting biodiversity in Costa Rica is not necessarily a new phenomenon. Costa Rica's system of national parks and equivalent reserves has saved countless species from the extinction records. INBio, however, seeks to inventory the species and preserve representative voucher specimens of each. It uses the national parks and forests to find the species and has developed twenty biodiversity field offices to aid in their processing. The institute's mission is to stem the tide of species endangerment in Costa Rica, which, according to a Fundación Neotrópica and Conservation International study, includes 157 "critically endangered" species, 325 "very threatened" species, and 278 "rare and vulnerable" species. But while Costa Rica was the first country in Central America to be party to the CITES treaty on listing and prohibiting the taking and trafficking of endangered species in 1974, poaching and illegal exports have continued. INBio is working to save what is left and to research and publicize the species' interconnectedness with the environment.[5]

The second step, knowing what's been saved, involves what journalist Chris Wille referred to as a "Noah's Ark—where INBio is identifying and cataloguing every living thing in the country." Gámez' goal is to have this completed by the year 2000. While this may seem insurmountable, especially considering Costa Rica's small number of field biologists and professional systematists, INBio has developed an innovative program using "parataxonomists" and local assistants. Parataxonomists are not trained scientists; they are university students, government employees, or most often local individuals who live near the wildlands being studied and become salaried collectors of flora and fauna. They work closely with professional taxonomists, and what they collect is processed into the INBio data banks. This system of using lay people to assist in collecting biological data was created by Daniel Janzen as part of the push in the 1980s for socioeconomic park uses and sustainable development in Guanacaste.[6]

By the early 1990s, INBio employed over thirty such individuals who were required to take a six-month training course in botany, entomology, and ecology. Chris Wille asserted that these employees "have gathered more species in the past few months than the Costa Rica Natural History Museum had collected in the last century." The *Tico Times* reported in 1992 that INBio had graduated its third class of parataxonomists — mainly local lay people who Dan Janzen, speaking at the graduation ceremony, said "instinctively" knew where to look for specimens. And INBio board member Carlos Valerio wrote that "our estimate is that a steady pool of 100 to 200 parataxonomists working through INBio for about ten years can put well over 95 percent of Costa Rica's diversity into our National Biodiversity Collections." He estimated that a full-time worker trapping insects could "conservatively" produce 500 "properly pinned specimens per day for twenty days per month, or 10,000 specimens per month."[7]

Insufficient time has lapsed to gauge accurately the success of the third step or goal, but some things are in place to show how saving biodiversity will work for the improvement of society. First, INBio has been an obvious economic boost in employing many scientists, lay parataxonomists, and field assistants. Yet even more economically hopeful is INBio's role in the developing industry called "chemical prospecting." Defined as "the notion that nature can teach chemists a few tricks about how to design drugs," medical and pharmaceutical research is taking on new meaning through chemical prospecting in tropical nations. Approximately one-half of the modern medicines in use today are derived from the natural world, with most of those coming from tropical forests. INBio and three universities (UCR, Cornell, and Strathclyde of Glasgow, Scotland) have arranged a joint research program to identify, study, and experiment with plant and insect extracts and to perform preliminary bioassays of chemical compounds. Analytical techniques like mass spectrometry and magnetic resonance spectroscopy are then used to determine the extracts' chemical structures for their possible pharmaceutical values. INBio will receive a 60 percent royalty from any such patentable compound or a 51 percent royalty from a compound that requires significant chemical modification. INBio, in turn, will release all profits generated through the program to conservation causes in Costa Rica.[8]

Much of this plan was originated by Thomas Eisner, a chemical ecologist at Cornell University and one of the world's foremost researchers of tropical medicines. Eisner believed that if pharmaceutical corporations could join up with tropical countries, both sides (and mankind in general) would benefit. One such company that agreed was Merck & Company of Rahway, New Jersey. In 1992–1993 Merck paid INBio $1 million for the opportunity to search for drugs that could possibly cure

Alzheimer's disease, high blood pressure, AIDS, and other maladies. In addition, Merck donated $135,000 in chemical extraction laboratory equipment to INBio and sent chemists there to help train INBio staff. The money generated by Merck was turned over to the Ministry of Natural Resources for support of Isla del Coco National Park.[9] To finance such an undertaking required government assistance and outside help. Initial support came from the Central Bank of Costa Rica, U.S. AID, the MacArthur Foundation, the Swedish government, Pew Charitable Trusts, and other foundations. Money from Merck also supports administrative costs.

Generating money for research is another INBio advantage. According to Gámez, National Museum personnel were at first "horrified" about chemical prospecting, but warmed to the idea in view of the economic benefit. Microbiologist Anna Sittenfeld, who heads INBio's biodiversity prospecting division, stated: "The idea is to create alternatives for economic development, and alternatives for jobs. Then there will be less pressure against the land that is now protected [and] benefits will accrue even if the prospectors fail to find a billion dollar drug in the rainforest."[10] Daniel Janzen agreed but warned that "if people say biodiversity has value then it will fall under the social rules that all other things that have value do. You bargain for it, you hide it, you steal it, you put it in the bank. It's no longer the toy of the English rich."[11] INBio, therefore, has established safeguards to ensure companies using forest products do not claim that the resources are synthetic to avoid paying royalties.

Still, the philosophy behind "selling nature" bothers some environmentalists. Ivannia Mora has asked what the price on natural resources should be, who is to determine it, and how some resources will be classified "invaluable" and others of "relative" value. To her, the program seemed like yet another case of rich, northern countries being able to buy their way to the natural resources they need at the expense of the struggling, developing countries of the South. Others have criticized how INBio has "ceded intellectual property rights" to Merck. Journalist John McPhaul pointed out that critics have questioned "the right of any private entity to exploit natural resources" and have petitioned the government to regulate biogenetic research in the country.[12]

But according to Alsio Piva, INBio's director of inventories, the critics have exaggerated the importance of the Merck deal. "Everyone has paid attention to the contract with Merck, perhaps because it's something new," Piva surmised, "but for us it represents only 20 percent of our budget for the year." He went on to point out that the deal was for two years only and involved a "relatively small number of genetic samples for which the company will retain no rights after the contract expires." Likewise, the contract is nonexclusive—INBio may contract with other companies. "If we are going to propose developing the country's genetic resources, it doesn't make much sense to think about trying to market medicinal herbs; we have to play in the big league," Piva concluded.[13]

Some critics find fault with INBio's novel "parataxonomist" program. In some ways INBio officials have been condescending or paternalistic regarding whom they hire as their search and collections assistants, and why. Note, for example, how INBio board member Carlos Valerio described the program: "It should be emphasized that the parataxonomists are not thought to be embarking on the first steps to becoming Ph.D. biologists. Rather they are learning a trade. . . . Experience is showing us that the parataxonomists view their new trade as an enlightened and intellectual step upward, and that they are truly moved up from a static position in society." Alsio Piva mentioned that "we don't expect them [the parataxonomists] to have the skills of scientists, but they will be excellent assistants."[14] But a question remains regarding what they might do with these skills after the proposed ten-year collections period is over. Will they be dumped or gainfully employed?

Currently INBio is involved with other ongoing projects in addition to biosystematics and chemical harvesting. Staff training, public biological literacy programs, wildlife management, and support for sustained agriculture and forestry are among its priorities. Likewise, INBio is serving as a model to help other countries develop a biodiversity survey. Representatives from Chile and China have made serious inquiries and have visited the institute. U.S. congressman James Scheuer of New York drafted a bill in 1992 to establish a biodiversity institute in the United States based on his staff's visit to INBio. And Gámez has visited Italy and East Africa with his message of how to protect and capitalize on biodiversity.

In conclusion, INBio is perhaps in some ways Costa Rica's most poignant manifestation of a national environmental awareness. As Luis Diego Gómez has written, "Biological diversity is the password in today's conservation." The realization that protecting the environment means first knowing as much as possible about it, and then using and marketing that information to benefit the country and pay its own way (without taxing the citizens of the country), is unique to Costa Rica in the tropics, and in the world it may be surpassed only by Australia. In addition to the economic spin-offs, the information from INBio is disseminated to various centers around the country, making it available to a wide range of users. In the meantime, Costa Rica's conserved areas are being used developmentally but safely in a manner that gains more public support than if they were merely fenced-off preserves. One writer referred to this as a kind of "biological OPEC" in which Costa Rica could control its resources on its own terms. But diversity research has implications beyond the boards of Costa Rica. The Smithsonian's Thomas Lovejoy accurately addressed this when he stated, "He who supposes that we live on a well explored planet is not only foolish but arrogant; the protection and investigation of our biological resources, especially those located in the tropics, should be an item of high priority on the human agenda."[15] INBio proves that it is a high priority in Costa Rica.

"Picking Up the Gauntlet"

If we examine the past, it is undeniable that every day a greater number of Costa Ricans . . . are picking up the gauntlet. What this tells us is that more persons are contributing to the forging of a better Costa Rica for this and future generations, as well as undertaking the role that corresponds to a civilized nation, resolved to safeguard its natural heritage and extraordinary culture, on this little piece of planet Earth.

Gerardo Budowski, "La eficacia del movimiento a favor de la conservación de los áreas silvestres"

This work has attempted to show the multidimensional history of conservation in Costa Rica. Research revealed that it was the combination of the country's unique biogeography, legacy of scientific inquiry, and reliance on primarily locally owned and relatively small agricultural units that provided the foundation for Costa Rica's conservation successes. But while the outlook on land stewardship for renewable natural resource use became skewed with the advent of developmental export agriculture—not to be omitted or analyzed lightly in a review of Costa Rican environmental history—the nation responded with a conservationist agenda. INBio's Rodrigo Gámez attributed the successes since 1969 to four principal factors: the opportunity that Costa Rica had to establish a system of protection "while there was still some time left to save substantial portions of the country from destruction"; the initial "enthusiasm and commitment" of a large percentage of the population; the "stability of an unarmed democracy and its satisfactory attention to the basic socioeconomic needs" of the people; and "the political support that conservation has received from the five administrations since the system was established." Luis Fournier emphasized the improvement of higher education (especially at the University of Costa Rica in the 1960s and early 1970s) and "the better dispensation of funds for scientific ecological research." All of this, he added, created "a better comprehension on the part of Costa Ricans about the practical importance of ecology."[1]

In tracking the emergence and development of this pattern, this work has attempted to show how the government and society in general have reacted to conservation concerns and what framework has been created for future environmental protection (agencies, NGOs, education, etc.). But there are pressures on this model that will test its very core. The most pronounced of these is the pressure of growth—demographic and economic.

While the population of Costa Rica historically has been low (and today is just over three million), the rate of growth is what worries social scientists. Jeffrey Leonard reported that by 1987 Costa Rica's density had reached 85 persons per square mile—the third most dense in the region, behind El Salvador and Guatemala. From 1960 to 1980 the country experienced the most dramatic demographic growth (4 percent a year), largely due to the government's excellent health care and resultant low mortality rate. By the 1990s the population density was 155 persons per square mile, despite having the third highest rate of birth control in the world, just after Singapore and Taiwan.[2]

Of course, growth means pressure on natural resources. The link was shown most graphically by Fournier, who directly matched population increases with the rate of deforestation. Others have discussed the long-term disadvantages of spiraling growth to both the environment and the economy. The goal, then, is for balance. Can Costa Rica rise to the challenge as it has in the past? Will the "seductions of the American way of life," as Raúl Prebisch referred to it, impede the work for sustainable development?[3]

These and other questions must be addressed by the public and the policy makers in Costa Rica. In fact, they are part of the larger picture of Costa Rica's grand contradiction: the juxtaposition of conservation with destruction. The literature is consistent about Costa Rica's admirable (and much publicized) work to protect one-fourth of the country while millions of other acres were being systematically deforested. "Paradise on the brink," "ecological contradiction," and "environmental myth" are the kind of pat terms so commonly used to describe this ironic condition. J. Robert Hunter went so far as to suggest that "Costa Rica is rapidly adopting a two-faced policy on environmental and conservation matters . . . [or] an almost anti-conservation trend." John Vandermeer and Ivette Perfecto's study perhaps best exemplifies this thinking:

> Costa Rica has been held up as one of the world's best examples of rainforest conservation. Its internationally recognized conservation ethic, its position of relative affluence, its democratic traditions, the remarkable importance of ecotourism to its national economy, its willingness to adopt virtually any and all programs of conservation promoted by Western experts make it the most likely place for the success of the traditional model of rainforest conservation. The fact that the model has been an utter failure in Costa Rica, where it had the greatest chance of success, calls the model itself into serious question.[4]

Will there be any natural areas outside of parks and preserves by the year 2020? Or will it be like Vandermeer and Perfecto predict, that Costa Rica's landscape "will be converted into isolated islands [national parks and biological reserves] surrounded by a sea of pesticide-drenched modern agriculture?" And even the word "model" for Costa Rica has been called into question. Marjorie Sun reported that "representatives of American conservation foundations shy away from calling Costa Rica a model for other countries because of its unusual political and social achievements." She quoted the Nature Conservancy's Geoffrey Barnard, who for many years was involved in the country's conservation efforts: "We hesitate to use the term 'model' [for Costa Rica] because it makes teeth grate in other developing countries." (And yet it was Barnard himself who only six years earlier had published an article with the title "Costa Rica: Model for Conservation in Latin America"!)[5]

But Hunter, Vandermeer, Perfecto, and others who assert that Costa Rica's "model" has failed have not considered the alternative. It does not appear that they have comparatively considered what Costa Rica's landscape (or economy, for that matter) would look like without its past conservation record. The Tilarán and Talamanca mountains no doubt would be completely denuded, if not by now, then soon into the twenty-first century. Endangered species would be extinct. The tropical dry forest would be gone from the globe. Some of the most beautiful shorelines might look like Torremolinos (Spain), Cancún (Mexico), or South Padre Island (Texas). Instead of green, Costa Rica would be a brown republic. No, the national park system, while not without challenges, has reversed the tide and protected places that can be studied for their biological and biogenetic riches for years to come. These places can be (and are) enjoyed by Ticos to understand and better appreciate their natural heritage and by foreigners to taste the wonders of the tropical world. An article that Mario Boza helped write perhaps best sums up this philosophy. "Robert Hunter is right to point out that we haven't found a panacea," the authors state. They continue:

> Tropical conservation projects are gambles. The Costa Rica casino has the best odds, so ecogamers place their bets here. There have been many failures, large and small, but conservationists should learn as much from failures as from successes. One expects failures in a laboratory; that's the way science proceeds. The culture and economy and confidence of Costa Rica can absorb these implosions, and the park system continues to protect a healthy gridwork of ecosystems. . . . While there is much in Costa Rica to appall, this republic and all of Central America is replete with little conservation miracles wrought by those with vision and dedication. And there is still room to dream and scheme big.[6]

Thus, picking up the gauntlet for a balanced, sustained, and environmentally protected Costa Rica is the agenda for the conservationist community and society as a whole. Costa Rica has an indisputable advantage in the framework that is already in place and that has made enormous strides in accomplishing this goal. Its emphasis on protecting wild areas, inventorying biodiversity, and educating the public will reap valuable rewards in the continuing process of preserving the environment. In addition, research must continue and new information must be constantly published. Existing parks and protected areas should be expanded and improved. Seventeen percent of national park land still belongs to private landowners. The government will have to reimburse them soon to consolidate park management and to strengthen local support. It will also have to hire more park guards and improve the enforcement of regulations. In 1997 the number of guards at Corcovado National Park, for example, dropped from sixty to thirteen. There are no guards at Baulas National Marine Park. And poaching has increased on the unprotected beaches of Tortuguero. "In some . . . parks we find what we call empty forest," Boza explained. "You see the forest, but there are no animals. They were hunted."[7]

New areas and small reserves of fragile environments should be developed. Many sectors of society should be involved in this process. Broad support is a requisite. Some sectors of society may have to change their traditional views of privately owned and developed land. The economic values of conservation must be further projected into society. Because the "pragmatism of economic man, and especially the pragmatism of the Latin culture," as Luis Diego Gómez and Jay Savage put it, cannot and should not be ignored in Costa Rica, compromises on the part of environmentalists may have to continue. Rodrigo Gámez concludes: "The Costa Rican park system has survived so far because three million people have their basic needs met. But what happens when we reach six million? The fact is that a park, in addition to protecting the species, has to be socially viable. And it may be that we will have to sacrifice some of conservation to be more socially acceptable."[8]

And Costa Rica's "conservation cartel" recognizes the challenges. Mario Boza has written that "future concerns for the national parks of Costa Rica include the economic situation, conservation education, the need to demonstrate the monetary value of conservation, population growth, the need for citizen involvement, and the need for effective environmental legislation." In a recent interview he remarked, "The government talks a lot about protected areas, biodiversity, sustainable development, but the practice is not so good." Tropical Science Center director Julio Calvo agreed, saying, "I think politicians have overestimated what we are doing in conservation. . . . We have not been able to stop deforestation or the pollution of our rivers." Boza has also advocated that a U.N. environmental organization be given power to set standards, "just as similar U.N. agencies now set international health and labor standards . . . [and] be empowered to infringe on the sovereignty of individual states in environmental matters."[9]

Alvaro Ugalde, now with the U.N.'s Environmental Program Office for Central America, concurs with Boza's assessment. On demographics, Ugalde fears that "Costa Rica will double its present population in twenty-five years, and I see no way to change that." Thus he has called for a system of "optimal parks" that would continue to protect representative selections of all biological regions, would protect biodiversity and genetic wealth, and "would strive to save all the parts without exception," although he admits that "the challenging question" here is "how to choose priorities when we cannot save all the parts." "How do we save parts that are becoming increasingly separated," he wondered, "the parks

of the next century will be shrunken, highly mixed fragments of nature."
Therefore, more "political battles" will ensue, the park staff will have to
be "more scientific and education oriented," and a "conservation philosophy" must continue to be "embedded in our societies as a new kind
of institution, heavily linked to education, to aspects of everyday life,
and to local economies."[10]

One way to stem the separation of parts that Ugalde fears is with the
continued success of the Mesoamerican Biological Corridor, or Paseo
Pantera. Mario Boza, who directs the project, has written that the Path of
the Panther "envisions a future landscape that would in theory allow a
cougar to prowl from the Yucatán to the Darien without leaving protected greenways," and he noted that the program has already sponsored
"dozens of promising ecoprojects in Central America."[11] One bright success was achieved when Nicaragua created the Sí-a-Paz ("Yes to Peace")
National Park on its extreme southern border that connects with Costa
Rica's large Barra del Colorado National Wildlife Refuge.

Alexander Bonilla lists six specific goals for the future: to reduce the
bureaucracy that produces redundancy in effort and slows conservation; to enforce management plans that already exist; to regulate urban
sprawl; to control slash and burn farming; to eliminate poaching; and to
reduce dependency on industrial agriculture. Luis Fournier stated that
the biggest challenge is to control the borders—to stem the tide of illegal immigrants pouring into Costa Rica (primarily from Nicaragua) who
"cause pressure" on protected areas. La Nación reported in 1992 that
there were 35,000 undocumented Nicaraguan immigrants who had "invaded" Costa Rica due to a lack of control along the northern border of
the country. Roxana Salazar, however, noted that most Nicaraguan immigrants are absorbed into the banana labor force ("their level of poverty
justifies their coming here") and are "not an ecological problem." Instead, she suggested that urban problems, pollution, and toxic industrial waste control are the most serious environmental concerns that the
country faces.[12]

The call is also out for people in the "developed" countries of the
North to do their part. Bonilla stated that "northerners have no right to
complain"—that their lifestyles must change to help protect endangered
ecosystems in places like Costa Rica. Vandermeer and Perfecto assert that
North Americans and Europeans are "slicing up the rain forest [of Costa
Rica] on [their] breakfast cereal" and that they should reconsider their

tastes and demands. And a recent study by Russell Greenberg, of the Smithsonian Institution's Migratory Bird Center, found that rapid expansion of unshaded coffee farms in Central America has accounted for an alarming drop in songbird numbers. Greenberg cites how Costa Rica has converted 40 percent of its coffee plantations to "sun coffee"—coffee plants without tree shade that live twelve to fifteen years, compared with "shade coffee" plants that live fifteen to fifty years and whose trees overhead shelter a diversity of passerines that winter in the South. His findings, however, show that the exponential rise in demand for "gourmet coffees" is good for the birds and the environment because they are shade-grown varieties. He, like Vandermeer and Perfecto, then, has called on North Americans to do their part and demand the gourmet blends.[13]

There are other innovative ideas in the works that could help make conservation more economically attractive and therefore more marketable to the public. It was reported in the summer of 1996 that the Costa Rican government had struck a deal to sell oxygen produced in rainforests to Norway. Paying ten dollars per ton, officials agreed to purchase an initial 200,000 tons to be shipped to Norway. *La Nación* hailed the deal as the first of its kind "to export environmental services in the entire world." René Castro, minister of environment and energy (MINAE), said the money from the sale would go to start a National Forestry Financing Fund and that MINAE would start looking for other international clients for its "environmental services."[14]

Costa Rica's latest environmental service is its creation of a kind of world carbon bank. It works through a "joint implementation system" with a private power company or public utility agency in another country that is having difficulty meeting standards for reduced carbon emissions. The utility may "purchase" reductions from Costa Rica via conservation easements (i.e., buying a tract of forest land to prevent it from being turned into pasture), or simply pay for a reforestation project. Thus the land becomes a capturer or sequesterer of carbon and the industry or utility has met its pollution requirements in a so-called "market of virtue."[15]

Such innovations, in the words of the World Wildlife Fund's Thomas Lovejoy, have made Costa Rica "a country of choice at the dawn of the age of biotechnology." Former president José María Figueres was in the forefront of the changes and worked to institute a nationwide energy policy to phase out the use of fossil fuels for power generation by 2010.

His aggressive energy program included levying a 15 percent national fuel tax (at the expense of one of the most unprecedented popularity drops in recent Costa Rican history) to pay for reforestation projects and to reduce emissions. Lovejoy explained that the program is "restoring the resource base while avoiding or reducing carbon emissions as only forests can"; thus "the savings of environmental protection [are] off-set[ting] its costs." And while Figueres suffered at the polls for such initiatives, Lovejoy believed he persevered because he was "convinced he should do the right thing for his country's economic growth and quality of life, and confident that this will in time be recognized." Figueres' conservation innovations and energy policies recently prompted U.S. Secretary of the Interior Bruce Babbitt to suggest that "the world needs a Costa Rica to show the way." [16] Time will tell if such directions continue in the administration of President Miguel Rodríguez, who was elected in 1998.

In addition to these prospects, some of Costa Rica's deforested pastures may be on the rebound. Forestry consultant James Barborak explained that "although in places like the Amazon it's appropriate to say that once you cut the forest down you may never get it back, that's obviously not the case with the fertile volcanic soils in most of Costa Rica." He pointed out that, for better or worse, much of the country is becoming urban—people are leaving areas of poor soil never suited for agriculture, and trees are beginning to crop up. "Ten years from now, an awful lot of Costa Rica's going to be in second growth," especially in places like the Nicoya Peninsula, he said.[17]

Costa Rica may be so on the environmental rebound that one of its prominent citizens has called on the whole country to be declared the first "world park." Robert Muller, chancellor of the University for Peace and a former assistant secretary general of the United Nations, stated in an interview that because of its working conservation system and lack of a military force, Costa Rica would be the prime country for such an experiment. He envisioned the Costa Rican World Park to be replete with an environmentally friendly monorail system, more national parks, efficient alternative energy use, culturally sensitive indigenous reserves, and other ideas that, to this author, smacked of Ernest Callenbach's *Ecotopia*. According to Muller, such a concept would attract a great deal of attention to world environmental problems and could be a financial boon to the nation. Cautioning against such idealism, however, Mario Boza and colleagues wrote an article entitled "Costa Rica Is a Laboratory, Not Ecotopia." In it they argued, "We haven't created Ecotopia in Costa Rica. . . . Conservation here, like everywhere, faces mile-high obstacles. Few of these impediments are strictly ecological; they are socioeconomic problems that are difficult to supersede or even measure."[18]

While Costa Rica is a long way from becoming a tropical ecotopia, it has been blessed with a variety of conservation successes in a short period of time. How those have occurred, the key individuals behind them, the stumbling blocks along the way, and the framework set to confront the environmental challenges of the future have been the topics of this book. Future research will have to qualify the long-range successes or shortcomings of Costa Rica's conservation program. But that the framework is in place is one of the most important considerations. And as a "model" (if that word dare be used), future research is wide open to measure conservation successes in other regional countries. Panama, for example, is ripe for research in this genre of conservation history. How that nation arguably has surpassed Costa Rica in national park and biological reserve designation (at least on paper) in an even shorter period of time deserves careful historical inquiry. Any conservation successes in tropical America are to be applauded for the biological wealth, natural heritage, and enjoyment they will preserve for future generations. Placing this green republic of Costa Rica in perspective, Luis Gómez and Jay Savage reminisced:

> We remember the bright blue skies, the white clouds, the almost black forests on the slopes of the volcanoes, the driving rain, the green complexity of the forest canopy viewed from a mountain slope and our own tininess within the forest's grasp. Can we truly believe that man is so foolish as to completely destroy this special world? We cannot let it be so! For once gone, something special and basic about ourselves will be gone too—and afterward man himself will not survive. ¡Viva Costa Rica![19]

List of Acronyms

ACs	Areas de Conservación (Conservation Areas; formerly URCs)
AECO	Asociación Ecologista Costarricense (Costa Rican Ecology Association)
ALA	Archives of the Legislative Assembly
ASCONA	Asociación para la Conservación de la Naturaleza (Association for the Conservation of Nature)
CATIE	Centro Agronómico Tropical de Investigación y Enseñanza (Tropical Agronomical Research and Higher Education Center)
CCC	Caribbean Conservation Corporation
CONAI	Consejo Nacional de Asuntos Indígenes (National Council for Indigenous Affairs)
CONICIT	Consejo Nacional de Investigaciones Científicas y Tecnológicas (National Science and Technology Research Council)
DGF	Dirección General Forestal (General Forestry Directorate)
EPOCA	Environmental Program on Central America

FAO	United Nations Food and Agriculture Organization
FECON	Federación Costarricense para la Conservación del Ambiente (Costa Rican Federation for the Conservation of the Environment)
FPN	Fundación de Parques Nacionales (National Parks Foundation)
ICE	Instituto Costarricense de Electricidad (Costa Rican Electricity Institute)
ICT	Instituto Costarricense de Turismo (Costa Rican Tourism Institute)
IDA	Instituto de Desarrollo Agrario (Agrarian Development Institute; formerly ITCO)
INBio	Instituto Nacional de Biodiversidad (National Biodiversity Institute)
INDERENA	Instituto de Recursos Naturales (proposed)
ITCO	Instituto de Tierras y Colonización (Lands and Colonization Institute; changed to IDA)
IUCN	International Union for the Conservation of Nature (changed to World Conservation Union)
MAB	United Nations Man and the Biosphere Program
MAG	Ministerio de Agricultura y Ganadería (Ministry of Agriculture and Livestock)
MINAE	Ministerio de Ambiente y Energía (Ministry of Environment and Energy; formerly MIRENEM)
MIRENEM	Ministerio de Recursos Naturales, Energía y Minas (Ministry of Natural Resources, Energy and Mines; changed to MINAE)
NGOs	Nongovernmental organizations
OFIPLAN	Oficina de Planificación (Office of Planning)
OTS	Organization for Tropical Studies
PEC	Partido Ecologista Costarricense (Costa Rican Ecology Party)
PLN	Partido de Liberación Nacional (National Liberation Party)
PUSC	Partido de Unidad Social Cristiana (Social Christian Unity Party)
RECOPE	Refinadora Costarricense de Petróleo (Costa Rican Oil Refinery)

SINAC	Sistema Nacional de Areas de Conservación (National System of Conservation Areas; formerly SPN)
SINAPROMA	Sistema Nacional de Protección y Mejoramiento Ambiental (National System of Environmental Protection and Improvement)
SPN	Servicio de Parques Nacionales (National Park Service; changed to SINAC)
TSC	Tropical Science Center
UCR	Universidad de Costa Rica (University of Costa Rica)
UNA	Universidad Nacional (National University)
UNED	Universidad Estatal a Distancia (National Open University)
UNEP	United Nations Environmental Programme
URCs	Unidades Regionales de Conservación (Regional Conservation Units; changed to ACs)
USNPS	U.S. National Park Service
WWF	World Wildlife Fund

2 The Presidents of the Republic of Costa Rica, 1928–1998

1928–1932	Cleto González Víquez
1932–1936	Ricardo Jiménez Oreamuno
1936–1940	León Cortés Castro
1940–1944	Rafael Angel Calderón Guardia
1944–1948	Teodoro Picado Michalski
1948–1949	José Figueres Ferrer
1949–1953	Otilio Ulate
1953–1958	José Figueres Ferrer
1958–1962	Mario Echandi Jiménez
1962–1966	Francisco Orlich Bolmarcich
1966–1970	José Joaquín Trejos
1970–1974	José Figueres Ferrer
1974–1978	Daniel Oduber Quirós
1978–1982	Rodrigo Carazo Odio
1982–1986	Luis Alberto Monge
1986–1990	Oscar Arias Sánchez
1990–1994	Rafael Angel Calderón Fournier
1994–1998	José María Figueres Olsen
1998–	Miguel Angel Rodríguez

The History of Controversy at Santa Rosa— A Besieged National Park

1856	William Walker and the Filibuster War
1930–1966	Santa Rosa owned by Nicaraguan dictator Anastasio Somoza García
1955	Somoza's Nicaraguan soldiers involved with border skirmishes at Santa Rosa, upon Somoza's orders
1969	Scandal 1: forty *precarista* (squatter) families move onto Playa Naranjo; Alvaro Ugalde in charge of removal
1969	Scandal 2: neighboring rancher moves his fences into park, grazes cattle, has support of friend and Guanacaste rancher Daniel Oduber, who as president of the Legislative Assembly moves to take Santa Rosa from the National Parks Department
1970	Scandal 3: MAG minister found running his cattle on Santa Rosa National Park's grassland savannas
1972	Scandal 4: severe regional drought causes MAG minister to allow area ranchers to cut hay in park
1978	President Carazo expropriates hacienda El Murciélago from Anastasio Somoza Debayle and adds it to Santa Rosa

1982	Scandal 5: Ministry of Public Service uses El Murciélago as training grounds for Nicaraguan Sandinistas (and later, Contras); soldiers cross over into Santa Rosa, use trees for target practice
1984	Scandal 6: U.S. Green Berets found training Nicaraguan Contras and special unit of Tico Guards (Relámpago Battalion) at El Murciélago
1986	Scandal 7: secret airstrip discovered built by U.S. special forces under guise of ecotourism outfit; strip used as part of Oliver North's plan to resupply Nicaraguan contras using drug money and arms-sales money from Iran
1994	Scandal 8: chemical pesticide runoff, from nearby agro-industrial cotton plantation owned by ALCORSA, found to be cause of wildlife mortality in Santa Rosa

4 *Anonymous Poem Regarding the Palo Verde National Park Controversy, Summer 1981*

Requiem por un parque

Entre decreto y decreto se acaban los parques,
los patos, los piches y el guayacán;
adiós PALO VERDE, no volveré a verte,
las aves que migran no te encontrán.

Hitoy, Barra Honda, Guayabo y Rincón,
tiritan de miedo por esta agresión,
por estos decretos que los elimina,
echando por tierra la conservación.

Traigo penas en el alma,
por las Pailas del Rincón;
cavernas de Barra Honda
bellezas de esta nación.

Que poca huella dejaron,
la ley y la convención;
con un decreto enterraron
tesoros de esta región.

Los parques hermosos hoy brindan sus bosques,
sus playas, sus ríos, montañas y el mar;
que poco aprecian la naturaleza,
esta indiferencia nos va a aniquilar.

Traigo penas en el alma,
por la Pailas del Rincón;
cavernas de Barra Honda
bellezas de esta nación.

Que poca huella dejaron,
la ley y la convención;
con un decreto enterraron
tesoros de esta región.

National Archives, SPN file 1090

Requiem for a Park

Between decree and decree the parks all die,
along with the ducks, the swans, and the guayacans,*
good-bye Palo Verde, I'll not see you again,
the migrating birds will never find you.

Hitoy, Barra Honda, Guayabo, and Rincón
shake in fear of this aggression,
and for these decrees that eliminate them,
taking the land from conservation.

I feel pains in my soul,
for Rincón Volcano,

for the caves of Barra Honda
and the beauty of this nation.

What small marks were left
by the law and the convention,
with one decree they buried
the treasures of this region.

The beautiful parks today offer their forests,
their beaches, their rivers, mountains and seas;
how little they value nature,
this indifference will annihilate us.

I feel pains in my soul,
for Rincón Volcano,
for the caves of Barra Honda
and the beauty of this nation.

What small marks were left
by the law and the convention,
with one decree they buried
the treasures of this region.

*a type of aquatic bird

The National Conservation Strategy for Sustainable Development

A. Objectives
1. To maintain essential ecological processes and life systems.
2. To preserve genetic diversity.
3. To enhance equity, social justice, and ethical values.
4. To develop sustainable utilization of natural resources.
5. To balance rural development and urban growth.
6. To raise public consciousness about conservation.
7. To ensure the sustainable utilization of ecosystems.
8. To manage nonrenewable resources for long-term benefit.
9. To establish population and immigration policies based on basic resource constraints for an acceptable standard of living.

B. Sectors
1. Agriculture
2. Water resources
3. Energy, industry
4. Pollution, health
5. Demography

6. Legislation
7. Urban planning
8. Education, research
9. National heritage issues
10. Fishing, coastal zones
11. Mining
12. Forestry, wildlands

Based on Julio C. Calvo, "The Costa Rican National Conservation Strategy for Sustainable Development: Exploring the Possibilities," *Environmental Conservation* 17, no. 4 (Winter 1990): 356.

6 Indigenous Population of Costa Rica by Region and Group

Zona Talamanca	
Talamanca Bribri	7,500
Keköldi	450
Talamanca Cabécar	2,200
Zona Cabécar	
Tayní	1,700
Telire	650
Bajo Chirripó	700
Nairi Awari	500
Chirripó	4,800
Zona Guaymí	
Abrojo	500
Conteburica	2,000
Coto Brus	1,500
Guaymí	150
Zona Norte	
Matambú	850
Guatuso	700

Zona Buenos Aires	
Ujarrás	2,000
Salitre	2,900
Cabagra	2,100
Curré	1,000
Boruca	2,000
Térraba	750
Zona Huétar	
Quitirrisí	800
Zapatón	900
Total	36,350

Source: CONAI, July 1996

NOTES

Preface

1. John B. Oakes, "Greening Central America," *New York Times,* 20 April 1988, p. A-23; proceedings of Central America Day are in Valerie Barzetti and Yanina Rovinski, eds., *Toward a Green Central America.*

2. Luis Fournier Origgi, *Ecología y desarrollo en Costa Rica,* p. 21. All translations from Spanish are mine.

3. María Eugenia Bozzoli de Wille, *El indígena costarricense y su ambiente natural;* Carolyn Hall, *Costa Rica;* Luis A. Tenorio Alfaro, *Las comunidades indígenas de Costa Rica.*

4. Karen Olsen Beck de Figueres, interview, 29 June 1992, Curridabat.

5. Estrella Guier, "La conservación como elemento educacional para el desarrollo," in *Primer Simposio de los Parques Nacionales y Reservas Biológicas,* p. 61; Fournier, *Ecología y desarrollo,* pp. 20-21.

6. Lane Simonian, *Defending the Land of the Jaguar,* p. xii.

Introduction

1. Tom Barry, *Costa Rica,* p. 27; Allen M. Young, *Field Guide to the Natural History of Costa Rica,* p. 32; Bill Weinberg, *War on the Land,* p. 100; H. Jeffrey Leonard, *Natural Resources and Economic Development in Central America,* p. 200.

2. Gabriel Ureña Morales, *Costa Rica,* p. 22.

3. Mario Boza, *Costa Rica National Parks,* p. 7; Fundación Neotrópica and Conservación Internacional, *Costa Rica: Evaluación de la conservación de los recursos biológicos,* pp. 113-122.

4. Chris Wille, "Tropical Treasures," *Panoscope,* March 1991, p. 16.

5. Hall, *Costa Rica,* p. 1; Henri Pittier, *Capítulos escogidos de la geografía física y prehistórica de Costa Rica;* G. Alvarado, "Centroamérica y las Antillas: Puente, barrera, y filtro biológico," *Geoistmo* 2, no. 1 (1988): 9.

6. Hall, *Costa Rica,* p. 1.

7. Leslie R. Holdridge, *Life Zone Ecology;* Leslie R. Holdridge, *Forest Environments in Tropical Life Zones;* Alexander Bonilla, *Situación ambiental de Costa Rica,* p. 9; Hall, *Costa Rica,* p. 1.

8. María Eugenia Bozzoli de Wille, interview, 19 July 1996, San Pedro. Dr. Bozzoli's new findings dispute her earlier demographic data in *El indígena*

costarricense, which were based on the standard work by Bishop Augusto Thiel, *Monografía de la población de la República de Costa Rica en el siglo XIX.*

9. *Tico Times,* 7 August 1992, p. 4.

10. Tenorio Alfaro, *Las comunidades indígenas,* p. 5; Virginia P. Laftwich, "Succession and Related Soil Changes in the Tropical Rainforest on the Osa Peninsula, Costa Rica," manuscript, 1972, National Archives, Servicio de Parques Nacionales series (hereafter cited as SPN), file 1357; William M. Denevan, "The Pristine Myth: The Landscape of the Americas in 1492," *Annals of the Association of American Geographers* 82, no. 3 (1992): 369–385; John W. Hoopes, "In Search of Nature: Imagining the Pre-Columbian Landscapes of Ancient Central America," working paper, Nature and Culture Colloquium, Hall Center for the Humanities, University of Kansas, 1996.

11. Jean Carriere, "The Crisis in Costa Rica: An Ecological Perspective," in *Environment and Development in Latin America,* ed. Redclift and Goodman, p. 188; Hall, *Costa Rica,* p. 59.

12. Carriere, "Crisis in Costa Rica," p. 188; L. D. Gómez and J. M. Savage, "Searchers on That Rich Coast," in *Costa Rican Natural History,* ed. Janzen, p. 2.

13. Amelia Smith Calvert and Philip Powell Calvert, *A Year of Costa Rican Natural History,* p. 328; Nicolo Gligo and Jorge Mello, "Notas sobre la historia ecológica de la América Latina," in *Estilos de desarrollo y medio ambiente en la América Latina,* ed. Sunkel and Gligo; Figueres interview.

14. Hall, *Costa Rica,* p. 29.

15. International Union for the Conservation of Nature, *United Nations List of National Parks and Equivalent Reserves;* FAO, *A Manual for National Parks Planning;* James Barborak, "El programa de planificación del Servicio de Parques Nacionales de Costa Rica," in *Primer Simposio de Parques Nacionales y Reservas Biológicas,* p. 116; Young, *Field Guide,* p. 29.

16. Figures are as of December 1995, SINAC offices, San José.

17. Fundación Neotrópica and Conservación Internacional, *Evaluación,* p. 4.

18. Law 4465, Ley Forestal, *Leyes, decretos, y resoluciones,* semester 2, vol. 2 (San José: Imprenta Nacional, 1969), p. 917; Mario Boza and Rolando Mendoza, *The National Parks of Costa Rica,* p. 27.

19. Ricardo Zeledón, ed., *Código ecológico,* pp. 201–227; Bonilla, *Situación,* p. 63.

20. Boza and Mendoza, *National Parks,* p. 15.

21. Luis Fournier Origgi, *Recursos naturales,* p. 92.

22. Mario Boza, testimony before Agriculture and Natural Resources Commission, Archives of the Legislative Assembly (hereafter cited as ALA), Law 7575, *Acta* (proceeding) 3, file 1, p. 62.

23. Boza and Mendoza, *National Parks,* p. 26; Oscar Arias Sánchez, "Palabras

del presidente de Costa Rica," in *La situación ambiental de Centro América y el Caribe,* ed. Hedström, p. 30.

I. A Legacy of Scientific Thought and Tropical Research

1. Mario Boza, *Los parques nacionales de Costa Rica,* p. 2.
2. Fournier, *Ecología y desarrollo,* p. 26.
3. Charles L. Stansifer, "Foreign Scientists in Costa Rica, 1845–1914," manuscript, 1989; Gómez and Savage, "Searchers," p. 2; Rodríguez, "Ciencias naturales," *La Nación,* 24 November 1969, p. 73.
4. Carl Hoffman, *Viajes por Costa Rica,* p. 24; Gómez and Savage, "Searchers," p. 2.
5. Stansifer, "Foreign Scientists," p. 4.
6. Carlos Meléndez Cheverri, introduction to Hoffman, *Viajes,* p. 19.
7. Stansifer, "Foreign Scientists," p. 6.
8. Gómez and Savage, "Searchers," p. 4; Pittier, as quoted in Bonilla, *Situación,* p. 9.
9. Marshall C. Eakin, "The Origin of Modern Science in Costa Rica: The Instituto Físico-Geográfico Nacional, 1887–1904," *Latin American Research Review* 34, no. 1 (Winter 1999): 123–150.
10. Calvert and Calvert, *A Year of Costa Rican Natural History,* pp. v, vii.
11. Alexander F. Skutch, *A Naturalist in Costa Rica,* p. 8.
12. Luis Fournier Origgi, *Desarrollo y perspectiva del movimiento conservacionista costarricense,* p. 41.
13. Omar Cruz Rodríguez, "Alberto Manuel Brenes Mora: Científico costarricense," *Biocenosis* 7, no. 1 (1990): 54–55; Gómez and Savage, "Searchers," p. 4.
14. Fournier, *Desarrollo y perspectiva,* p. 55.
15. Alexander F. Skutch, *A Naturalist on a Tropical Farm,* p. 34.
16. Fournier, *Desarrollo y perspectiva,* p. 53.
17. For insight into Dr. Wille's writings and research, see Alvaro Wille Trejos, *Corcovado, meditaciones de un biólogo: Un estudio ecológico.*
18. Gerardo Budowski, interview, 18 July 1996, Curridabat.
19. The survey is found in SPN file 698.
20. Elizabeth Royte, "Imagining Paseo Pantera," *Audubon* 94, no. 6 (November–December 1992): 74–80.
21. Joseph Tosi Olin, "A Brief History of the Tropical Science Center's Monteverde Cloud Forest Preserve, 1972–1992," pp. 1–3.
22. Ibid., pp. 2, 8; Victor Dwyer, "Cheap Conservation at $25 an Acre," *Macleans,* 4 April 1988, p. 52.
23. SPN file 724; visitation figure is from TSC office, Monteverde, Costa

Rica; quotation is from Tosi, "Brief History," p. 9; speciation figures are from Joseph Franke, *Costa Rica's National Parks and Preserves,* p. 120.

24. Franke, *Costa Rica's National Parks and Preserves,* p. 121.

25. David Clark, "La Selva Biological Station: A Blueprint for Stimulating Tropical Research," in *Four Neotropical Rainforests,* ed. Gentry, p. 9.

26. J. Christopher Brown, "The OTS: The Development of Its Relationship with Costa Rica over Three Decades," pp. 2–8; Clark, "La Selva," p. 16; Gómez and Savage, "Searchers," p. 8.

27. Quoted in Laura Tangley, "The OTS," *BioScience* 38:6 (June 1988): 384.

28. Gómez and Savage, "Searchers," p. 8; speciation figures are from Norman Myers, "Tropical Deforestation and a Mega-Extinction Spasm," in *Conservation Biology: The Science of Scarcity and Diversity,* ed. Soulé, p. 397.

29. Rodrigo Gámez, introduction to Lucinda A. McDade et al., eds., *La Selva: Ecology and Natural History of a Neotropical Rainforest,* p. vii.

30. Clark, "La Selva," p. 16; Charles Schnell to Grace Solano, 24 October 1983, SPN file 1206.

31. Darryl Cole-Christensen, personal communication, 5 June 1997; and information from OTS North American Headquarters in Durham, N.C., 10 November 1997.

32. Cole-Christensen, personal communication; Beatrice Blake and Anne Becher, *The New Key to Costa Rica,* pp. 245–246.

33. Clark, "La Selva," p. 21.

34. Gómez and Savage, "Searchers," p. 10. For more on the links between scientific study and preservation, see Catherine Christen, "Tropical Field Ecology and Conservation Initiatives on the Osa Peninsula, Costa Rica, 1962–1973," in *Twentieth-Century Science beyond the Metropolis, Vol. 3: Nature and Environment.*

35. Budowski interview.

36. Mario Boza, Diane Jukofsky, and Chris Wille, "Costa Rica Is a Laboratory, Not Ecotopia," *Conservation Biology* 9, no. 3 (June 1995): 684.

2. The Environmental Problem

1. Bozzoli de Wille, *El indígena costarricense;* Tenorio Alfaro, *Las comunidades indígenas.*

2. Hall, *Costa Rica,* p. 2.

3. Bozzoli de Wille, *El indígena costarricense,* p. 79.

4. Hall, *Costa Rica,* p. 83; Alfred W. Crosby, *Ecological Imperialism,* p. 134. Quotation is from Michael Redclift and David Goodman, eds., *Environment and Development in Latin America,* p. 10.

5. Hall, *Costa Rica,* p. 1.

6. Fournier, *Recursos naturales,* p. 15.

7. Bonilla, *Situación.*

8. William C. Holliday, Jr., "Profit and Progress, Pesticides and Poisonings: The Sustainability and Environmental Impact of Costa Rican Banana Agriculture, 1900–1990" (M.A. thesis, University of Kansas, 1997), p. 103; *La Nación,* 1 April 1993, p. 12A.

9. Holliday, "Profit and Progress," p. 107; see also Steve Marquardt, "Green Havoc: Environment, Labor, and the State in Costa Rica's Pacific Banana Industry, 1938–84" (Ph.D. dissertation, University of Washington, 1999).

10. John Augelli, "Modernization of Costa Rica's Beef Cattle Economy: 1950–1989," *Journal of Cultural Geography* 9, no. 2 (Spring/Summer 1989): 82.

11. Reinaldo Carcanholo, "La industrialización centroamericana y el patrón del despilfarro: El caso de Costa Rica," in *Problemas del desarrollo de América Latina y el Caribe,* ed. Funes.

12. Hoffman, *Viajes por Costa Rica,* p. 97.

13. *La Prensa Libre,* 26 November 1969, p. 18; Norman Myers, "The Hamburger Connection," *Ambio* 10, no. 1 (1981): 3–8.

14. Leonard, *Natural Resources,* p. 216; George M. Guess, "Bureaucracy and the Unmanaged Forest Commons in Costa Rica," Working Paper, no. 1, University of New Mexico, Division of Public Administration, 1979, p. 31.

15. Susan E. Place, "Export Beef Production and Development Contradictions in Costa Rica," *Tjidschrift voor Economische en Sociale Geografie* 76, no. 4 (1985): 295.

16. Place, "Export Beef," p. 295. Cattle figures are from Augelli, "Modernization," p. 82.

17. Hall, *Costa Rica,* p. 87; Carriere, "Crisis in Costa Rica," p. 188; Julio C. Calvo, "The Costa Rican National Conservation Strategy for Sustainable Development," *Environmental Conservation* 17, no. 4 (Winter 1990): 355; George M. Guess, "Pasture Expansion, Forestry, and Development Contradictions: The Case of Costa Rica," *Studies in Comparative International Development* 14, no. 1 (Spring 1979): 42–55.

18. Carriere, "Crisis in Costa Rica," p. 187; Arias, "Palabras del presidente," p. 300; John H. Vandermeer and Ivette Perfecto, "Slicing Up the Rain Forest on Your Breakfast Cereal," *The Humanist* 55, no. 5 (1995): 26; Leonard, *Natural Resources,* p. 119; Barry, *Costa Rica,* p. 73.

19. Pasture expansion figures are from Augelli, "Modernization," p. 88; road expansion figures are from Leonard, *Natural Resources,* p. 212.

20. B. E. Lemus, *Costa Rica Crisis: Desafío para el desarrollo,* p. 109; Hall, *Costa Rica,* p. 1994. Wood import estimate is from Calvo, "Costa Rican National Conservation Strategy," p. 355.

21. Skutch, *A Naturalist in Costa Rica,* pp. 37–38.

22. Carriere, "Crisis in Costa Rica," p. 188.

23. Weinberg, *War on the Land,* p. 106.

24. Beatriz Villarreal M., *El precarismo rural en Costa Rica, 1960–1980,* p. 100; Daniel Janzen, *Guanacaste National Park,* p. 82; Brown, "The OTS," p. 12; Dwyer, "Cheap Conservation," p. 52.

25. Virginia P. Laftwich, "Succession and Related Soil Changes in the Tropical Rainforest on the Osa Peninsula, Costa Rica," manuscript, SPN file 1357, p. 11.

26. Raúl Prebisch, "Biosfera y desarrollo," in *Estilos de desarrollo y medio ambiente en la América Latina,* ed. Sunkel and Gligo, p. 86.

27. Craig McFarland et al., "Establishing, Planning, and Implementation of a National Wildlands System in Costa Rica," in *National Parks, Conservation, and Development,* ed. McNeeley and Miller, p. 593; Augelli, "Modernization," p. 77.

28. Vandermeer and Perfecto, "Slicing," p. 25.

29. As reported in *La Nación,* 1 April 1993, p. 12A.

30. Vandermeer and Perfecto, "Slicing," p. 26; *La Nación,* 1 April 1993, p. 12A; S. A. Lewis, "Banana Bonanza: Multinational Fruit Companies in Costa Rica," *Ecologist* 22, no. 6 (1992): 289–290.

31. Jorge Cortés, interview, 15 July 1996, San Pedro.

32. *Tico Times,* 17 July 1992, p. 5.

33. *La Nación,* 1 April 1993, p. 12A; *Tico Times,* 3 July 1992, p. 1.

34. *Tico Times,* 3 July 1992, p. 1; *Tico Times,* 4 July 1992, p. 28; Boza, Jukofsky, and Wille, "Costa Rica Is a Laboratory," p. 685; Cortés interview. See also L. Corrales, "Programa de Certificacíon ECO-O.K.," Project Overview—Proyecto Banano ECO-O.K., Rainforest Alliance/Fundacíon Ambio, San José, 1994.

35. Luis Fournier Origgi, interview, 19 July 1996, San Pedro.

36. Bonilla, interview; Salazar, interview, 23 July 1996, San José.

37. Vandermeer and Perfecto, "Slicing," p. 25.

38. Guess, "Pasture Expansion," pp. 47, 44; Place, "Export Beef," p. 294. For the environmental impact of livestock in Guanacaste Province, see Gonzalo Cortés, "El impacto ambiental de la actividad ganadera en Guanacaste," *Biocenosis* 7, no. 1 (1990): 21–23.

39. Place, "Export Beef," p. 294; Guess, "Pasture Expansion," p. 44.

40. Hall, *Costa Rica,* p. 151. Quotation is from McFarland et al., "Establishing," p. 593.

41. Barry, *Costa Rica,* p. 37.

42. Carlos Campos, "Costa Rica: En busca de alternativas," in *La situación ambiental,* ed. Hedström, p. 179.

43. McFarland et al., "Establishing," p. 592.

44. Leonard, *Natural Resources,* p. 119.

45. Fournier, *Ecología y desarrollo,* p. 309; Hall, *Costa Rica,* p. 122; Wolfgang A. Hein, "Costa Rica y Nicaragua: Políticas ambientales desde perspectiva comparativa," in *La situación ambiental,* ed. Hedström, p. 277.

46. Weinberg, *War on the Land,* p. 113; *La Nación,* 20 March 1991, p. 4.

47. Fournier, *Ecología y desarrollo,* p. 153.

48. Hall, *Costa Rica,* p. 194.

49. Fournier interview.

3. The Conservationist Response

1. Fournier, *Desarrollo y perspectiva,* p. 44.

2. Quoted in ibid., p. 45.

3. Ibid., p. 46.

4. Law 13 (10 January 1939), Articles 1, 2, and 4, ALA.

5. Ana María Tato, "Legislación de parques nacionales," manuscript, 1982, SPN file 698.

6. The delegate, José A. Torres Morreira from the Ministry of Agriculture and Industries, is quoted in Fournier, *Desarrollo y perspectiva,* p. 48.

7. Ibid., pp. 48–49.

8. Law 1540, Article 14, as printed in Bonilla, *Situación,* p. 61; Fournier, *Desarrollo y perspectiva,* p. 49.

9. Tato, "Legislación," p. 1.

10. Law 2790 (18 July 1961), Articles 1, 2, 8, and 4, ALA.

11. Ibid., Articles 6 and 7.

12. Law 2790 (18 July 1961), *Acta* 1, file 1, ALA.

13. Both laws ratifying these conventions are in Ricardo Zeledón, ed., *Código ecológico,* pp. 37–76.

14. Program, Primer Congreso Nacional sobre Conservación de Fauna Silvestre, San José, 914–919 (July 1980), SPN file 719.

15. Law 7174, as printed in Zeledón, ed., *Código ecológico,* pp. 88–97.

16. James P. Rowles, *Law and Agrarian Society in Costa Rica,* pp. 9–11.

17. Ibid., pp. 211–212.

18. Law 2825 (2 October 1961), Chapters I, III, and VII, ALA.

19. Weinberg, *War on the Land,* pp. 107–110.

20. Quoted in David Rains Wallace, *The Quetzal and the Macaw,* p. 7.

21. Quoted in ibid., p. 8.

22. Wallace, *Quetzal,* p. 9; Weinberg, *War on the Land,* p. 108.

23. Budowski to Wessberg, 27 July 1971, SPN file 888.

24. Mario Boza, *Guía de los parques nacionales de Costa Rica,* pp. 6–7; Boza and Mendoza, *National Parks,* p. 24; Weinberg, *War on the Land,* p. 117; Wallace, *Quetzal,* pp. 15–16.

25. David Carr, "A Comprehensive Analysis of the Development of Costa Rica's National Park System: Draft Prospectus," manuscript, 1980, SPN file 896, p. 2; Fournier, *Desarrollo y perspectiva,* p. 62.

26. Guillermo Yglesias, testimony at hearings on Law 4465, *Acta* 1 (19 August 1968), dossier 3515, file 1, ALA; Fournier interview.

27. Yglesias to Legislative Assembly, 14 June 1968, Law 4465, *Acta* 1, dossier 3515, file 1, ALA.

28. Law 4465, Ley Forestal, Articles 1, 2, 9, 10, 15, 18, 74, 75, 80, 81, 93, 98, and 99, *Leyes, decretos, y resoluciones,* semester 2, vol. 2 (San José: Imprenta Nacional, 1969), pp. 908–910.

29. Ibid., p. 908; Yglesias testimony, pp. 5–8.

30. Yglesias testimony, pp. 37, 38–42.

31. Hearings on Law 4465, *Acta* 2 (21 August 1968), dossier 3515, file 1.

32. Ibid.

33. Hearings, *Actas* 3 and 4 (22 August 1968), dossier 3515, file 1.

34. Hearings, *Actas* 1 (19 August 1968), 2 (21 August 1968), 95 (16 December 1968), and 100 (3 May 1969), dossier 3515, file 1.

35. Law 4465, dossier 3515, file 2, ALA.

36. *La Prensa Libre,* 25 November 1969, p. 6.

37. Law 4465, dossier 3515, file 2, ALA. Curiously, the ALA does not have the register of debate from the final few weeks of the law's consideration, the vote tally, or the register of how each *diputado* voted.

38. *La Prensa Libre,* 24 November 1969, p. 21.

39. *La Nación,* 25 November 1969, p. 57; *La Nación,* 27 November 1969, p. 42; *La República,* 25 November 1969, p. 13; *La Nación,* 27 November 1969, p. 44.

4. The Development of National Parks and Other Protected Areas

1. Robert Cahn, "Parks Bloom in Poorer Nations," *Christian Science Monitor,* 20 September 1972, p. 19; Boza, quoted in Wallace, *Quetzal,* p. 15; Miller, quoted in Robert Cahn and Patricia Cahn, "Treasure of Parks for a Little Country That Really Tries," *Smithsonian* 10, no. 6 (September 1979): 64–75.

2. Cahn, "Parks Bloom," p. 19; John Milton and Harold Prowse, "International Short Course," National Archives, SPN file 59.

3. Milton and Prowse, "International Short Course"; Wallace, *Quetzal,* pp. 16–17.

4. Boza, *Los parques nacionales,* p. 2.

5. Quoted in Cahn and Cahn, "Treasure," p. 69.

6. Ugalde, quoted in Wallace, *Quetzal,* p. 17; Mario Boza, "Conservation in Action: Past, Present, and Future of the National Park System in Costa Rica," *Conservation Biology* 7, no. 2 (June 1993): 240.

7. Young, *Field Guide,* p. 29; Boza, "Conservation in Action," p. 241.

8. Mario Boza, "Costa Rica: A Case Study of Strategy in the Setting Up of National Parks in a Developing Country," in *Proceedings of the Second World Conference on National Parks,* ed. Elliot, p. 189.

9. Figueres interview.

10. Quoted in Wallace, *Quetzal,* p. 18.

11. Cahn and Cahn, "Treasure," p. 69; Wallace, *Quetzal,* pp. 27–28.

12. Cahn and Cahn, "Treasure," p. 69; Boza, quoted in Wallace, *Quetzal,* p. 19.

13. Wallace, *Quetzal,* p. 19.

14. Boza, "Conservation in Action," p. 240.

15. *La República,* 22 March 1971, p. 10.

16. Ibid.; *La Nación,* 21 March 1971, p. 42; Rogers C. B. Morton to Mario Boza, 2 February 1971, SPN file 890.

17. Boza to Budowski, 23 November 1970, SPN file 888; Tato, "Legislación," pp. 2–3.

18. Quoted in Wallace, *Quetzal,* p. 29.

19. Figueres interview.

20. Ibid.

21. Ibid.; Wallace, *Quetzal,* p. 30; Guillermo Cruz to Julio Calleja, 23 June 1972, SPN file 65.

22. Figueres interview.

23. Fournier, *Desarrollo y perspectiva,* p. 14; Wallace, *Quetzal,* pp. 33–34.

24. Boza, "Conservation in Action," pp. 240–241.

25. Robert Bridges to Mario Boza, 28 December 1971, SPN file 888.

26. "Pilot Study of Potential Park Sites and Reserve Areas throughout Costa Rica," SPN file 888, pp. 1–2.

27. Mario Boza to Myron Sutton, 10 May 1971 and 24 August 1971, SPN file 890.

28. "Resumen de la historia del Servicio de Parques Nacionales," SPN file 852, pp. 8–9.

29. Boza to Sutton, 13 June 1971, SPN file 890.

30. Boza to Budowski, 27 January 1971, SPN file 888.

31. *La Nación,* 8 June 1971, p. 29; "Resumen de la historia," p. 9; Boza, "Conservation in Action," p. 241.

32. Information on these three volunteers is from letters about their projects in SPN files 888 and 890.

33. Vaughan to Budowski, 18 August 1971, SPN file 888; Boza to U.S. Fish and Wildlife Service, 5 August 1971, SPN file 890.

34. Boza, "Costa Rica: A Case Study," p. 185; SPN file 890; Kirk Koepsel, telephone interview, 13 August 1992.

35. Mario Rojas to Gilberto Ugalde, 6 June 1971, SPN file 1207.

36. Boza to Budowski, 15 June 1971, SPN file 888.

37. Cahn, "Parks Bloom," p. 19; Wallace, *Quetzal,* p. 30.

38. Cahn, "Parks Bloom," p. 19; Fournier, *Ecología y desarrollo,* p. 92.

39. Boza to Nicholls, 19 August 1971; Nicholls to Boza, 6 October 1971, SPN file 888.

40. Boza, "Costa Rica: A Case Study," p. 185; Cahn, "Parks Bloom," p. 19.

41. Boza and Mendoza, *National Parks*, p. 25; Wallace, *Quetzal*, pp. 46–49.

42. Wallace, *Quetzal*, p. 50.

43. Bonilla, *Situación*, p. 61; Boza, "Conservation in Action," p. 241.

44. Various correspondence, SPN files 890 and 1292.

45. SPN files 59, 891, and 1282.

46. Boza, "Conservation in Action," p. 240.

47. Quoted in Wallace, *Quetzal*, pp. 34–35.

48. Wallace, *Quetzal*, p. 19; Cahn and Cahn, "Treasure," p. 70.

49. Mario Boza, interview, 9 July 1996, San Pedro; Cahn and Cahn, "Treasure," p. 70; Wallace, *Quetzal*, p. 19.

5. The Oduber Years

1. Quoted in Cahn and Cahn, "Treasure," p. 70.

2. Wallace, *Quetzal*, p. 54; Boza and Mendoza, *National Parks*, p. 25.

3. Ugalde, quoted in Wallace, *Quetzal*, p. 823; Young, *Field Guide*, p. 29.

4. Boza, *Guía*, pp. 8–20.

5. Fournier, *Desarrollo y perspectiva*, p. 66; Wallace, *Quetzal*, pp. 76–78.

6. Christopher Vaughan, *Parque Nacional Corcovado*, p. 31; Gary Hartshorn, "Plants: Introduction," in *Costa Rican Natural History*, ed. Janzen, p. 133.

7. Vaughan, *Parque Nacional Corcovado*, pp. 15–20; Weinberg, *War on the Land*, p. 108; Wallace, *Quetzal*, pp. 56–57. The full account of the dilemma between economics and preservation is found in Catherine Christen, "Development and Conservation on Costa Rica's Osa Peninsula, 1937–1977" (Ph.D. dissertation, Johns-Hopkins University, 1994).

8. Quoted in Weinberg, *War on the Land*, pp. 108–109; see also Wallace, *Quetzal*, pp. 59–65.

9. *La República*, 21 August 1975, p. 1; Wallace, *Quetzal*, p. 69.

10. Cahn and Cahn, "Treasure," p. 70; Wallace, *Quetzal*, p. 70.

11. Cahn and Cahn, "Treasure," p. 70; Ugalde to Ken Thelan, 31 May 1976, SPN file 1282.

12. León and Budowski, quoted in Wallace, *Quetzal*, pp. 80–81; visitation figure is from Servicio de Parques Nacionales, as cited in Bonilla, *Situación*, p. 137.

13. Miscellaneous correspondence in SPN file 892; Boza and Mendoza, *National Parks*, p. 25; Cahn and Cahn, "Treasure," p. 70.

14. Garihan-Ugalde correspondence, SPN files 892 and 893.

15. Law 6084, file 1, ALA.

16. Francisco Terán Valls to Edwin Múñoz Mora, 19 July 1972, and Asociación de Estudiantes de Biología to Múñoz, 22 July 1972, ALA, ibid.

17. Statement of Mario Boza to the Comisión de Asuntos Sociales, Law 6084, *Acta* 181 (13 November 1973), file 1, ALA.

18. Tato, "Legislación," pp. 3–5.

19. Cahn and Cahn, "Treasure," p. 71; Tato, "Legislación," p. 2; Wallace, *Quetzal,* p. 40.

20. Cahn and Cahn, "Treasure," p. 71.

21. SPN records, cited in Bonilla, *Situación,* p. 137; miscellaneous correspondence, SPN file 892.

22. Ugalde to Editor-in-Chief of the *Washingtonian,* 19 April 1977, SPN file 892.

23. Ugalde to Ken Thelan, 31 May 1976, and Ugalde to Robert C. Milne, 18 August 1976, SPN file 1282.

24. Alvaro Ugalde, "Proyecto: Ley de Creación del Instituto de Recursos Naturales y Conservación Ambiental," 27 January 1976, SPN file 19; Fournier, *Desarrollo y perspectiva,* p. 67; Boza, quoted in Wallace, *Quetzal,* p. 78.

25. Ugalde, "Proyecto," pp. 2–3.

26. SPN files 892 and 893.

27. SPN file 852; Oduber, in Andrew Reding, "Voices from Costa Rica," *World Policy Journal* 3, no. 2 (1986): 328–329.

6. Carazo and the Economy

1. Carriere, "Crisis in Costa Rica," p. 192; Rodrigo Carazo, *Carazo: Tiempo y marcha,* p. 513; Calvo, "Costa Rican National Conservation Strategy," p. 355.

2. "El programa de parques nacionales durante la administración Carazo," SPN file 852, pp. 8–9; Carazo, *Tiempo y marcha,* p. 479; Boza, *Guía,* pp. 18–98.

3. Rodrigo Carazo Odio, interview, 29 June 1992, Escazú; Carazo, *Tiempo y marcha,* pp. 17–21; Carazo, prologue to Boza and Mendoza, *National Parks,* p. 6.

4. Carazo, *Tiempo y marcha,* p. 18; Carazo interview.

5. Argentina Molina Morris, interview, 29 February 1992, Chicago; Carazo, *Tiempo y Marcha,* p. 513.

6. World Bank and Central Bank of Costa Rica data, in Carazo, *Tiempo y marcha,* pp. 504–512; Thomas Lovejoy, "El teatro ecológico y el drama sociológico," in *Primer Simposio de Parques Nacionales y Reservas Biológicas,* p. 160.

7. James Barborak, "El programa de planificación del Servicio de Parques Nacionales de Costa Rica," in *Primer Simposio de Parques Nacionales y Reservas Biológicas,* p. 117; José R. Mora to Michael Wright, 18 January 1982, SPN file 1098; Alvaro Ugalde, interview, 25 June 1992, San José.

8. Fournier, *Desarrollo y perspectiva,* p. 74; José María Rodríguez, quoted in Wallace, *Quetzal,* p. 93.

9. Ugalde interview; AID Loan Project no. 515-0145, SPN file 1336; Boza, "Conservation in Action," p. 245.

10. Fundación de Parques Nacionales, By-Laws, SPN file 698; "Account Records, 1981," SPN file 1098.

11. Archie Carr to Mario Boza, 11 May 1982, and Rafa Mora to Alvaro Ugalde, 11 June 1982, SPN file 1098.

12. "Posibles miembros honorarios," SPN file 1098; Rodrigo Carazo to Emilio Garnier, 11 January 1982, SPN file 852.

13. Carazo interview; Wallace, *Quetzal,* p. 89; Boza, *Los parques nacionales,* p. 66; Franke, *Costa Rica's National Parks and Preserves,* p. 161.

14. Franke, *Costa Rica's National Parks and Preserves,* p. 161; Boza, *Los parques nacionales,* p. 66.

15. Jorge Astacio to José María Rodríguez, 28 May 1980, SPN file 754; Michael Kaye to Rodrigo Carazo, 18 January 1982, and Carazo to Kaye, 20 January 1982, SPN file 852; Goinez to Carazo, 2 March 1982, SPN file 1098; Erdal Osturk to Carazo, 12 December 1981, and SPN denial, 18 March 1982, SPN file 852.

16. Fernando Fonseca to SPN, 16 July 1982, SPN file 734.

17. From Franke, *Costa Rica's National Parks and Preserves,* p. 162; Cortés interview.

18. Figueres interview; Carazo interview.

19. Margot Hornblower, "Protecting Resources in an Oasis of Democracy," *Washington Post,* 4 April 1982, p. A-18.

20. Carazo, *Tiempo y marcha,* p. 297; "El programa de parques," pp. 2–3.

21. Rafa Mora to Michael Wright, 18 January 1982, SPN file 1098; Wallace, *Quetzal,* pp. 89–90.

22. Wallace, *Quetzal,* pp. 84–85.

23. Quoted in ibid., pp. 86–87.

24. Portions of the interview are in Wallace, *Quetzal,* pp. 84–87.

25. Ugalde to Wright, 11 January 1979, SPN file 905.

26. "El programa de parques," pp. 3, 5, 9.

27. Morris interview; Carazo to Fonseca, 24 September 1981, and Carazo to Odio Benito, 24 September 1981, SPN file 941.

28. Luis Diego Gómez to Carazo, 2 March 1982, SPN file 1098; Clark, "La Selva," p. 16.

29. Carazo, Declaration of Palo Verde National Park, Executive Decree no. 1154-A, 13 June 1980, SPN file 1090.

30. Nidia Rodríguez, "Reserva de la Biosfera La Amistad," *Biocenosis* 7, no. 1 (1990): 30–32; Carazo, *Tiempo y marcha,* p. 479.

31. "El programa de parques," p. 6; Presidential Agreement Establishing La Amistad, April 1981, SPN file 941.

32. "El programa de parques," pp. 6–7.

33. Boza, *Guía,* p. 98.

34. "Inventorio de los recursos naturales y culturales y la característica socio-económica y elaboración del plan de manejo y desarrollo del prosupuesto Parque Internacional La Amistad, Costa Rica–Panama," SPN file 941.

35. Mora to Wright, 18 January 1982, SPN file 1098.

36. Presidential decree, SPN file 941; Silberman, quoted in *Tico Times*, p. 37; Presidential decree, SPN, 19 March 1982, p. 1; Budowski, quoted in Wallace, *Quetzal*, p. 97.

37. Carazo, *Tiempo y marcha*, p. 478; Wallace, *Quetzal*, p. 97.

38. Kaye to Carazo, 18 January 1982, and Silberman to P. H. C. Lucas, 29 March 1982, SPN file 852.

39. Boza, quoted in *Tico Times*, 15 October 1982, p. 1.

40. "Manual para el manejo y la administración de las áreas del SPN," SPN file 698; Barborak, "El programa de planificación," p. 107; Vaughan, *Parque Nacional Corcovado*, p. 24; Salazar to Rodríguez, 22 October 1980, SPN file 707.

41. Quoted in Hornblower, "Protecting Resources," p. A-18.

42. Weinberg, *War on the Land*, p. 105.

43. Carazo to Hernán Sáenz, 7 June 1979, SPN file 819; Yadira Mena et al., "Investigación: Educación ambiental," SPN file 700.

44. George Reiger, "A New Beginning," *Field and Stream* 86, no. 9 (January 1982): 70.

45. See *Primer Simposio de Parques Nacionales y Reservas Biológicas* (San José: Editorial UNED, 1982); "El programa de parques," p. 6.

46. Decree no. 12194-0P (January 1981), SPN file 859.

47. Program information, SPN files 724, 1037, and 1255.

48. Ugalde, quoted in Wallace, *Quetzal*, p. 99; Boza and Mendoza, *National Parks*, p. 25.

49. Figueres interview.

50. Quoted in Hornblower, "Protecting Resources," p. A-18.

51. Quoted in Reding, "Voices from Costa Rica," p. 335.

52. *La Nación*, 3 July 1981, p. 9-A.

53. Villarreal M., *El precarismo rural*, pp. 100–101.

54. Quoted in Reding, "Voices from Costa Rica," pp. 333–334.

55. Carazo, introduction to Boza and Mendoza, *National Parks*, p. 7.

56. *La Nación*, 27 July 1981, p. 2-A.

57. Tato to Carazo, 25 May 1981, SPN file 1090.

58. Boza and Rodríguez to Carazo, 27 May 1981, SPN file 1090.

59. Freer to Tato, 24 June 1981, SPN file 1090; *La Nación*, 9 July 1981, p. 4-A.

60. Executive Decree no. 12.765-A, 2 July 1981, SPN file 1090.

61. Bonilla to Carazo, 1 July 1981, and Carazo to Bonilla, 7 August 1981, SPN file 1090.

62. *La Nación*, 6 July 1981, p. 6-A.

63. *La Nación*, 9 July 1981, p. 4-A; *La República*, 14 July 1981, p. 15.

64. *La Nación*, 14 July 1981, p. 18-A; *La República*, 23 July 1981, p. 4.

65. *La Nación*, 15 July 1981, pp. 6-A, 14-A.

66. *La Nación*, 17 July 1981, p. 8-A.

67. *La República*, 17 July 1981, p. 3.

68. *La Nación,* 19 July 1981, p. 1-A; *La Nación,* 12 July 1981, p. 4-A.

69. *La Nación,* 18 July 1981, p. 8-A.

70. Letters, petitions, and poem are in SPN file 1090.

71. *La Nación,* 22 July 1981, p. 19-A; "El programa de parques nacionales durante la administración Carazo," SPN file 852; *La Nación,* 24 July 1981, p. 34-A.

72. *La República,* 23 July 1981, p. 24; Boza interview.

73. *La República,* 24 July 1981, p. 5.

74. ALA, Ley 80, *Acta* 51 (2 August 1981), pp. 13–14.

75. Ibid., pp. 14–15, 25–26, 28.

76. Ibid., pp. 28, 31.

77. Court events and records are in Bonilla, *Situación,* pp. 149–155.

78. Ugalde to Bonilla, 3 February 1982, as reprinted in Bonilla, *Situación,* pp. 169–170.

79. More research is needed on the rice growers' sudden decision. There is nothing on it in the Palo Verde file in SPN file 1090. The information here is from Boza interview.

80. Boza interview.

81. Alexander Bonilla, "Segregación del Parque Nacional Palo Verde," SPN file 1090.

7. The Monge Administration

1. Quoted in Wallace, *Quetzal,* p. 98.

2. Morales to Rodríguez, 21 June 1982, SPN file 806; "The Nature Conservancy," SPN file 1098; Ugalde to Luis Alberto Monge, 11 May 1982, and Ugalde to Doris de Monge, 17 May 1982, SPN file 852.

3. Ugalde, quoted in Wallace, *Quetzal,* p. 99; Ugalde to Manuel Carballo, 13 October 1982, SPN file 1098; Ugalde to Monge, 22 February 1983.

4. Fundación de Parques Nacionales, "Plan de prioridades," SPN file 1098; Tato to Rodríguez, 16 November 1982, SPN file 698.

5. Wallace, *Quetzal,* p. 101; Tato to Rodríguez, 16 November 1982, SPN file 689.

6. Ugalde to Junta Directiva de FNP, 18 May 1982, and Ugalde to Stone, 5 November 1982, SPN file 1098; WWF to Varela, 20 December 1984, SPN file 901.

7. Memo from Boza to FPN Staff, 13 July 1983, SPN file 1201; "Toward Environmental Advocacy in Costa Rica: A National Environmental Awareness Program," 1 September 1983, SPN file 1201.

8. Yuill to Ugalde, 12 October 1983, SPN file 1206.

9. Wallace, *Quetzal,* pp. 105–106, 150.

10. Boza Guadamuz to Monge, 27 September 1982, and Rodríguez to Viria Jiménez, 13 December 1982, SPN file 852.

11. Ministry of Industry, Energy, and Mines, "Proyecto de control y empadronamiento de oreros en la Península de Osa y Punta Barica," August 1983, SPN file 790; Wallace, *Quetzal,* p. 135; permit information, SPN files 789 and 790; Weinberg, *War on the Land,* p. 110.

12. "Proyecto de control," pp. 1, 4, 26; Ley de protección de medio ambiente, *Acta* 155 (31 October 1983), dossier 7853, SPN file 770.

13. Quoted in Wallace, *Quetzal,* p. 134.

14. Weinberg, *War on the Land,* p. 110.

15. Ugalde to Manuel Carballo (Office of the Presidency), 13 October 1982, SPN file 1098.

16. Ibid.

17. "La educación forestal a nivel universitario," 14 October 1982, SPN file 851; "Informe anuario," 13 October 1983, SPN file 804.

18. Bonilla, *Situación,* p. 221.

19. Ibid., p. 230; Bonilla, interview, 22 July 1996, San José.

20. Bonilla, *Situación,* p. 266.

21. Weinberg, *War on the Land,* p. 112; Hein, "Costa Rica y Nicaragua," p. 275.

22. Weinberg, *War on the Land,* p. 117.

23. Andrew Reding, "Costa Rica: Democratic Model in Jeopardy," *World Policy Journal* 3, no. 2 (Spring 1986): 310–311; Weinberg, *War on the Land,* pp. 117–118; Rodrigo Carazo, *Tiempo y marcha,* pp. 297–298; Reding, "Voices from Costa Rica," p. 331.

24. Joshua Karliner, "Contragate: The Environmental Connection," *EPOCA Update,* Summer 1987, pp. 4–9. The complete history of Costa Rica's links with the contra affair is found in Martha Honey, *Hostile Acts.*

25. Weinberg, *War on the Land,* pp. 119–120.

26. Karliner, "Contragate," p. 9; Weinberg, *War on the Land,* p. 119.

27. Wallace, *Quetzal,* pp. 153, 185–186.

8. Restructuring and Decentralizing Conservation

1. Janzen, *Guanacaste,* p. 13.

2. Quoted in Constance Holden, "Regrowing a Dry Tropical Forest," *Science* 234, no. 4778 (14 November 1986): 810; Thomas A. Lewis, "Daniel Janzen's Dry Idea," *International Wildlife* 19, no. 1 (January–February 1989): 34.

3. Janzen, *Guanacaste,* p. 9.

4. Ibid., p. 81.

5. Quoted in Holden, "Regrowing," p. 809; Lewis, "Dry Idea," p. 36.

6. Janzen, *Guanacaste,* p. 9; Holden, "Regrowing," p. 809.

7. Quoted in Marjorie Sun, "Costa Rica's Campaign for Conservation," *Science* 29, no. 4846 (18 March 1988): 1368; Lewis, "Dry Idea," p. 36; Holden, "Regrowing," p. 809. The theory of community-based conservation is dis-

cussed thoroughly in D. Western and R. M. Wright, eds., *Natural Connections.*

8. Sun, "Costa Rica's Campaign," p. 1368; Lewis, "Dry Idea," p. 36.

9. Holden, "Regrowing," p. 810.

10. Sun, "Costa Rica's Campaign," p. 1367.

11. Calvo, "Costa Rican National Conservation Strategy," p. 357; Barry, *Costa Rica,* p. 33; Sun, "Costa Rica's Campaign," p. 1367; Bonilla, quoted in Weinberg, *War on the Land,* p. 114.

12. Quoted in Sun, "Costa Rica's Campaign," p. 1367.

13. Sergio Salas, "La planificación del sector turismo," in *Primer Simposio de Parques Nacionales y Reservas Biológicas,* p. 28; Daniel Janzen, "The Eternal External Threat," in *Conservation Biology: The Science of Scarcity and Diversity,* ed. Soulé, p. 302.

14. Janzen, *Guanacaste,* p. 9; Weinberg, *War on the Land,* p. 120.

15. Weinberg, *War on the Land,* p. 121.

16. Ibid., p. 110.

17. Bonilla interview.

18. Eric Ulloa, interview, 25 June 1992, San José.

19. Wallace, *Quetzal,* p. 182.

20. Calvo, "Costa Rican National Conservation Strategy," p. 356.

21. Carriere, "Crisis in Costa Rica," p. 186; Katiana Murillo, "Use Capacity Maps: A Guide for Land Ordering in Costa Rica," *Neotrópica* 5, no. 2 (1996): 5–7.

22. Quoted in Sun, "Costa Rica's Campaign," p. 1367.

23. Ibid., p. 1368; Weinberg, *War on the Land,* pp. 115–116.

24. Law 7032, *Acta* 1, dossier 9600, 18 September 1983 and 14 November 1983, pp. 31, 155, ALA.

25. Roxana Salazar, *Legislación y ecología en Costa Rica,* p. 163. I thank Roxana Salazar and Leonel Núñez (director of the ALA) for explaining this matter to me.

26. Roxana Salazar, interview, 23 July 1996, San José; Fournier interview.

27. ALA, Law 7174, dossier 10940, pp. 1, 2, 65.

28. Ibid., pp. 3, 6, 64, 68, 85, 97.

29. Cited in Weinberg, *War on the Land,* p. 124.

30. ALA, Law 7575, file 1, *Actas* 2 and 3 of Special Commission, pp. 12, 39, 54–58.

31. Ibid., pp. 58–63.

32. Ibid., pp. 72–77, 97.

33. Ibid., *Acta* 5, p. 168; *Acta* 22, pp. 706–708.

34. Ibid., *Acta* 5, p. 168; Boza, quoted in Wallace, *Quetzal,* pp. 188–191.

35. *Tico Times,* 3 April 1992, p. 1; *Tico Times,* 19 June 1992, p. 1; conference information from Earth Council brochures at headquarters in San José.

36. *La Nación,* 26 June 1992, p. 15-A.

37. *Tico Times,* 3 April 1992, p. 1; 5 June 1992, p. 1.

38. *Tico Times,* 5 June 1992, p. 1.

39. Interviews with Earth Council staff, 17 July 1996, San José; miscellaneous Earth Council brochures.

40. Salas, "La planificación," p. 28; Carriere, "Crisis in Costa Rica," pp. 193–194.

41. Ulloa interview, 25 June 1992.

42. Miscellaneous SINAC brochures.

43. Alvaro León, interview, 11 July 1996, San José.

44. Anselmo Flores Reyes, interview, 19 July 1996, San José.

45. Eric Ulloa, interview, 4 July 1996, San José; René Castro Salazar, "Proyecto de reestructura del Ministerio de Recursos Naturales, Energía y Minas," MINAE, n.d., p. 200.

46. Salazar interview; Fournier interview.

47. Cortés interview; Budowski interview; Bonilla interview.

48. Boza interview; Madeline Carvajal, interview, 9 July 1996, San José; Luis Paniagua, interview, 8 July 1996, Curridabat.

49. ALA, Law 757, file 11, *Acta* 117 of Plenary Session, p. 3761.

50. Ibid., p. 3862.

51. Calvo and Hay, quoted in *Tico Times,* 28 February 1998, p. 1.

52. John Burnett, "Deforestation Is Threatening Costa Rican Wilderness," *Latin American Data Base* 3, no. 2 (15 January 1998): 2–3.

9. Environmental Education

1. Guier, "La conservación," p. 63; Salazar, *Legislación,* p. 207. For further details, see Rolando Mendoza, "Hacia una fundamentación teórica de la educación ambiental," *Biocenosis* 7, no. 1 (1990): 2–5.

2. Salazar, *Legislación,* p. 208.

3. Guier, "La conservación," p. 65.

4. Luko Quirós, "El movimiento conservacionista," in *La situación ambiental,* ed. Hedström, p. 309.

5. "CORENAMA, Objetivos Generales," in SPN file 778; Alvaro Ugalde to Jorge Falla, 12 November 1984, SPN file 778.

6. Guier, "La conservación," p. 62.

7. Ibid., pp. 66–68; Fournier, *Desarrollo y perspectiva,* p. 19.

8. *Tico Times,* 5 June 1992, p. 10.

9. *New York Times,* 29 May 1992, p. A-6.

10. Gómez and Savage, "Searchers," p. 10.

11. Gerardo Budowski, "La eficacia del movimiento a favor de la conservación de los áreas silvestres," in *Primer Simposio,* pp. 275–276.

12. Boza, "Costa Rica: A Case Study," p. 189; Douglas Cuillard, "La interpre-

tación en los parques nacionales: Una forma directa de crear conciencia conservacionista," in *Primer Simposio,* p. 121.

13. Yadira Mena et al., "Investigación: Educación ambiental," SPN report, SPN file 700, pp. 1, 11–13.

14. Taller Regional Mesoamericano information, SPN file 1255.

15. Course syllabus, SPN file 778.

16. 1983 Annual Report, SPN file 804.

17. Kirk Koepsel, telephone interview, 13 August 1992; Peace Corps, "Manual sobre interpretación y educación ambiental," SPN file 1255; Guier, "La conservación," p. 68; Susan Place, "The Impact of National Park Development on Tortuguero, Costa Rica," *Journal of Cultural Geography* 9, no. 1 (Fall–Winter 1988): 47.

18. Carazo interview; Boza, "Costa Rica: A Case Study," p. 183; Boza, "Conservation in Action," p. 246; Budowski, "La eficacia," p. 166.

19. Koepsel, telephone interview; Figueres interview.

20. Petitions, 22 November 1984, SPN file 778.

21. Carlos Sandi to Alvaro Ugalde, 7 November 1984, SPN file 778; Weinberg, *War on the Land,* p. 123.

22. The papers are in Jeffrey A. McNeeley and Kenton R. Miller, eds., *National Parks, Conservation, and Development.*

23. Janzen, *Guanacaste,* p. 13.

24. Fournier interview; Budowski interview.

25. Bonilla interview; Orlando Castillo, interview, 22 July 1996, Zapote.

10. The Nongovernmental Approach

1. FECON, *Directorio de organizaciones, instituciones, y consultores en el sector de recursos naturales en Costa Rica,* pp. vii–xvi.

2. Bonilla, *Situación,* p. 83; brochure from ASCONA office.

3. Bonilla, *Situación,* pp. 129–237; Ugalde interview; Weinberg, *War on the Land,* p. 114.

4. Koepsel telephone interview; Bonilla, *Situación,* pp. 230–233; Bonilla interview.

5. AECO, "Nuestro perfil," manuscript, n.d., pp. 1–2; AECO, "Proyecto de desarrollo institucional," manuscript, 1995, pp. 9–21.

6. AECO, "Nuestro perfil," pp. 1, 3; FECON, *Directorio,* p. 29; León interview, 11 July 1996, San José.

7. *Tico Times,* 5 June 1992, p. 10.

8. Boza, "Conservation in Action," p. 246.

9. Ugalde interview; Quirós, "El movimiento conservacionista," p. 311; Weinberg, *War on the Land,* p. 109.

10. Bonilla interview.

11. Carlos Brenes Castillo, "Costa Rica: Desarrollo forestal campesino," in *La Situación ambiental,* ed. Hedström, p. 169.

12. Hall, *Costa Rica,* p. 194; Lemus, *Costa Rica Crisis,* pp. 109–110.

13. *Tico Times,* 5 June 1992, p. 10; Weinberg, *War on the Land,* pp. 106–107.

14. Campos, "Costa Rica," pp. 177–179; Weinberg, *War on the Land,* p. 103; Brenes Castillo, "Desarrollo forestal," p. 169.

15. William Soto, introduction to *El indígena costarricense,* by Bozzoli de Wille, p. 6; Bozzoli de Wille, *El indígena costarricense,* p. 8; Bozzoli de Wille, interview, 25 June 1992, San Pedro.

16. Mario Alvarado Sánchez, interview, 19 July 1996, San José.

17. FECON, *Directorio,* pp. 75, 18, 66; Alvarado interview.

18. Flores Reyes interview.

19. "Talamanca's Sweet Success," *Nature Conservancy* 47, no. 1 (January–February 1997): 14–15.

20. Ibid.; Alvarado interview.

21. Juan Carlos Crespo and Doris Ortiz, quoted in Wallace, *Quetzal,* pp. 176, 178; Alvarado interview.

22. Alvarado interview; *Tico Times,* 12 June 1992, p. 24; *Tico Times,* 10 July 1992, p. 4.

23. Alvarado interview; "Marcha Indígena Nacional" agenda, CONAI office; *Al Día,* 15 July 1996, p. 3.

24. *Al Día,* 15 July 1996, p. 3.

25. Alvarado interview; Budowski interview.

11. Ecotourism for Economic Growth

1. Boza, *Guía,* p. 6; Carole Hill, "The Paradox of Tourism in Costa Rica," *Cultural Survival Quarterly* 14:1 (1990): 16–18.

2. Quoted in Tamara Budowski, "Ecotourism Costa Rican Style," in *Toward a Green Central America,* ed. Barzetti and Rovinski, p. 48.

3. Quoted in Wallace, *Quetzal,* p. 15.

4. Banco Central and ICT figures, as reported in Hill, "Paradox," p. 14; Budowski, "Ecotourism," p. 52; John Burnett, "Once an Eco-Paradise, Costa Rican Parks Are Falling on Hard Times," *Latin American Data Base* 3, no. 1 (8 January 1998): 3.

5. Hill, "Paradox," p. 16.

6. Budowski, "Ecotourism," pp. 55–56.

7. Cited in Yanina Rovinski, "Private Reserves, Parks, and Ecotourism in Costa Rica," in *Nature Tourism,* ed. Whelan, pp. 54–55; Wallace, *Quetzal,* pp. 119–120.

8. Rovinski, "Private Reserves," p. 56. Slogans are from billboards and advertisements in travel magazines.

9. Katiana Murillo, "Tourism with an Environmental Conscience," *Neotrópica* 2, no. 5 (1996): 18–19.

10. Law 1917, Article 4, cited in Salazar, *Legislación,* pp. 197–198.

11. Hill, "Paradox," p. 16; Rovinski, "Private Reserves," pp. 50–51.

12. Rovinski, "Private Reserves," pp. 51–52; Jan G. Laarman, "A Survey of Return Visits to Costa Rica by OTS Participants and Associates," working paper, North Carolina State University, 1987.

13. Compiled from Rovinski, "Private Reserves," p. 41; "Santuario Biológico del Bosque Nublado de Monteverde," manuscript, 1978, SPN file 811; Tosi Olin, "Brief History"; and current records from the Monteverde office.

14. Salazar, *Legislación,* p. 200; Burnett, "Once an Eco-Paradise," p. 2.

15. *Tico Times,* 2 April 1993, special supplement, p. 15.

16. Rovinski, "Private Reserves," pp. 46–47.

17. Agency ads and brochures; Rovinski, "Private Reserves," p. 47.

18. Rovinski, "Private Reserves," p. 49; Marenco ads.

19. Rovinski, "Private Reserves," p. 49.

20. Horizontes ads; Rovinski, "Private Reserves," p. 47.

21. Budowski, "Ecotourism," p. 52; Barry, *Costa Rica,* p. 81; ICT ads.

22. Boza to Budowski, 11 January 1972, SPN file 888; Ugalde, quoted in Wallace, *Quetzal,* p. 118; Ugalde interview.

23. Budowski, "Ecotourism," p. 53.

24. Place, "Impact of National Park Development," p. 47. Information on Poás Volcano is from Alexander Bonilla, *Situación,* p. 252. I thank Scot Vink for assistance with the number crunching at Corcovado National Park.

25. Rovinski, "Private Reserves," p. 56.

26. Gámez, quoted in *New York Times,* 29 May 1992, p. A-6; Place, "Impact of National Park Development," p. 47; Ulloa interview, 25 June 1992.

27. Hill, "Paradox," p. 18; *Tico Times,* 5 June 1992, p. 24; Salazar, *Legislación,* pp. 195–196.

28. *La Prensa Libre,* 18 October 1991, p. 2.

29. Ibid., p. 6.

30. Anacristina Rossi, *La loca de Gandoca;* Cortés interview.

31. *Tico Times,* 17 January 1992, pp. 1, 10.

32. *La Nación,* 31 March 1993, p. 2-A; *Tico Times,* 2 April 1993, p. 5. I thank Dr. Jorge Cortés for alerting me to this matter.

33. Kaye, quoted in Wallace, *Quetzal,* p. 123; Rovinski, "Private Reserves," pp. 57, 42.

34. León interview, 11 July 1996; Budowski interview; Fournier interview. I thank Martha Honey for alerting me to the private reserve dilemma.

35. FECON, *Directorio,* p. 10; SINAC, Regulation Guidelines, July 1996, SINAC office.

36. Ad supplement in *LACSA's World,* 1994, pp. 73–75; *Tico Times,* 14 May

1993 to 2 July 1993; J. Robert Hunter, "Is Costa Rica Truly Conservation-Minded?" *Conservation Biology* 8, no. 2 (June 1994): 592.

37. Rovinski, "Private Reserves," p. 52.

38. *Tico Times,* 24 January 1992, p. 25; Blake and Becher, *The New Key,* pp. 36–38.

39. *La Nación,* 28 June 1996, p. 13-A; *La Nación,* 2 July 1996, p. 14-A.

40. *Tico Times,* 4 March 1988, p. 24; Law 7575, *Acta* 117 (29 January 1996), file 113764, ALA.

41. Bonilla, *Situación,* p. 135.

12. The National Biodiversity Institute

1. "Instituto Nacional de Biodiversidad de Costa Rica, INBio," brochure, INBio office, Santo Domingo.

2. Quoted in Laura Tangley, "Cataloging Costa Rica's Biodiversity," *BioScience* 40, no. 9 (October 1992): 633.

3. INBio brochure.

4. Wallace, *Quetzal,* pp. 152–153; Rodrigo Gámez, "Development, Preservation of Tropical Biological Diversity, and the Case of Costa Rica," *International Agricultural Update* 5, no. 1 (1990): 3; Rodrigo Gámez, "Biodiversity Conservation through Facilitation of Its Sustainable Use," *Tree* 6, no. 12 (December 1991): 377. The credo is cited in Chris Wille, "Tropical Treasures," *Panoscope,* March 1991, p. 15.

5. Fundación Neotrópica and Conservación Internacional, *Evaluación,* p. 5; Kathryn S. Fuller and Byron Swift, *Latin American Wildlife Trade Laws,* p. 145.

6. Wille, "Tropical Treasures," p. 15.

7. Ibid.; *Tico Times,* 10 July 1992, p. 11; Carlos E. Valerio G., "INBio: A Pilot Project in Biodiversity," *ASC Newsletter,* 20, no. 2 (April 1992): 104.

8. Leslie Roberts, "Chemical Prospecting: Hope for Vanishing Ecosystems," *Science* 256 (26 May 1992): 1142; Lynn Llewellyn, "Tropical Deforestation and the Threat to Biodiversity," in *Methods for Social Analysis in Developing Countries,* ed. Finsterbach et al., p. 207; Christopher Joyce, "Prospectors for Tropical Medicines," *New Scientist,* October 1991, pp. 37–39.

9. Roberts, "Chemical Prospecting," p. 1142.

10. Gámez, quoted in Joyce, "Prospectors," p. 38; Sittenfeld, quoted in Roberts "Chemical Prospecting," p. 1143.

11. Quoted in Joyce, "Prospectors," p. 39.

12. Ivannia Mora, "Costa Rica: Naturaleza en venta," *Aportes,* March 1992, p. 22; John McPhaul, "Negotiating Costa Rica's Rich Biodiversity," *Latinamerica Press* 24, no. 34 (17 September 1992): 4. I thank John Simmons for bringing these criticisms to my attention.

13. Quoted in McPhaul, "Negotiating," p. 4.

14. Valerio, "INBio," p. 104; Piva, quoted in McPhaul, "Negotiating," p. 4.

15. Luis Diego Gómez, "Preserving Biological Diversity," in *Tropical Rainforests: Diversity and Conservation,* ed. Almeda and Pringle, p. 125; Joyce, "Prospectors," p. 36; Lovejoy, "El teatro ecológico, p. 160.

Conclusion

1. Gámez, "Development," p. 3; Fournier, *Ecología y desarrollo,* p. 33.

2. Leonard, *Natural Resources,* p. 198; Hall, *Costa Rica,* p. 99.

3. Fournier, *Desarrollo y perspectiva,* p. 14; Prebisch, "Biosfera y desarrollo," p. 87.

4. Hunter, "Is Costa Rica Truly Conservation-Minded?" p. 595; Vandermeer and Perfecto, "Slicing," p. 30.

5. Sun, "Costa Rica's Campaign," p. 1366; Geoffrey Barnard, "Costa Rica: Model for Conservation in Latin America," *Nature Conservancy News* 32, no. 4 (July–August 1982): 7–11.

6. Boza, Jukofsky, and Wille, "Costa Rica Is a Laboratory," pp. 684–685.

7. Burnett, "Once an Eco-Paradise," pp. 1–2.

8. Gómez and Savage, "Searchers," p. 10; Gámez, quoted in *New York Times,* 29 May 1992, p. A-6.

9. Boza, "Conservation in Action," pp. 239, 246; Boza and Calvo, as quoted by Burnett, "Once an Eco-Paradise," p. 2.

10. Alvaro F. Ugalde, "An Optimal Park System," in *Conservation for the Twenty-first Century,* ed. Western and Pearly, pp. 145–147.

11. Boza, Jukofsky, and Wille, "Costa Rica Is a Laboratory," p. 685.

12. Bonilla, *Situación,* p. 64; Fournier interview, 19 July 1996; *La Nación,* 17 August 1992, p. 10-A; Salazar interview.

13. Bonilla interview; Vandermeer and Perfecto, "Slicing," pp. 24–25; Greenberg study, cited in *Lawrence (Kansas) Journal-World,* 30 January 1997, pp. 1-A, 8-A.

14. *La Nación,* 21 July 1996, p. 18-A.

15. Thomas Lovejoy, "Lesson from a Small Country," *Washington Post,* 22 April 1997.

16. Ibid.

17. Quoted in Wallace, *Quetzal,* pp. 199–200.

18. Robert Muller, interview, 20 July 1996, University for Peace near Ciudad Colón; Boza, Jukofsky, and Wille, "Costa Rica Is a Laboratory," p. 685. See also Ernest Callenbach, *Ecotopia.*

19. Gómez and Savage, "Searchers," p. 10.

BIBLIOGRAPHY

Archival Sources

Archivo de la Asamblea Legislativa. San José, Costa Rica. Records of debates, proceedings, hearings, and legislative enactments for:
Ley 13, Ley General de Terrenos Baldíos, 1939
Ley 2790, Ley de Conservación de la Fauna Silvestre, 1961
Ley 2825, Ley de Tierras y Colonización, 1961
Ley 4465, Ley Forestal, 1969
Ley 6084, Ley de Creación del Servicio de Parques Nacionales, 1977
Ley 7032, Reformas de la Ley Forestal, 1986
Ley 7174, Reformas de la Ley Forestal, 1990
Ley 7317, Ley de Conservación de Vida Silvestre, 1992
Ley 7575, Ley Forestal (new), 1996
Archivo Nacional de Costa Rica. Zapote, Costa Rica. Servicio de Parques Nacionales series, files 650–1300, 1970–1989.

Newspapers

Al Día (San José, C.R.)
Christian Science Monitor (Boston, Mass.)
El Diario de Costa Rica (San José, C.R.)
La Nación (San José, C.R.)
La Prensa Libre (San José, C.R.)
La República (San José, C.R.)
New York Times (New York, N.Y.)
Tico Times (San José, C.R.)
Washington Post (Washington, D.C.)

Books, Articles, Manuscripts

AECO (Asociación Ecologista Costarricense). "Nuestro perfil." Manuscript, n.d.
———. "Proyecto de desarrollo institucional." Manuscript, 1995.
Allen, P. H. *The Rainforests of Golfo Dulce.* Gainesville: University of Florida Press, 1956.
Almeda, Frank, and Catherine M. Pringle, eds. *Tropical Rainforests: Diversity and Conservation.* San Francisco: California Academy of Sciences, 1988.
Alvarado, G. "Centroamérica y las Antillas: Puente, barrera, y filtro biológico." *Geoistmo* 2, no. 1 (1988): 9–25.

Ameringer, Charles D. *Don Pepe: A Political Biography of José Figueres of Costa Rica.* Albuquerque: University of New Mexico Press, 1978.

Anderson, Roger. "Ecotourism in Costa Rica: Environmental Friendly or Harmful?" Paper presented at Eighth Biennial Conference of the American Society for Environmental History, Las Vegas, Nevada, 8–11 March 1995.

Arias Sánchez, Oscar. "Palabras del presidente de Costa Rica en la XVII Asamblea General de la Unión Internacional para la Conservación de la Naturaleza y los Recursos Naturales." In *La situación ambiental en Centro América y el Caribe,* ed. Ingemar Hedström. San José: Editorial DEI, 1989.

Augelli, John P. "Costa Rica's Frontier Legacy." *Geographical Review* 77, no. 1 (January 1987): 1–16.

———. "Modernization of Costa Rica's Beef Cattle Economy: 1950–1989." *Journal of Cultural Geography* 9, no. 2 (Spring/Summer 1989): 77–91.

Barborak, James. "El programa de planificación del Servicio de Parques Nacionales de Costa Rica." In *Primer Simposio de Parques Nacionales y Reservas Biológicas* (proceedings). San José: Editorial UNED, 1982.

Barnard, Geoffrey. "Costa Rica: Model for Conservation in Latin America." *Nature Conservancy News* 32, no. 4 (July/August 1982): 6–12.

Barry, Tom. *Costa Rica: A Country Guide.* Albuquerque: Inter-Hemispheric Education Research Center, 1991.

Barzetti, Valerie, and Yanina Rovinski, eds. *Toward a Green Central America: Integrating Conservation and Development.* West Hartford, Conn.: Kumarian Press, 1992.

Basic Documents, University for Peace. San José: Imprenta Nacional, 1981.

Beebe, Spencer. "A Model for Conservation." *Nature Conservancy News* 34, no. 1 (January/February 1984): 4–8.

Blake, Beatrice, and Anne Becher. *The New Key to Costa Rica.* San José: Publications in English, 1991.

Bonilla, Alexander. *Situación ambiental de Costa Rica.* San José: Instituto del Libro/Ministerio de Cultura, Juventud, y Deportes, 1985.

———. *Un oleoducto en Costa Rica: Todo lo que debe saber pero no se ha dicho.* San José: ASCONA, 1983.

Bonilla, Alexander, and Tobías A. Meza Ocampo. *Problemas de desarrollo sustentable en América Central: El caso de Costa Rica.* San José: Editorial Alma Mater, 1994.

Boza, Mario. "Conservation in Action: Past, Present, and Future of the National Park System in Costa Rica." *Conservation Biology* 7, no. 2 (June 1993): 239–247.

———. "Costa Rica: A Case Study of Strategy in the Setting Up of National Parks in a Developing Country." In *Proceedings of the Second World Conference on National Parks,* ed. Sir Hugh Elliot. Morges, Switzerland: IUCN, 1974.

———. *Costa Rica National Parks.* Madrid: INCAFO, 1987.

————. "El sistema de parques nacionales de Costa Rica: Una década de desarrollo." CIDA Miscellaneous Publications, no. 1. San José, 1981.

————. *Guía de los parques nacionales de Costa Rica.* San José: Fundación de Parques Nacionales, 1984.

————. *Los parques nacionales de Costa Rica.* San José: SPN, 1978.

Boza, Mario, Diane Jukofsky, and Chris Wille. "Costa Rica Is a Laboratory, Not Ecotopia." *Conservation Biology* 9, no. 3 (June 1995): 684–685.

Boza, Mario, and Rolando Mendoza. *The National Parks of Costa Rica.* Madrid: INCAFO, 1981.

Bozzoli de Wille, María Eugenia. *El indígena costarricense y su ambiente natural: Usos y adaptaciones.* San José: Editorial Porvenir, 1986.

————. *Los recursos naturales de la Costa Rica del año 2000.* San José: Ministerio de Cultura, Juventud, y Deportes, 1977.

Brenes, Olga Emilia. "La situación ambiental de Costa Rica." In *Ecología y política en América Latina,* ed. Tomás Guerra. San José: CEDAL, 1984.

Brenes Castillo, Carlos. "Costa Rica: Desarrollo forestal campesino." In *La situación ambiental en Centro América y el Caribe,* ed. Ingemar Hedström. San José: Editorial DEI, 1989.

Browder, John O., ed. *Fragile Lands in Latin America: Strategies for Sustainable Development.* Boulder: Westview Press, 1989.

Brown, J. Christopher. "The OTS: The Development of Its Relationship with Costa Rica over Three Decades." Manuscript, 1990.

Budowski, Gerardo. *La conservación como instrumento para el desarrollo.* San José: Editorial UNED, 1985.

————. "La eficacia del movimiento a favor de la conservación de los áreas silvestres: Una opinión desde adentro." In *Primer Simposio de los Parques Nacionales y Reservas Biológicas* (proceedings). San José: Editorial UNED, 1982.

————. "Perceptions of Deforestation in Tropical America: The Last 50 Years." In *Changing Tropical Forests: Historical Perspectives on Today's Challenges in Central and South America,* ed. Harold K. Steen and Richard P. Tucker. Durham, N.C.: Forest History Society, 1992.

————. "Scientific Imperialism." *Unasylva* 27, no. 107 (1975): 24–30.

Budowski, Tamara. "Ecotourism Costa Rican Style." In *Toward a Green Central America,* ed. Valerie Barzetti and Yanina Rovinski. West Hartford, Conn.: Kumarian Press, 1992.

Burnett, John. "Deforestation Is Threatening Costa Rican Wilderness." *Latin American Data Base* 3, no. 2 (15 January 1998): 1–3.

————. "Once an Eco-Paradise, Costa Rican Parks Are Falling on Hard Times." *Latin American Data Base* 3, no. 1 (8 January 1998): 1–3.

Cahn, Robert. "An Interview with Alvaro Ugalde." *Nature Conservancy News* 34, no. 1 (January/February 1984): 8–18.

——. "Parks Bloom in Poorer Nations." *Christian Science Monitor,* 20 September 1972, p. 19.

Cahn, Robert, and Patricia Cahn. "Treasure of Parks for a Little Country That Really Tries." *Smithsonian* 10, no. 6 (September 1979): 64–75.

Callenbach, Ernest. *Ecotopia.* Berkeley: Banyon Tree Books, 1975.

Calvert, Amelia Smith, and Philip Powell Calvert. *A Year of Costa Rican Natural History.* New York: Macmillan, 1917.

Calvo, Julio C. "The Costa Rican National Conservation Strategy for Sustainable Development: Exploring the Possibilities." *Environmental Conservation* 17, no. 4 (Winter 1990): 355–358.

Campos, Carlos. "Costa Rica: En busca de alternativas." In *La situación ambiental en Centroamérica y el Caribe,* ed. Ingemar Hedström. San José: Editorial DEI, 1989.

Carazo, Rodrigo. *Carazo: Tiempo y marcha.* San José: Editorial UNED, 1989.

Carcanholo, Reinaldo. "La industrialización centroamericana y el patrón del despilfarro: El caso de Costa Rica." In *Problemas del desarrollo de América Latina y el Caribe,* ed. Julio César Funes. Caracas: AEALC, 1982.

Carr, Archie F. *The Windward Road: Adventures of a Naturalist on Remote Caribbean Shores.* New York: Alfred Knopf, 1956.

Carr, David. "A Comparative Analysis of the Development of Costa Rica's National Park System: Draft Prospectus." Manuscript, 1980. National Archives, SPN file 896.

Carriere, Jean. "The Crisis in Costa Rica: An Ecological Perspective." In *Environment and Development in Latin America: The Politics of Sustainability,* ed. Michael Redclift and David Goodman. Manchester: Manchester University Press, 1991.

Castro Salazar, René. "Proyecto de reestructura del Ministerio de Recursos Naturales, Energía, y Minas." Manuscript, n.d.

Chacón, I., J. García, and E. Guier. *Introducción a la problemática ambiental costarricense: Principios básicos y posibles soluciones.* San José: Editorial UNED, 1990.

Chase, Alston. "The Janzen Heresy." *Conde Nast Traveller,* November 1989, pp. 122–127.

Chaverri, Adelaida. "Análisis de un sistema de reservas biológicas privadas en Costa Rica." Master's thesis, University of Costa Rica/CATIE, 1979.

Christen, Catherine. "Development and Conservation on Costa Rica's Osa Peninsula, 1937–1977: A Regional Case Study of Historical Land Use Policy and Practice in a Small Neotropical Country." Ph.D. dissertation, Johns-Hopkins University, 1994.

——. "Tropical Field Ecology and Conservation Initiatives on the Osa Peninsula, Costa Rica, 1962–1973." In *Twentieth-Century Science beyond the Metropolis. Vol. 3: Nature and Environment.* Paris: UNESCO, 1995.

Clark, David. "The Search for Solutions: Research and Education at the La Selva

Station and Their Relation to Ecodevelopment." In *Tropical Rainforests: Diversity and Conservation,* ed. Frank Almeda and Catherine M. Pringle. San Francisco: California Academy of Sciences, 1988.

———. "La Selva Biological Station: A Blueprint for Stimulating Tropical Research." In *Four Neotropical Rainforests,* ed. Alwyn Gentry. New Haven: Yale University Press, 1991.

Corrales, L. "Programa de Certificación ECO-O.K." Project Overview, Proyecto Banano ECO-O.K. Rainforest Alliance/Fundación Ambio, San José, 1994.

Cortés, Gonzalo. "El impacto ambiental de la actividad ganadera en Guanacaste." *Biocenosis* 7, no. 1 (1990): 21–23.

Cortés, Jorge. "Situación actual de los arrecifes coralinos de Costa Rica." Centro de Investigación en Ciencias del Mar y Limnología, University of Costa Rica, 1989.

Crosby, Alfred W. *Ecological Imperialism: The Biological Expansion of Europe, 900–1900.* Cambridge: Cambridge University Press, 1986.

Cruz Rodríguez, Omar. "Alberto Manuel Brenes Mora: Científico costarricense." *Biocenosis* 7, no. 1 (1990): 54–55.

Cuillard, J. Douglas. "La interpretación en los parques nacionales: Una forma directa de crear conciencia conservacionista." In *Primer Simposio de Parques Nacionales y Reservas Biológicas* (proceedings). San José: Editorial UNED, 1982.

Dean, Warren. "The Tasks of Latin American Environmental History." In *Changing Tropical Forests: Historical Perspectives on Today's Challenges in Central and South America,* ed. Harold K. Steen and Richard P. Tucker. Durham, N.C.: Forest History Society, 1992.

Denevan, William M. "The Pristine Myth: The Landscape of the Americas in 1492." *Annals of the Association of American Geographers* 82, no. 3 (1992): 369–385.

———, ed. *The Native Population of the Americas in 1492.* 2d ed. Madison: University of Wisconsin Press, 1992.

Dengo Obregón, Jorge Manuel. "Recursos naturales." In *Proceedings of the Symposium La Costa Rica del Año 2000.* San José: Ministerio de Cultura, Juventud, y Deportes, 1977.

Dwyer, Victor. "Cheap Conservation at $25 an Acre." *Macleans,* 4 April 1980, p. 52.

Eakin, Marshall C. "The Instituto Físico-Geográfico Nacional and the Development of Science in Costa Rica, 1887–1904." Honors thesis, University of Kansas, 1975.

———. "The Origin of Modern Science in Costa Rica: The Instituto Físico-Geográfico Nacional, 1887–1904." *Latin American Research Review,* 34, no. 1 (Winter 1999): 123–150.

Edgar, Blake. "Seeds of Change in the Dry Forest." *Pacific Discovery* 42, no. 4 (Fall 1989): 22–37.

Estrada, Numa R. "La eficiencia económica de la migración rural en Costa Rica." In *Problemas del desarrollo de América Latina y el Caribe,* ed. Julio César Funes. Caracas: AEALC, 1982.

FAO. *A Manual for National Parks Planning.* Rome: FAO, 1976.

FECON. *Directorio de organizaciones, instituciones y consultores en el sector de recursos naturales en Costa Rica.* San José: FECON, 1994.

Fournier Origgi, Luis. *Desarrollo y perspectiva del movimiento conservacionista costarricense.* San José: Editorial UCR, 1991.

———. *Ecología y desarrollo en Costa Rica.* San José: Editorial UNED, 1981.

———. *Recursos naturales.* San José: Editorial UNED, 1983.

Fournier Origgi, Luis, and María E. Herrera de Fournier. "Importancia científica, económica y cultural de un sistema de pequeñas reservas naturales en Costa Rica." *Agronomía Costarricense* 3, no. 1 (March 1979): 53–55.

Francis, David R. "Natural-Resource Losses Reduce Costa Rican GNP Gains." In *Tropical Rainforests: Latin American Nature and Society in Transition,* ed. Susan E. Place. Wilmington, Del.: Scholarly Resources, 1993.

Franke, Joseph. *Costa Rica's National Parks and Preserves.* Seattle: The Mountaineers, 1993.

Fuller, Kathryn S., and Byron Swift. *Latin American Wildlife Trade Laws.* 2d ed. Washington, D.C.: World Wildlife Fund, 1985.

Fundación Neotrópica and Conservación Internacional. *Costa Rica: Evaluación de la conservación de los recursos biológicos.* San José: Fundación Neotrópica, 1988.

Gámez, Rodrigo. "Biodiversity Conservation through Facilitation of Its Sustainable Use: Costa Rica's National Biodiversity Institute." *Tree* 6, no. 12 (December 1991): 377–378.

———. "Development, Preservation of Tropical Biological Diversity, and the Case of Costa Rica." *International Agricultural Update* 5, no. 1 (1990): 1–4.

Gámez, Rodrigo, and Alvaro Ugalde. "Costa Rica's National Park System and the Preservation of Biodiversity: Linking Conservation with Socio-economic Development." In *Tropical Rainforests: Diversity and Conservation,* ed. Frank Almeda and Catherine M. Pringle. San Francisco: California Academy of Sciences, 1988.

Gligo, Nicolo. "El estilo de desarrollo agrícola de la América Latina de la perspectiva ambiental." In *Estilos de desarrollo y medio ambiente en la América Latina,* ed. Osvaldo Sunkel and Nicolo Gligo. Mexico City: Fondo de Cultura Económica, 1980.

Gligo, Nicolo, and Jorge Mello. "Notas sobre la historia ecológica de la América Latina." In *Estilos de desarrollo y medio ambiente en la América Latina,* ed. Osvaldo Sunkel and Nicolo Gligo. Mexico City: Fondo de Cultura Económica, 1980.

Gómez, Luis Diego. "Preserving Biological Diversity: The Case of Costa Rica." In *Tropical Rainforests: Diversity and Conservation,* ed. Frank Almeda and Catherine M. Pringle. San Francisco: California Academy of Sciences, 1988.

Gómez, Luis Diego, and J. M. Savage. "Searchers on That Rich Coast: Costa Rican Field Biology, 1400–1980." In *Costa Rican Natural History,* ed. D. H. Janzen. Chicago: University of Chicago Press, 1983.

González, Rodrigo. "Establecimiento y desarrollo de reservas forestales en Costa Rica." *Agronomía Costarricense* 3, no. 2 (September 1979): 161–166.

González Flores, L. F. *Historia de la influencia extranjera en el desenvolvimiento educacional y científico de Costa Rica.* San José: Editorial Costa Rica, 1976.

Gudmundson, Lowell. *Costa Rica before Coffee: Society and Economy on the Eve of the Export Boom.* Baton Rouge: Louisiana State University Press, 1986.

Guess, George M. "Bureaucracy and the Unmanaged Forest Commons in Costa Rica (or Why Development Does Not Grow on Trees)." Working Paper, no. 1, University of New Mexico, Division of Public Administration, 1979.

———. "Pasture Expansion, Forestry, and Development Contradictions: The Case of Costa Rica." *Studies in Comparative International Development* 14, no. 1 (Spring 1979): 42–55.

Guier, Estrella. "La conservación como elemento educacional para el desarrollo." In *Primer Simposio de los Parques Nacionales y Reservas Biológicas* (proceedings). San José: Editorial UNED, 1982.

Guzmán, Hector M. "Restoration of Coral Reefs in Pacific Costa Rica." *Conservation Biology* 5, no. 2 (June 1991): 189–194.

Hall, Bill, and Joshua Karliner. "A Forgotten War: The Assault on Central America's Environment." *Greenpeace* 12, no. 4 (1987).

Hall, Carolyn. *Costa Rica: A Geographical Interpretation in Historical Review.* Boulder: Westview Press, 1985.

———. *El café y el desarrollo histórico geográfico de Costa Rica.* San José: Editorial Costa Rica, 1976.

Hartshorn, Gary. "Plants: Introduction." In *Costa Rican Natural History,* ed. Daniel Janzen. Chicago: University of Chicago Press, 1983.

Hartshorn, Gary, et al. *Costa Rica: Country Environmental Profile, a Field Study.* San José: Trejos Hermanos, 1982.

Heckadon, Stanley. "Central America: Tropical Land of Mountains and Volcanoes." In *Toward a Green Central America: Integrating Conservation and Development,* ed. Valerie Barzetti and Yanina Rovinski. West Hartford, Conn.: Kumarian Press, 1992.

Hein, Wolfgang A. "Costa Rica y Nicaragua: Políticas ambientales desde una perspectiva comparativa." In *La situación ambiental en Centro América y el Caribe,* ed. Ingemar Hedström. San José: Editorial DEI, 1989.

Herrera S., Wilberth. *Costa Rica: Mapa-guía de la naturaleza.* Heredia, C.R.: INCAFO Costa Rica, 1992.

Hill, Carole. "The Paradox of Tourism in Costa Rica." *Cultural Survival Quarterly* 14, no. 1 (1990): 14–19.

Hoffman, Carl. *Viajes por Costa Rica.* San José: Ministerio de Cultura, Juventud, y Deportes, 1976.

Holden, Constance. "Regrowing a Dry Tropical Forest." *Science* 234, no. 4778 (14 November 1986): 809–810.

Holdridge, Leslie R. *Forest Environments in Tropical Life Zones.* New York: Pergamon Press, 1971.

———. *Life Zone Ecology.* San José: Tropical Science Center, 1964.

Holliday, William C., Jr. "Profit and Progress, Pesticides and Poisoning: The Sustainability and Environmental Impact of Costa Rican Banana Agriculture, 1900–1990." Master's thesis, University of Kansas, 1997.

Honey, Martha. *Hostile Acts: United States Policy in Costa Rica in the 1980s.* Gainesville: University of Florida Press, 1994.

Hoopes, John W. "In Search of Nature: Imagining the Pre-Columbian Landscapes of Ancient Central America." Working Paper, Nature and Culture Colloquium, Hall Center for the Humanities, University of Kansas, 1996.

Hopkins, Jack W. "Saving Costa Rica's Environment." *Hemisphere* 2, no. 1 (Fall 1989): 17–18.

Hornblower, Margot. "Protecting Resources in an Oasis of Democracy." *Washington Post,* 4 April 1982, p. A-18.

Hunter, J. Robert. "Is Costa Rica Truly Conservation-Minded?" *Conservation Biology* 8, no. 2 (June 1994): 592–595.

International Union for the Conservation of Nature. *The IUCN Directory of Neotropical Protected Areas.* Dublin: Tycooly International Publishing, 1982.

———. *United Nations List of National Parks and Equivalent Reserves.* Brussels: Hayez Publishers, 1971.

Janzen, Daniel. "Complexity Is in the Eye of the Beholder." In *Tropical Rainforests: Diversity and Conservation,* ed. Frank Almeda and Catherine M. Pringle. San Francisco: California Academy of Sciences, 1988.

———. "Costa Rican Parks: A Researcher's View." *Nature Conservancy News* 34, no. 1 (January/February 1984): 22–23.

———. "The Eternal External Threat." In *Conservation Biology: The Science of Scarcity and Diversity,* ed. Michael E. Soulé. Sunderland, Mass.: Sinauer and Associates, 1983.

———. "The Evolutionary Biology of National Parks." *Conservation Biology* 3, no. 2 (June 1989): 109–110.

———. *Guanacaste National Park: Tropical, Ecological and Cultural Restoration.* San José: Editorial UNED, 1986.

———. "Investigaciones biológicas en el parque nacional Corcovado, Costa Rica." In *Primer Simposio de Parques Nacionales y Reservas Biológicas* (proceedings). San José: Editorial UNED, 1982.

———. "Tropical Dry Forests: The Most Endangered Major Tropical Ecosystem." In *Biodiversity,* ed. E. O. Wilson. Washington, D.C.: National Academy Press, 1988.

Joyce, Christopher. "Prospectors for Tropical Medicines." *New Scientist,* October 1991, pp. 36–40.

Karliner, Joshua. "Central America: Political Ecology and U.S. Foreign Policy." In *Tropical Rainforests: Latin American Nature and Society in Transition,* ed. Susan E. Place. Wilmington, Del.: Scholarly Resources, 1993.

———. "Contragate: The Environmental Connection." *EPOCA Update,* Summer 1987, pp. 4–9.

Kutay, Kurt. "Cahuita National Park, Costa Rica: A Case Study in Living Cultures and National Park Management." In *Resident Peoples and National Park Management,* ed. Patrick C. West and Steven R. Brechin. Tucson: University of Arizona Press, 1991.

Laarman, Jan G. "A Survey of Return Visits to Costa Rica by OTS Participants and Associates." Working Paper, North Carolina State University, 1987.

Laarman, Jan G., and Richard R. Perdue. "Science Tourism in Costa Rica." *Annals of Tourism Research* 16, no. 2 (1989): 205–215.

———. "Tropical Tourism as Economic Activity: OTS in Costa Rica." FPEI Working Paper, no. 33. Southeastern Center for Forest Economics Research, North Carolina State University and Duke University, 1988.

Laftwich, Virginia P. "Succession and Related Soil Changes in the Tropical Rainforest on the Osa Peninsula, Costa Rica." Manuscript, 1972. National Archives, SPN file 1357.

Lee, David N. B., and David J. Snepender. "Ecotourism Assessment of Tortuguero, Costa Rica." *Annals of Tourism Research* 19, no. 2 (1992): 367–370.

Lehmann, Mary Pamela. "Deforestation and Changing Land-Use Patterns in Costa Rica." In *Changing Tropical Forests: Historical Perspectives on Today's Challenges in Central and South America,* ed. Harold K. Steen and Richard P. Tucker. Durham, N.C.: Forest History Society, 1992.

Lemus, B. E. *Costa Rica Crisis: Desafío para el desarrollo.* San José: CERTEDI, 1985.

Leonard, H. Jeffrey. *Natural Resources and Economic Development in Central America.* Washington, D.C.: International Institute for the Environment and Development, 1987.

Lewis, S. A. "Banana Bonanza: Multinational Fruit Companies in Costa Rica." *Ecologist* 22, no. 6 (1992): 289–290.

Lewis, Thomas A. "Daniel Janzen's Dry Idea." *International Wildlife* 19, no. 1 (January/February 1989): 34–37.

Leyes, decretos, y resoluciones. 2 vols. San José: Imprenta Nacional, 1969.

Llewellyn, Lynn. "Tropical Deforestation and the Threat to Biodiversity: New Directions in Social Assessment." In *Methods for Social Analysis in Developing Countries,* ed. K. Finsterbach et al. Boulder: Westview Press, 1990.

López Ocampo, Juan Diego, and Rodolfo Meono Soto. *Guía verde de Costa Rica.* Alajuela, C.R.: Guías de Costa Rica, 1992.

Lovejoy, Thomas. "Lesson from a Small Country." *Washington Post,* 22 April 1997, p. 5.

———. "El teatro ecológico y el drama sociológico." In *Primer Simposio de Parques Nacionales y Reservas Biológicas* (proceedings). San José: Editorial UNED, 1982.

Margolis, Kenneth. "La Zona Protectora." *Nature Conservancy News* 36, no. 1 (January/February 1986): 22–23.

Marquardt, Steve. "Green Havoc: Environment, Labor, and the State in Costa Rica's Pacific Banana Industry, 1938–84." Ph.D. dissertation, University of Washington, 1999.

Matos, Felipe. "Ayuda para conservar: El papel de las fundaciones internacionales y otras organizaciones privadas." In *Primer Simposio de los Parques Nacionales y Reservas Biológicas* (proceedings). San José: Editorial UNED, 1982.

McDade, Lucinda A., et al., eds. *La Selva: Ecology and Natural History of a Neotropical Rainforest.* Chicago: University of Chicago Press, 1994.

McFarland, Craig, et al. "Establishing, Planning, and Implementation of a National Wildlands System in Costa Rica." In *National Parks, Conservation, and Development: The Role of Protected Areas in Sustaining Societies,* ed. Jeffrey A. McNeeley and Kenton R. Miller. Washington, D.C.: Smithsonian Institution, 1984.

McLarney, William O. "Guanacaste: The Dawn of a Park." *Nature Conservancy News* 38, no. 1 (January/February 1988): 11–16.

McNeeley, Jeffrey A., and Kenton R. Miller, eds. *National Parks, Conservation, and Development: The Role of Protected Areas in Sustaining Societies.* Washington, D.C.: Smithsonian Institution, 1984.

McPhaul, John. "Negotiating Costa Rica's Rich Biodiversity." *Latinamerica Press* 24, no. 34 (17 September 1992): 4.

Mendoza, Rolando. "Ecoturismo en Costa Rica." *Biocenosis* 3 (1986): 14–16.

———. "Hacia una fundamentación teórica de la educación ambiental." *Biocenosis* 7, no. 1 (1990): 2–5.

Meza Ocampo, Tobías A. *Areas silvestres de Costa Rica.* San Pedro, C.R.: Alma Mater, 1988.

Meza Ocampo, Tobías A., and Alexander Bonilla. *Areas naturales protegidas en Costa Rica.* San José: Editorial Tecnológica de Costa Rica, 1990.

Miller, Kenton R. *Planificación de parques nacionales para el desarrollo en Latinoamérica.* Madrid: FEPMA, 1980.

Moffet, Mark W. *The High Frontier: Exploring the Tropical Rainforest Canopy.* Cambridge, Mass.: Harvard University Press, 1994.

Mora, Ivannia. "Costa Rica: Naturaleza en venta." *Aportes,* March 1992, pp. 22–23.

Murillo, Katiana. "Tourism with an Environmental Conscience." *Neotrópica* 2, no. 5 (1996): 18–19.

———. "Use Capacity Maps: A Guide for Land Ordering in Costa Rica." *Neotrópica* 2, no. 5 (1996): 5–7.

Myers, Norman. "The Hamburger Connection: How Central America's Forests Became North America's Hamburgers." *Ambio* 10, no. 1 (1981): 3–8.

———. "Tropical Deforestation and a Mega-Extinction Spasm." In *Conservation Biology: The Science of Scarcity and Diversity,* ed. Michael E. Soulé. Sunderland, Mass.: Sinauer and Associates, 1986.

Myers, Norman, and Richard Tucker. "Deforestation in Central America: Spanish Legacy and Northern American Consumers." *Environmental Review* 11, no. 1 (1987): 55–72.

Nations, James D., and Daniel I. Komer. "Indians, Immigrants, and Beef Exports: Deforestation in Central America." *Cultural Survival Quarterly* 6, no. 2 (1982): 8–12.

———. "Rainforests and the Hamburger Society." *Ecologist* 17, no. 4–5 (1987): 161–167.

Perry, David. *Life above the Jungle Floor.* San José: Don Perro Press, 1986.

Picado Chacón, M. *Vida y obra del Dr. Clodomiro Picado.* San José: Editorial Costa Rica, 1964.

Pierce, Susan M. "Environmental History of La Selva Biological Station: How Colonization and Deforestation of Sarapiquí Canton, Costa Rica, Have Altered the Ecological Context of the Station." In *Changing Tropical Forests: Historical Perspectives on Today's Challenges in Central and South America,* ed. Harold K. Steen and Richard P. Tucker. Durham, N.C.: Forest History Society, 1992.

Pittier, Henri. *Capítulos escogidos de la geografía física y prehistórica de Costa Rica,* 2d ed. San José: Imprenta Nacional, 1942; originally published in 1901.

Place, Susan E. "Export Beef Production and Development Contradictions in Costa Rica." *Tjidschrift voor Economische en Sociale Geografie* 76, no. 4 (1985): 288–298.

———. "The Impact of National Park Development on Tortuguero, Costa Rica." *Journal of Cultural Geography* 9, no. 1 (Fall/Winter 1988): 37–53.

———. "Nature Tourism and Rural Development in Tortuguero, Costa Rica." *Annals of Tourism Research* 18 (1991): 186–210.

Porras Z., Anabelle, and Beatriz Villarreal M. *Deforestación en Costa Rica: Implicaciones sociales, económicas y legales.* San José: Editorial Costa Rica, 1986.

———. *La legislación ambiental en Costa Rica.* San José: Editorial Papiro, 1982.

Prebisch, Raúl. "Biosfera y desarrollo." In *Estilos de desarrollo y medio ambiente en la América Latina,* ed. Osvaldo Sunkel and Nicolo Gligo. Mexico City: Fondo de Cultura Económica, 1980.

Pringle, Catherine M. "The History of Conservation Efforts and Initial Exploration of the Lower Extension of Parque Nacional Braulio Carrillo, Costa Rica." In *Tropical Rainforest: Diversity and Conservation,* ed. Frank Almeda and Catherine M. Pringle. San Francisco: California Academy of Sciences, 1988.

Quesada, Carlos. *Estrategía de conservación para el desarrollo sostenible en Costa Rica.* San José: MIRENEM, 1990.

Quirós, Luko. "El movimiento conservacionista: Nuevas rutas o viejas pautas?" In *La situación ambiental en Centro América y el Caribe,* ed. Ingemar Hedström. San José: Editorial DEI, 1989.

Ramírez, S., and T. Maldonado, eds., *Desarrollo socio-económico y el ambiente natural en Costa Rica: Situación actual y perspectivas.* San José: Fundación Neotrópica, 1988.

Raven, Peter. "Braulio Carrillo and the Future: Its Importance to the World." In *Tropical Rainforests: Diversity and Conservation,* ed. Frank Almeda and Catherine M. Pringle. San Francisco: California Academy of Sciences, 1988.

Redclift, Michael, and David Goodman, eds. *Environment and Development in Latin America: The Politics of Sustainability.* Manchester: Manchester University Press, 1991.

Reding, Andrew. "Costa Rica: Democratic Model in Jeopardy." *World Policy Journal* 3, no. 2 (Spring 1986): 301–315.

———. "Voices from Costa Rica." *World Policy Journal* 3, no. 2 (Spring 1986): 317–345.

Reiger, George. "A New Beginning." *Field and Stream* 86, no. 9 (January 1982): 68–70.

Roberts, Leslie. "Chemical Prospecting: Hope for Vanishing Ecosystems." *Science* 256 (26 May 1992): 1142–1143.

Rodríguez, Nidia. "Reserva de la Biosfera La Amistad." *Biocenosis* 7, no. 1 (1990): 30–32.

Rossi, Anacristina. *La loca de Gandoca.* San José: EDUCA, 1996.

Rovinski, Yanina. "Private Reserves, Parks, and Ecotourism in Costa Rica." In *Nature Tourism: Managing for the Environment,* ed. Tensie Whelan. Washington, D.C.: Island Press, 1991.

Rowles, James P. *Law and Agrarian Reform in Costa Rica.* Boulder: Westview Press, 1985.

Royte, Elizabeth. "Imagining Paseo Pantera." *Audubon* 94, no. 6 (November–December 1992): 74–80.

Salas, Sergio. "La planificación del sector turismo, recreación y el sistema de áreas silvestres." In *Primer Simposio de Parques Nacionales y Reservas Biológicas* (proceedings). San José: Editorial UNED, 1982.

Salazar, Roxana. *Actividad bananera en Costa Rica: Análisis legal e institucional.* San José: Fundación Ambio, 1993.

———. *Legislación y ecología en Costa Rica.* San José: Libro Libre, 1991.

Salazar, Roxana, Jorge A. Cabrera-Medaglia, and Alvaro López Mora, eds. *Biodiversidad: Políticas y legislación a la luz del desarrollo sostenible.* San José: Fundación Ambio, 1995.

Salazar, Roxana, et al. *Diversidad biológica y desarrollo sostenible.* San José: Euroamericana de Ediciones, 1993.

Salvin, Osbert, and F. Ducane Godman, eds. *Biologia Centrali-Americana.* London: Taylor and Francis, 1879–1904.

Samper Kutschbach, Mario. *Generations of Settlers: Rural Households and Markets on the Costa Rican Frontier, 1850–1935.* Boulder: Westview Press, 1990.

Sánchez, Marco Vinicio. *El oleoducto en Costa Rica: Aspectos ambientales y geopolíticos.* San José: SIAP, 1984.

Savage, Jay Mathers. *Introducción a la herpetofauna de Costa Rica.* Oxford, Ohio: Society for the Study of Amphibians and Reptiles, 1986.

Seligson, Mitchell. *Peasants of Costa Rica and the Development of Agrarian Capitalism.* Madison: University of Wisconsin Press, 1980.

Shane, Douglas R. *Hoofprints in the Forest: Cattle Ranching and the Destruction of Latin America's Tropical Forests.* Philadelphia: Institute for the Study of Human Issues, 1986.

Silberman, Murray. "Los parques nacionales en el siglo XXI." In *Primer Simposio de Parques Nacionales y Reservas Biológicas* (proceedings). San José: Editorial UNED, 1982.

Simonian, Lane. *Defending the Land of the Jaguar: A History of Conservation in Mexico.* Austin: University of Texas Press, 1995.

Skutch, Alexander F. *The Imperative Call: A Naturalist's Quest in Temperate and Tropical America.* Gainesville: University Presses of Florida, 1979.

———. *A Naturalist in Costa Rica.* Gainesville: University of Florida Press, 1971.

———. *A Naturalist on a Tropical Farm.* Berkeley: University of California Press, 1980.

Stansifer, Charles L. "Foreign Scientists in Costa Rica, 1845–1914." Manuscript, 1989.

———. "Reflections on Early Costa Rican Exceptionalism." Paper delivered at Second Inter-American Relations Conference, 12 October 1996, Jacksonville, Fla.

Stephens, John L. *Incidents of Travel in Central America, Chiapas, and Yucatán.* 2 vols. New York: Harper and Brothers, 1841.

Stiles, F. Gary, and Deborah Clark. "Conservation of Tropical Rain Forest Birds: A Case Study from Costa Rica." *American Birds* 1, no. 3 (Fall 1989): 420–427.

Stiles, F. Gary, and Alexander Skutch. *Birds of Costa Rica.* Ithaca, N.Y.: Comstock Publishing, 1989.

Stone, Donald E. "The Organization for Tropical Studies (OTS): A Success Story in Graduate Training and Research." In *Tropical Rainforests: Diversity and Con-*

servation, ed. Frank Almeda and Catherine M. Pringle. San Francisco: California Academy of Sciences, 1988.

Sun, Marjorie. "Costa Rica's Campaign for Conservation." *Science* 29, no. 4846 (18 March 1988): 1366–1369.

Sunkel, Osvaldo. "La interacción entre los estilos de desarrollo y el medio ambiente en la América Latina." In *Estilos de desarrollo y medio ambiente en la América Latina,* ed. Osvaldo Sunkel and Nicolo Gligo. Mexico City: Fondo de Cultura Económica, 1980.

Takacs, David. "Costa Rica's National Institute of Biodiversity: Where Biologists Transform Science, Conservation, Nature, and 'Nature.'" Paper presented at the Eighth Biennial Conference of the American Society of Environmental History, Las Vegas, 8–11 March 1995.

———. *The Idea of Biodiversity: Philosophies of Paradise.* Baltimore: Johns Hopkins University Press, 1996.

"Talamanca's Sweet Success." *Nature Conservancy* 47, no. 1 (January/February 1997): 14–15.

Tangley, Laura. "Cataloguing Costa Rica's Biodiversity." *BioScience* 40, no. 9 (October 1992): 633–636.

———. "The OTS." *BioScience* 38, no. 6 (June 1988): 375–385.

Tato, Ana María. "Legislación de parques nacionales." Manuscript, 1982. National Archives, SPN file 698.

Tenorio Alfaro, Luis A. *Las comunidades indígenas de Costa Rica.* San José: Imprenta Nacional, 1988.

Thiel, Bishop Augusto. *Monografía de la población de la República de Costa Rica en el siglo XIX.* 2d ed. San José: Editorial Costa Rica, 1977.

Tosi Olin, Joseph. "A Brief History of the Tropical Science Center's Monteverde Cloud Forest Preserve, 1972–1992." Paper presented on the occasion of the Twentieth Anniversary of the Monteverde Cloud Forest Preserve. Monteverde, 1992.

Ugalde, Alvaro F. "An Optimal Park System." In *Conservation for the Twenty-first Century,* ed. David Western and Mary C. Pearl. New York: Oxford University Press, 1989.

Ureña Morales, Gabriel. *Costa Rica: La Suiza de Centroamérica.* Paris: Delroisse, 1977.

Valerio G., Carlos E. "INBio: A Pilot Project in Biodiversity." *ASC [Association of Systematics Collections] Newsletter* 20, no. 2 (April 1992): 101–105.

———. *La biodiversidad biológica de Costa Rica.* San José: Editorial Heliconia, 1991.

Vandermeer, John H., and Ivette Perfecto. *Breakfast of Biodiversity: The Truth about Rainforest Destruction.* Oakland: Food First Books, 1995.

———. "Slicing Up the Rainforest on Your Breakfast Cereal." *The Humanist* 55, no. 5 (1995): 24–30.

Vaughan, Christopher. *Parque Nacional Corcovado: Plan de manejo y desarrollo.* Heredia, C.R.: Editorial UNA, 1981.

Villarreal M., Beatriz. *El precarismo rural en Costa Rica, 1960–1980: Orígenes y evolución.* San José: Editorial Papiro, 1983.

———. *Precarismo campesinado y democracia.* San José: FLACSO, 1992.

Wallace, David Rains. "Communing in Costa Rica." *Wilderness,* Summer 1988, pp. 52–54.

———. *The Quetzal and the Macaw: The Story of Costa Rica's National Parks.* San Francisco: Sierra Club Books, 1992.

Weinberg, Bill. *War on the Land: Ecology and Politics in Central America.* London: Zed Books, 1991.

Western, D., and R. M. Wright, eds. *Natural Connections: Perspectives in Community-Based Conservation.* Washington, D.C.: Island Press, 1994.

Wille, Chris. "Tropical Treasures." *Panoscope,* March 1991, pp. 15–16.

Wille Trejos, Alvaro. *Corcovado, meditaciones de un biólogo: Un estudio ecológico.* 2d ed. San José: Editorial UNED, 1987.

Young, Allen M. *Field Guide to the Natural History of Costa Rica.* San José: LACSA, 1981.

Zeledón, Ricardo, ed. *Código agrario.* San José: Editorial Porvenir, 1985.

———, ed. *Código ecológico.* San José: Editorial Porvenir, 1992.

Interviews

Alvarado Sánchez, Mario (department coordinator, CONAI), San José, 19 July 1996.

Bonilla, Alexander (cofounder and past president, ASCONA; independent environmental consultant), San José, 22 July 1996.

Boza, Mario (past director, National Park Service; former presidential adviser; project coordinator, Mesoamerican Biological Corridor Foundation, CCC), San Pedro de Montes de Oca, C.R., 9 July 1996.

Bozzoli de Wille, María Eugenia (anthropologist, University of Costa Rica), San Pedro de Montes de Oca, C.R., 25 June 1992 and 19 July 1996.

Budowski, Gerardo (past director, IUCN; senior advisor to the director general, CATIE; trustee, WWF; director, Natural Resources Program, University for Peace; president, Worldwide Ecotourism Society), Curridabat, C.R., 18 July 1996.

Carazo Odio, Rodrigo (former president, Republic of Costa Rica, 1978–1982; founder, University for Peace), Escazú, C.R., 29 June 1992.

Carvajal Agulo, Madeline (official, Fundación de Parques Nacionales), San José, 9 July 1996.

Castillo, Orlando (historian; archivist, National Archives; environmentalist), Zapote, C.R., 22 July 1996.

Cortés, Jorge (marine biologist, University of Costa Rica), San Pedro de Montes de Oca, C.R., 15 July 1996.

Figueres, Karen Olsen Beck de (former First Lady of Costa Rica, 1970–1974), Curridabat, C.R., 29 June 1992.

Flores Reyes, Anselmo (president, Térraba Integral Indigenous Development Association), San José, 19 July 1996.

Fournier Origgi, Luis (forestry ecologist, University of Costa Rica), San Pedro de Montes de Oca, C.R., 19 July 1996.

Koepsel, Kirk (former Peace Corps volunteer working with ASCONA in Costa Rica, 1981–1983; associate representative, Sierra Club Northern Plains Regional Office, Sheridan, Wyo.) by telephone, 13 August 1992.

León, Alvaro (director, AECO), San José, 11 July 1996.

Morris, Argentina Molina (former personal secretary for President Rodrigo Carazo), Chicago, 29 February 1992.

Morris, Fred (past director, *Mesoamérica* and the Center for Mesoamerican Studies), Chicago, 29 February 1992.

Muller, Robert (chancellor, University for Peace; former assistant secretary general, United Nations), Ciudad Colón, C.R., 20 July 1996.

Paniagua, Luis (official, Fundación Neotrópica), Curridabat, C.R., 8 July 1996.

Salazar, Roxana (environmental attorney; author), San José, 23 July 1996.

Ugalde, Alvaro (past director, National Park Service), San José, 25 June 1992.

Ulloa, Eric (former assistant to the director, Ministry of Natural Resources, Energy, and Mines), San José, 25 June 1992 and 4 July 1996.

INDEX